MAKE PUB-STYLE
DRAFT BEER AT HOME

BREW LIKE -A- PRO

DAVE MILLER

Storey Publishing

The mission of Storey Publishing is to serve our customers by
publishing practical information that encourages
personal independence in harmony with the environment.

Edited by Margaret Sutherland and Nick Kaye
Art direction by Jessica Armstrong
Cover and book design by MacFadden & Thorpe

Front cover photograph by © Lara Ferroni
Inside front and inside back cover photography by Mars Vilaubi
Photograph on page 99 provided by the author
Illustrations by Steve Sanford

Indexed by Christine R. Lindemer, Boston Road Communications

Storey Publishing
210 MASS MoCA Way
North Adams, MA 01247
www.storey.com

Printed in the United States by Versa Press
10   9   8   7   6   5   4   3   2   1

Library of Congress Cataloging-in-Publication Data

Miller, David G., 1945–
  Brew like a pro / by Dave Miller.
      pages cm
  Includes bibliographical references and index.
  ISBN 978-1-61212-050-8 (pbk. : alk. paper)
  ISBN 978-1-60342-852-1 (e-book)
  1. Brewing. I. Title.
TP570.M46 2012
663'.3—dc23
                                    2012032601

Dedication

I dedicate this book to the memory of George Fix. To have been his friend is reward enough for my involvement in our common endeavor. George ended his inscription in my copy of his book with, "P.S. God smiles on those who brew beer." I believe that.

Requiem aeternam dona ei, Domine, et lux perpetua luceat ei.

Acknowledgments

I want to thank the members of the Music City Brewers for their help with a project that became part of this book. I appreciate the continued camaraderie of the St. Louis Brews. Josh Garrett, a dedicated home-brewer who was once my assistant and is now chief brewer at Blackstone Restaurant & Brewery in Nashville, gave me the benefit of his experience during the writing of this book.

I owe a debt of gratitude to my first employers, Tom Schlafly and Dan Kopman of the Saint Louis Brewery. They gave me a chance to prove I could make beer that people would buy. I am also grateful to Kent Taylor and Stephanie Weins, owners of Blackstone Restaurant & Brewery, where I worked from 1994 until my retirement in 2008. Throughout my career, I was fortunate to work for people who love good beer.

I want also to thank all the many teachers I have been privileged to learn from during the course of my life as a brewer. My instructors at Siebel must be mentioned, and then the brewing team at Schlafly, especially Stephen Hale and James Ottolini. Lastly I thank Greg Noonan, whom I knew only slightly but who through his writing taught me almost as much as anyone.

CONTENTS

HOW I GOT HERE

For those of you who do not know me, I guess I need to tell you a little about myself and my involvement in the world of craft beer. I started out as a homebrewer, but after about 15 years I "turned pro" and pretty much got away from the hobby side. I quickly discovered that brewing in a pub is a tough job, even for a young man. It requires lifting and lugging heavy sacks, crouching and kneeling on hard floors, filling (by hoe and shovel) and moving cartloads of wet spent grain, and much other heavy labor. For a middle-aged man, as I was at the start, it was a test of dedication. Every night I came home tired and sore, and the last thing I wanted to think about on my days off was making beer.

It took a year of retirement from professional brewing before my interest began to revive. This book is a field report of my reentry into homebrewing. A lot changed in homebrewing while I was away. I hope I am not being presumptuous in saying that I had something to do with that.

I made my first batch of homebrew in 1976. It was a typical recipe of the time, made with a 2½-pound can of "malt extract" (actually partly corn syrup), 4 pounds of corn sugar, half a 4-ounce brick of compressed "kettle hops" (lacking a scale, I just cut the brick in half — it was brown all the way through), a 1-ounce bag of "finish hops" (loose in a plastic bag, a little greener than the hop brick), and a packet of "lager yeast" (origin/manufacturer unspecified).

The result was just what you would expect. It smelled more like cider than beer. It was thin as water, with barely a hint of malt character, and had a bitterness level that was way out of balance with its ultralight body. I took a bottle to the owner of the local shop where I had purchased the ingredients, and he poured some into a glass, swirled it around, sniffed and tasted, and with a laugh announced, "That's good beer."

That should have been the end of the story. For the life of me I cannot explain why I persisted, but I did. I read every book I could find on the subject of homebrewing, profiting little from most of them, but eventually discovering *The Big Book of Brewing*, written by an Englishman named Dave Line. This chap had the temerity to suggest that homebrewers can, and should, take the trouble to make their beer from malted barley and other grains, just as commercial brewers do. That set me off.

In 1981 I won Homebrewer of the Year at the AHA (American Homebrewers Association) national competition, with a Dutch pilsner that today, I'm sure, would not make it out of the first round. But that was then, and the award confirmed what I already knew: that Dave Line was right. All-grain brewing, as it is still called in the homebrew world, is the way to make beer.

Then and Now

Homebrewing has come a long way since then. As the craft beer movement has taken off, the marketplace has responded to the corresponding growth of the hobby, and today homebrewers have access to just about everything available in the line of ingredients, including fresh hops of all varieties, every type of malted barley, and dozens of strains of yeast from breweries all over the world. In that respect, the playing field has been leveled. The best beers that I have tasted in homebrew competitions are beers that practically any professional brewer, including me, would be proud to sell.

Likewise, the information explosion has benefited the hobby just as it has so many other pursuits. Books, magazines, and websites abound. Once I got the itch to homebrew again, I read a lot of the new material. I got excited by the prospects of quick, simple, all-grain brewing using products and techniques that promised commercial-quality results with little effort and a minimum of equipment. In fact, my initial plan was to use only low-cost off-the-shelf gear, permitting myself just one exception: a lauter tun that I decided to build because the design I preferred is not available ready-made.

Some of you may be surprised to hear this. You might think the natural course would be to get a nice single-tier brewing "rack," as I call them, and go to town with it. Maybe you have seen these systems — a welded frame, three big kettles, three burners and a gas rail, three pumps, and yards of beautiful stainless piping. No doubt I could have been turning out good beer within days of taking delivery.

But I've *done* that. I worked with brewpub systems for nearly 17 years, first at The Saint Louis Brewery (makers of Schlafly) and then at Blackstone Restaurant & Brewery in Nashville. While they were not as flexible in some ways as the best homebrewers' racks, the gear was pretty much on the same level. I wanted to do something different. I have always had a minimalist streak, which I suppose is a euphemism for being cheap. I blanch at the prices of these "ready-to-brew" systems. I wanted to demonstrate, first of all to myself, that you don't need all that to make first-class beer.

The Limits of Simplicity

Then I started brewing. My first batch, brewed using the simple methods and equipment I wanted so much to champion, was from every point of view a disaster. Using the finest ingredients, including yeast from my former place of employment, I made a beer that was not worth drinking.

To be clear — it was not undrinkable, nor was it infected. But it was not worth drinking. A comparison with the pub beer that shared space in my beer fridge proved that beyond a doubt.

Things got a little better after that, as I corrected some deficiencies in the methods I was using. By the time I had made and flushed a few batches, I realized that simplicity can be taken too far. You compromise the quality of your wort. And bad wort makes bad beer.

As I continued to brew, I found that in order to improve the beer, I had to either modify a piece of equipment, or rethink how I was using it, or replace it with a new one. And in every case, these changes in equipment and procedure led in one direction, which was (as I should have expected) doing things the way I had done them when I was a professional.

Suffice it to say I recognized anew the merit of the typical pub brewery, which instances a series of design decisions that have been gradually worked out to make high-quality results possible with a minimum investment in floor space and capital.

This is not to say that every pub brewer makes the best use of his machinery. And not all pub breweries are, by any means, up to standard as far as equipment goes. I have seen systems so ramshackle that it seemed impossible to make good beer with them. Sometimes I have been surprised at how good the beer actually was — a tribute to the skill of the operator.

This also is not to say that I ended up with a miniature replica of the Blackstone brewery. What I attempted to do was to achieve the same functionality, in terms of process, ease of operation, and safety. The next two chapters explain what I was shooting for, and my design criteria and decisions.

Looking back, I don't know why I was surprised at the results I got from my first batches. After all, I'm the guy who turned his back on extract brewing and implored countless others to do the same, precisely because the simplicity of the process is bought at the price of low-quality wort.

The Place (or Lack Thereof) of Malt Extract

I am not saying that I have never tasted a good beer that was made from malt extract. I have. I have even tasted a few that deserved, and got, medals from judging panels that I sat on. But for every beer of this caliber, I have tasted dozens that were mediocre despite being free of infection and other typical flaws. Their downfall was the unmistakable "extract note" that is quite different from the malt flavor of beer that is made in the traditional way.

Where does this "extract note" come from? And why do some, though few, extract beers seem to escape it? These are questions that have puzzled me for years. So far, the best answer I have found is that the process of vacuum evaporation is the culprit. I won't go too far into the technical side of it, but the creation of malt extract syrup requires an extreme degree of concentration; the product is about 80 percent solids, compared with 12 percent for an average wort. The end result is a syrupy substance that has been darkened and caramelized and is, apparently, highly unstable. It begins to deteriorate as soon as it is made. To paraphrase what Dr. Johnson said about Scotsmen, then, something may be made of a malt extract — if it be caught young.

The trouble is that catching it young — and I mean within a few weeks of its manufacture — is highly problematic. Nobody is putting "born on" dates on packages of malt extract. And the alternative to syrup — spray-dried granular malt extract — seems scarcely any better. True, almost all the moisture has been removed, and that should make it more stable. But the drying process itself is a further insult. How all this will balance out in any particular case, such as a trial making the same recipe from one particular package of dry extract and one particular package of syrup, is unpredictable. It depends on the age of the samples in question and on manufacturing conditions, which may not be the same from one maker to another or even from one batch to another.

The only thing you can be sure of is this: the more a particular beer style depends on a clean malt flavor, the less suitable it is to being made from extract. Your best chance for a good result is probably something like a porter, with its caramel and roasted grain notes, or a well-hopped amber ale. Even here, of course, if the extract is old or otherwise defective, your beer will suffer. But you have a chance. On the other hand, if you are trying to make a pilsner or a wheat beer, forget it. The freshest extract in the world will not give a creditable result.

Those are the facts, and here's my conclusion: extract brewing is a blind alley. It is a good introduction to the brewing process, and I still recommend that everyone make a few batches of extract beer to get familiar with boiling, hopping, cooling, fermenting, and packaging. As an educational exercise it is useful. But look on it in that light. Don't think you will be able to make consistently good beer with this method, and don't get sidetracked into a series of brews where you try different brands of ingredients in the hope of improving your results.

In this book I am not going to go into extract brewing. I did that in some of my older books, and there are others with plenty of information and recipes. Some are listed in Resources (see page 255). I have not made a batch of extract beer in 20 years, and I did not go back into homebrewing with that in mind. What I wanted was to make beer as good as I made at work, and for that I'd need a plan.

Blueprint to Brew

As I said, my goal was simple: make beer similar to the beer I made at the pub.

That immediately dictated some choices, the most obvious of which is all-grain brewing. Almost as clear was another, which I have never questioned or regretted. I state it here as a bit of advice to you.

Dear Reader:

Don't waste an hour or a dollar on bottling.

Pub beer is draft beer, and draft beer is best because it is the freshest and subjected to the fewest insults after it is made.

Draft beer is unpasteurized, and it is kept cold from the end of fermentation until it reaches its destination in the stomach of a happy beer lover.

Draft beer is served from kegs.

Therefore, the first thing you should get is not a kettle or a fermenter, but a draft beer system, including a few kegs and a refrigerator.

As it happens, I already had a draft beer system before I went back into homebrewing, because my "pension" from Blackstone is, basically, unlimited free beer. All I need to do is take an empty keg in for a refill and pick it up the next day. That puts some light on the length of time it took me to go back into brewing. If I had been lacking good fresh beer, it would have happened a lot sooner.

So, here I am telling you to spend a few hundred bucks on a draft system, right up front. For most homebrewers it is one of the last things they pony up for. I say, do it now. Money spent on a draft system repays you from the start. De-labeling, cleaning, and sanitizing 50 bottles (enough for a 5-gallon batch) is a wet, nasty job that takes hours. Filling bottles is almost as tedious. I was a bottling homebrewer for 17 years, and I clearly remember the day I brought home my first keg as a day of liberation. Believe me: Money and time spent on bottles is a waste. At best you will be able to pass them along to a new brewer, and all that does is perpetuate the cycle of misery.

Allow me to present my case for investing in a draft system:

▸ FIRST: A refrigerator has other uses besides beer service. It helps you make better, cleaner-tasting beer. It facilitates post-fermentation crash cooling and clarification.

▸ SECOND: It allows you to brew year-round without buying large quantities of ice. Year-round brewing is part of the game. If you want fresh beer, you have to make it fresh.

▸ THIRD: A draft system has value even if you don't persist in the hobby, or if time constraints keep you from producing all the beer you want. Many brewpubs and some micros will gladly fill customers' kegs and, in fact, at Blackstone we have a fair number of regular customers who set up a draft system with no intention of making their own beer. And if worse comes to worst and you revert to buying bottled beer, you can sell the kit and caboodle and get most of your money back.

▸ FOURTH: Brewing is always exciting, an essay in a wonderful art; bottling is drudgery. It is also low-paying work. A draft system is much more cost effective, easily paying for itself with the time you'll save by not bottling your beer. Even if you figure your time is worth only three dollars an hour, a draft beer system will pay for itself in 20 batches of beer. Bottling is worthwhile only if there is nothing you would rather do with your leisure time. I have yet to meet a homebrewer who got into the hobby because he wanted to clean and fill bottles.

That's it. Taking it together, I believe the case for "going draft" is as compelling as the one for going all-grain.

I know that the course advocated here is not the one most of us took into homebrewing. This includes me. But it is the best.

As to what "going all-grain" involves, that is pretty much the subject of the next few chapters. For the benefit of those who are not familiar with the process of making beer, I will start with a brief overview; then we will look at how pub breweries are set up and operated, with the idea of doing the same thing at home, on a smaller scale.

My emphasis here is on practical procedures rather than brewing science. My goal was to limit theoretical discussion as much as possible. There are a number of good books, listed in Resources, that delve into the "whys" in a systematic way; I think anybody who gets serious about brewing will want to read them. But too much information, right at the start, can be an obstacle. It makes brewing seem like something only a chemist could master, and that is far from the truth.

On the other hand, there are some endeavors in which a certain amount of technical discussion cannot be avoided, and in which a willingness to deal with basic math is indispensable. Brewing is one of them. Before you buy one piece of equipment, read through the next few chapters and try to decide whether making your own beer would really be enjoyable for you. If, on the other hand, you have already gotten into this great hobby, then I hope you will use them as a guide to refining your craft.

The emphasis on practical procedures means that, when we come to specifics later on in the book, I am writing about the way I make beer at home. My preferences and habits are on display and, of course, they will not suit everyone. I try to mention some alternatives along the way, but if I am going to keep it simple and straightforward, I really have no choice but to focus on what I know firsthand. However, there are some limitations that come with this. The most obvious has already been mentioned: I am not going to go into extract brewing at all.

What sets this book apart from others you will find is simply that it reflects a different view of homebrewing. When I first turned pro, I tended to look at the process from a homebrewer's perspective. In my return to homebrewing, I find myself looking at it from a pub brewer's perspective. I think my experience has given me a better idea of what is truly necessary and what is just "nice to have" in a home brewery.

In the interests of full disclosure, there is another area where my perspective comes into play. Take a look at the chapter on recipes (chapter 8). I am what you might call a "beer classicist." You may like all the latest permutations and inventions, many of which march under the banner of "extreme beer" — imperial pilsners, double weizenbocks, honey goat cheese cranberry ale, and so on. I do not. Give me a well-balanced Märzen, a rich roasty oatmeal stout, or a tangy witbier, and I ask for nothing else. If you have read the well-known *New Yorker* article on craft brewing from a few years back (see Resources), I can say it simply: I'm with Garrett Oliver. If you like humongous beers, or monstrously hoppy beers, or monstrously hoppy humongous beers, well, you'll need to look elsewhere for information about them.

I do believe that a beginner should focus on the classic styles at first, regardless of personal preference; they require the greatest care and are least forgiving of errors. If you can brew a good Kölsch, a hundred-IBU quadruple IPA is a walk in the park. Years ago my friend Steve Fried (the longtime brewmaster at McGuire's in Pensacola, Florida) gave the keynote address at a homebrewers' conference. He concluded with a reminder that process is more important than your bill of ingredients.

I can't reproduce what he said word for word, but this is a paraphrase, as best I can recall:

HOMEBREWERS ASK ME FOR RECIPES. HERE'S YOURS:

8 pounds of malt

1 ounce of hops

1 packet of yeast

Keep making it until it tastes the same every time.

My recipes are a little more specific, but I hope you get the idea. Consistency is the ultimate test, even for a homebrewer. You don't have to meet customer expectations, but you do need to master the techniques that are required if you expect to make good beer every time.

Beer 101

If you are already familiar with the brewing process, you may want to skip this section and go on to the next chapter. My intent here is to give a very brief, basic outline of brewing — sufficient, I hope, to make the remainder of the book intelligible to those who have never made a batch of beer.

Beer is a fermented beverage. What does that mean? Basically, fermentation is the metabolic process by which yeast takes sugar and splits it into alcohol and carbon dioxide. This, of course, is what beer makers and drinkers are interested in. You might call me a yeast farmer. My job is to produce sugar solution and feed it to my yeast.

There are lots of ways to create a sugar solution, but if we want to make beer — as opposed to wine or sake or mead or some other beverage — then the main source of our sugar must be malted grain, specifically malted barley, which is usually just called malt. The making of malt is a difficult task in its own right: the raw barley must be soaked, sprouted, and then dried in a kiln (a hot-air oven). Each of these steps is exacting, and changes to time, temperature, and other variables can make a large difference in the outcome. Likewise, the breed (or strain) of barley and its exact constituents play a role. This is not the place for a detailed listing of the basic types of malt and their characteristics, but if you have never brewed before, you need to understand that malt is not all alike: different malts have vastly different colors, flavors, and other properties. In the modern world, malting usually is a separate industry that supplies standardized products to the breweries, which are their customers. Only a few breweries still maintain their own malting departments.

The reason brewers need malt, rather than some other type of grain, is quite simple. Malt contains enzymes that can break down starch into sugar. In fact, the difference between beer and other fermented drinks comes down to this: the main sugar source is malted grain whose starch has been broken down into fermentable sugars by the action of its own enzymes.

So, how do we accomplish this breakdown? We make a *mash*. That is, we crush (*mill*) the barley malt, then mix it with water in a kettle or other vessel, and heat it to around 150°F, a temperature at which the starch will be quickly and efficiently reduced to maltose and other sugars. Ordinarily, a stand of one hour at conversion temperature is more than enough to complete the process.

The next step is to separate, or strain, the newly created sugar solution — which is now called *wort* — from the husks and other remaining grain solids. In a good mash, about 80 percent of the grain (by weight) will convert to sugar and other soluble matter, but the other 20 percent needs to be removed, for the sake of both flavor and aesthetics (clarity). This is done in a vessel called a *lauter tun*, and the process is known as *lautering*. The lauter tun is fitted with a straining device — usually a slotted false bottom. Once the mash has been moved to the lauter tun, a valve beneath the false bottom is opened and the wort is drawn off and returned to the surface of the grain bed. As this recirculation continues, a filter bed forms and the wort will gradually clarify. When the wort is judged sufficiently clear, recirculation ends and the wort is run into a kettle. However, much of the wort will remain trapped in the spent grain solids, so after drawing off as much liquid as possible, the grain bed is usually rinsed, or *sparged*, with hot water. Sparging greatly increases efficiency and, for a normal-strength beer, can allow recovery of 90 percent or more of the sugar formed during mashing.

After the full volume of wort has been collected in the brew kettle, it is brought to a boil and boiled for one to two hours. During this time *hops* are added. The hop is a bitter herb, and one of the main purposes of boiling is to dissolve the hop resins and impart their characteristic flavor to the wort (and beer). Other purposes of boiling are to concentrate the wort, to deepen its color slightly, and most important, to sterilize it. We want to make sure that our carefully selected brewer's yeast has no competition from bacteria or other organisms. Along with careful cleaning and sanitizing practices, the boil is the brewer's primary weapon in the battle for clean-tasting beer.

After the boil is over, the hops and *trub* (coagulated protein) are separated from the hot wort. Depending on the form of the hops, one of two methods is used. Hop pellets break up into fine powder in the kettle and can be removed by whirlpooling; however, if whole leaf hops have been employed, they must be strained out in a vessel called a *hop back* or *hop jack*, which often resembles a shallow lauter tun. In any case, after kettle solids have been removed, the wort is sent to a cooling device, where it is dropped to room temperature (or lower) and then moved on to the fermenting tank, where yeast is pitched and the transformation from wort to beer will take place.

In the fermenter, yeast is added (the brewer's term is *pitched*) and the yeast begins to multiply and also to ferment. Fermentation can take anywhere from three to ten days, depending on temperature and other factors. Over the first one to three days, it builds to a peak, and then gradually tapers off. When the yeast has turned all the wort sugar into alcohol and carbon dioxide, the beer may need a period of aging to allow the spent yeast to complete its work by reducing some of its intermediate by-products (this is called *maturation*), and also to settle out. At the end of this step the beer is basically ready. It may require carbonation and/or clarification before it can be put in a package (for example, a keg) and served, but once the maturation is done and the yeast is removed, the flavor has reached its peak. Beer is not like wine: it does not improve in the bottle, and it is best drunk young. The only exceptions are very strong beers that still contain some live yeast. Storage conditions greatly influence the rate of deterioration. Besides time, the enemies of beer are heat, motion, and oxygen. The more air in the package, the shorter the shelf life will be.

TO SUMMARIZE, THE STEPS IN MAKING BEER ARE:

1. Milling the malt

2. Mashing

3. Lautering and sparging

4. Boiling the wort

5. Cooling

6. Yeast pitching and fermentation

7. Maturation and clarification

8. Packaging

Packaging is the final step before consumption. It is easier to keep air levels low in a larger container, which is one reason kegs are usually preferable; however, the main reason is that it is much easier to clean and sanitize a single 5-gallon keg (for example) than to do the same to 50 bottles. The only drawback is difficulty of handling.

Each of these steps requires dedicated equipment. In the next chapter we will look at how the brewing process is implemented in a brewpub, where space and capital must be kept to a minimum, without sacrificing quality.

2

AN INSIDE LOOK AT A PUB BREWERY

Now that I've given you a basic overview of the brewing process, let's take a field trip to see how that process is implemented on a small commercial scale. It bears noting that unlike large breweries, brewpubs are, in a sense, home-brewing writ large. The relatively small size of the operation allows a single brewer to run the show, being intimately involved in each and every step of the process.

The best way to get an understanding of small-scale brewing is to take a tour of the brewery, looking at each piece of equipment in order, and examining its role. So we'll start with a list of all the equipment you will find in a brewpub, organized by its place in the process. Few, if any, breweries will have every item on the list, but each represents a function that somehow has to be performed in order to transform malt, water, and hops into beer.

BREWPUB EQUIPMENT

- Malt mill*
- Grist case*
- Grain auger*
- Water treatment system
- Hot liquor back and associated pump*
- Grist hydrator and water mixing manifold
- Mash mixer*
- Mash/lauter tun and associated pump
- Grant*
- Kettle/whirlpool combination and associated pump

To heat the kettle, either:

    → Gas-fired burner, or

    → Low-pressure steam boiler and piping system

- Glycol chiller and associated reservoir and pump
- Cold liquor back and associated pump*
- Heat exchanger (wort cooler) assembly
- Fermentation tanks
- Lager tanks*
- Filter*
- Serving tanks
- Walk-in cooler*
- Draft beer system including CO_2 tank(s), pressure regulators, lines, and taps
- CIP (clean-in-place) and transfer pump(s), hoses, and fittings

indicates optional items

What, you might ask, does each of these things do?

The **malt mill** crushes the barley malt to prepare it for mashing. It is listed here as optional because, while somebody has to do this, it need not be the brewer. Many pubs buy malt precrushed from their suppliers. This is cheaper in the short run and cuts down on the space requirement for the brewery. It may also be necessary in some localities because codes do not permit milling of grain in the building. Precrushed malt does not necessarily compromise the quality of the finished product.

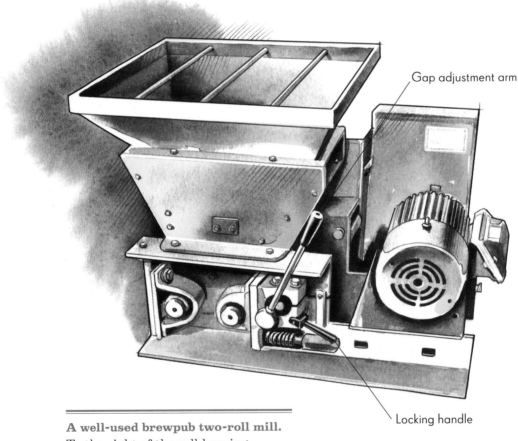

Gap adjustment arm

Locking handle

A well-used brewpub two-roll mill.
To the right of the roll-bearing
blocks is the gap adjustment arm
and locking handle.

The advantage of owning a mill is that it gives the brewer control of his crush and the ability to adjust for different types of malt. It is also cheaper in the long haul. Most pubs use the simplest type of mill, which consists of a single pair of iron or steel rolls that rotate against one another and crush the grain between them. While more elaborate mills can improve the crush somewhat, a two-roll mill is good enough to permit brewhouse efficiencies of 90 percent or more.

The *grist case* is just a special conical-bottomed bin for storing the crushed malt until it is time to start brewing. It is listed as optional because it is sometimes possible to locate the mill directly above the mash tun and crush it as the mash is being mixed. This requires two people, but it can be done.

The *grain auger* (there may be several) moves the grain to the mill, or from the grist case to the grist hydrator. If you can arrange your equipment vertically and store the grain on the same level as the mill, you can do without any augers.

The *water treatment system* is as elaborate as necessary, depending on how good or bad the municipal water is. A minimum setup would be a sediment filter to remove solid particles, and a carbon filter to remove disinfectant chemicals — chlorine or chloramine — before the water is used for brewing.

The *hot liquor back* is a tank that serves as a reservoir for hot brewing water (liquor) during sparging and perhaps at other times as well. The vessel may be heated directly, or it may just be insulated, in which case the water must be heated in the brew kettle and moved to the back before the kettle is required for boiling the wort. As long as you are brewing only one batch per day, a heated back is not necessary and is seldom found in pubs that have a gas-fired kettle. Many brewpubs save space by locating the hot liquor back directly below the mash/lauter tun.

The *grist hydrator* (see page 18) mixes hot brewing liquor with the crushed malt as they are both fed into the mash tun. Few brewpub mash tuns have motorized rakes, and the volume of mash in a typical brewpub makes it impossible to manually stir the grain thoroughly into the water. Balls of dry grist, a direct loss of malt sugar, are inevitable. Every particle of grain must be wetted, and the easiest way to do this is by some device that actively or passively mingles them in a small chamber before they reach the mash tun.

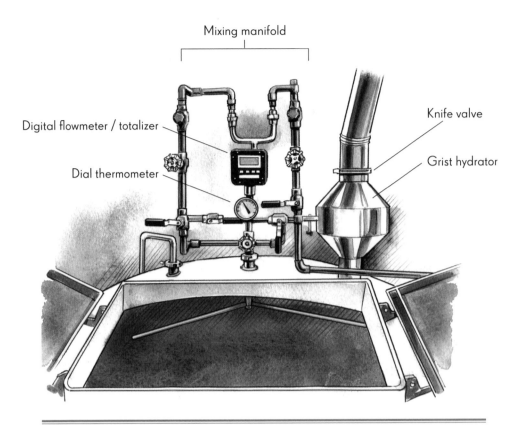

Mixing manifold

Digital flowmeter / totalizer

Dial thermometer

Knife valve

Grist hydrator

Top view of a pub brewery mash/lauter tun. The grist hydrator is to the right and the mixing manifold, which feeds tempered water, to the left. Note the dial thermometer and the digital flowmeter/totalizer, which keeps a running tally of water. This makes it possible to add in precise quantities of mash liquor.

The grist hydrator typically includes a ***mixing station***, which is a large pipe tee with valves to control the flow of hot and cold treated water into the common inlet. It will also have a thermometer and a flowmeter that allows the brewer to adjust the water flow rate. The flowmeter helps the brewer to control the water-grain mix ratio. If there's not enough water, the grist will not be wetted; if there is too much, the mash temperature will be too high, and malt enzymes will be destroyed. A knife valve atop the hydrator can be used to control the rate at which the grist is fed. The water valves are used to control both water temperature and flow rate.

Some microbreweries have a separate mash tun, sometimes called a **mash mixer**, with a heated bottom and/or sides and a large motorized paddle to stir the contents. The paddle ensures even temperatures throughout. This allows the brewer to rest or raise the temperature at will. It also, at least in theory, might allow you to do without a grist hydrator. You could bring water into the bottom of the vessel while grist drops in the top and let the paddle do the mixing. In practice, the mash mixers I have seen are fitted with a grist hydrator.

The **mash/lauter tun** is by far the most common choice for pub breweries. It combines two separate brewing steps, but the design limits the system's possibilities. The mash must be mixed at saccharification (starch conversion) temperatures. This is called single-infusion mashing. The vessel depends on insulation and the sheer mass of the contents to hold temperature in the proper range for the hour or so that is required.

The reason you cannot heat a mash/lauter tun is that it is, basically, a lauter tun with a grist hydrator fitted on the top. The primary feature of the vessel is the screen false bottom that acts as a strainer and makes it possible to clarify the wort. However, it also makes it impossible to get a smooth, even temperature rise. Steam injection might be an alternative, but, in fact, almost no mash/lauter tuns are heated.

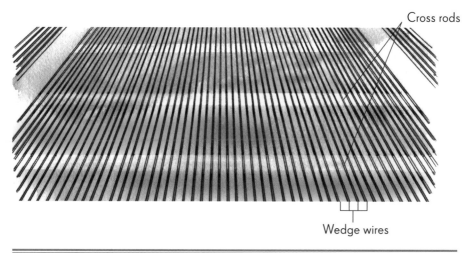

Cross rods

Wedge wires

Wedge-wire screen. A close-up of the wedge-wire screen false bottom fitted to a brewpub mash/lauter tun. Note the cross rods welded to the underside for support and spacing.

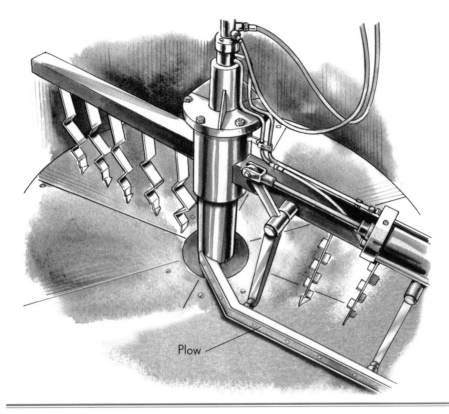

Plow

Lauter rakes. Rake assembly of a modern lauter tun. Rakes are the key to uniform drainage of large, modern lauter tuns. The rakes cut the bed continuously during runoff and sparging. In this illustration the plow is lowered, as it would be for pushing the grain out the spent grain chute.

This is something pub brewers simply learn to live with. It may be the most serious compromise we face in our process.

Still, while the limitations are real, they should not be overstated. Hundreds of award-winning brews come out of such vessels. Mash mixers and step mashing may make it possible to produce a more stable beer, but as long as the product stays close to home — which it obviously does in a pub — then with modern, well-modified malt, the single-infusion mash method is quite adequate.

The lauter tun always incorporates a *recirculation arm* (also called a *vorlauf arm*), and a *sparge arm*. The first of these, as its name implies, is used to recirculate the wort prior to runoff. This is how the wort is clarified. Dirty, husk-laden wort is pumped from below the

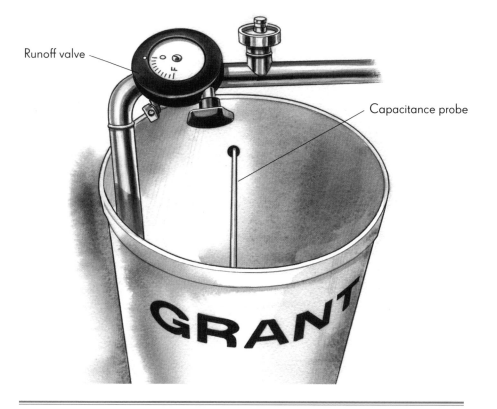

Runoff valve

Capacitance probe

Grant. Grant assembly in a pub brewery. The rod across the middle of the grant is a capacitance probe, which turns the lauter pump on and off. A speed control would work just as well and is far more practical in a home brewery, although it requires the operator to keep an eye on the wort level in the grant.

---

screen bottom and deposited on top of the mash. As this continues, the mash compresses slightly and forms a filter bed, and the wort becomes clear. When it is running clear, recirculation is stopped and the wort is pumped into the kettle. Then the wort is sparged or rinsed to wash out the sugar. The sparge arm is a pipe with holes drilled in it to spray hot water on top of the mash.

The ***grant*** is a small vessel for receiving the wort that strains through the screen at the bottom of the lauter tun. I call it optional, but it is actually quite simple and beneficial. Remember that the object of lautering is to clarify the wort. The grant provides a convenient sample and collection point. The alternative to a grant is direct piping with a sight glass in the line. This is all right in a brewpub, because a pump is needed for recirculation in any case. But eliminating the grant also means the pump is sucking on the mass of spent grain sitting in the lauter tun, a prospect that makes some brewers queasy. Direct piping also requires more valves and other fittings in addition to the sight glass.

The combination *kettle/whirlpool* is another instance of compromise for the sake of saving space and keeping costs down. One reason bigger breweries have a separate whirlpool is so they can get more brews through the kettle, which is a more expensive piece of equipment — in fact the second most expensive in the brewery. Only the lauter tun costs more. However, there also are other reasons for preferring a separate whirlpool.

The kettle should be able to deliver a good rolling boil, and a good evaporation rate — at least seven percent per hour. This is a real problem in many brewpubs. The kettle must also be large enough to have a good headspace for foam, because kettles are prone to boiling over, another problem for many pubs.

One compromise that the kettle/whirlpool demands is that only pellet hops are used. Whole hops cannot be separated by the whirlpool action and normally require a separate strainer, called the *hop back* or *hop jack*. With a flat-bottomed kettle it is possible to get around this limitation, but that imposes other penalties.

The most serious problem with the kettle/whirlpool is that it uses a centrifugal pump to recirculate the hot wort and get it spinning. The shearing action of the impeller tends to chop up the hot break — the flaky particles that form during the boil. Small break particles tend to hang in suspension rather than settle to the bottom, so the net result is that more hot break is carried out of the kettle and ends up in the fermenter. This is undesirable as it can lead to accelerated staling and other flavor defects. If a kettle/whirlpool is used, then the pump should be as large as is practical with as slow an impeller rotation as possible, and it should be run only long enough to develop a good spin. These precautions minimize shearing of the trub particles.

In larger breweries, the whirlpool is usually set below the kettle so that the wort can drop into it by gravity. The feed pipe enters at a tangent so that the wort is set spinning as the whirlpool tank fills.

The *gas-fired burner*, if selected, is integral with the kettle in most instances. Usually a blower burner swirls the flame into a closed combustion chamber below the flat-bottomed kettle. The combustion chamber is lined with insulation to prevent the flame from burning through the chamber wall. This heating method is called *direct-fire*. The disadvantages include fire and a gas pipe in the brewery, and a very hot kettle bottom, which makes scorching wort more likely than with steam. Nonetheless, it is usually the cheapest option and the one most common in smaller pubs. Steam makes economic sense if you want to heat your hot liquor back as well as the kettle. Electric heating is strictly a last resort for a brewpub, because it is much more expensive than gas.

The **glycol chiller** (process chiller) is a key piece of equipment in any brewpub, and probably represents the biggest difference between commercial and home brewing in terms of capabilities. Basically it is no different from an air conditioner, except that it cools a water-glycol (antifreeze) solution rather than air, and circulates it using a pump rather than a blower. Output temperature is usually 25 to 30°F, which makes it possible to cool down the jacketed fermenting and other tanks to near-freezing temperatures. The circulating glycol system makes it possible, with thermostatic control circuitry and solenoid valves, to automatically switch the glycol feed to any given tank on and off, so as to maintain any preset temperature within the tank. This is pretty much a requirement when one has several different brews going at once in different stages of the process.

For a pub brewer, the biggest problem with the glycol chiller is reliability. Even well-engineered systems tend to break down more frequently than other refrigeration equipment. And when the glycol goes down, you cannot brew, and all the fermenting beer — and possibly all the beer on tap — is at risk. If it cannot be repaired within 24 hours, you are facing catastrophe.

Larger breweries build redundancy into their chilling systems. They calculate the maximum cooling requirement and then divide it among several chillers. If any one of them breaks down, the others can carry the load. Unfortunately most pubs cannot afford to do things this way. Their ability to make and sell beer is at the mercy of one often cantankerous piece of machinery. The glycol chiller is responsible for most of the subliminal anxiety that is part of a pub brewer's psyche.

So all in all, it is just as well that there is no true equivalent to the glycol chiller in a home brewery.

The **cold liquor back** is a mirror image of the hot liquor back. It holds cold water for chilling the hot wort down to fermentation temperature after the whirlpool. I call it optional for two reasons: First, in some places, the water supply is cold enough year-round that wort can be cooled at least to ale-brewing temperatures; and second, there is an alternative strategy for dealing with cooling that is available in warm climates. This is to use the glycol chiller directly for supplemental cooling. See the discussion of two-stage heat exchangers, below, for details.

For breweries that cannot rely on cold tap water for all their wort cooling, a cold liquor back is desirable. It spreads out the cooling load so that a smaller glycol chiller can be specified, and it allows you to chill the wort with a smaller volume of water.

The **heat exchanger** is a key piece of equipment in any brewery. Wort needs to be cooled quickly, and the counterflow heat exchanger is by far the best way to do this. The operating principle of any heat exchanger is what the name suggests: to remove heat from one substance by transferring it to another. In a brewery the hot substance is wort; the cold substance is either water or glycol solution, or in the case of some two-stage heat exchangers, both. Regardless of the physical design, in any counterflow heat exchanger the hot wort flows through a closed passage in one direction. At the same time the coolant flows through an adjacent passage in the opposite direction. The two passages share a common wall, and this wall (generally metal) conducts heat from the wort to the coolant.

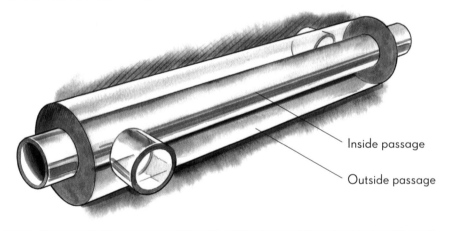

Inside passage

Outside passage

Tubular heat exchanger. The illustration shows the scheme of a tube-in-shell heat exchanger, a type that is still very commonly used. Hot wort flows through the tube (inside passage) while coolant flows counter to it through the shell (outside passage). Heat is conducted through the tube wall to the colder liquid.

Counterflow is not the only way to transfer heat, but it is by far the most efficient, in terms of time and coolant volume required. In a brewpub, the type of counterflow heat exchanger used is almost always the plate and frame, which has the smallest physical size for the area of transfer surface.

The one inescapable limitation of heat exchangers is coolant temperature. In most parts of the United States municipal water runs warm in the summer. Obviously you can't cool wort to 65 to 70°F (normal ale fermentation temperature) with 80°F water, hence the requirement

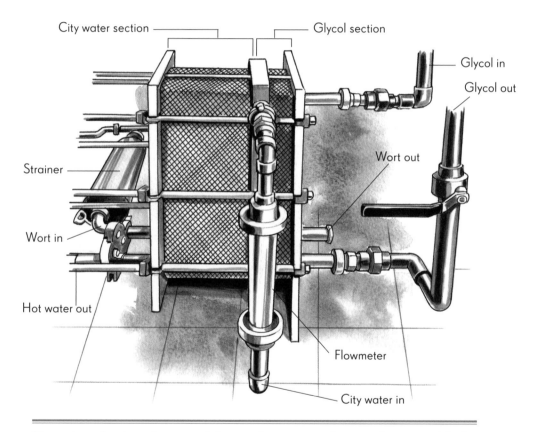

Two-stage heat exchanger. A brewpub two-stage heat exchanger, with the city water section on the left and glycol on the right. The flowmeter on the water side intake helps avoid wasted water — on this unit flow rates above 20 gallons per minute contribute very little additional cooling.

for either a cold liquor back or a two-stage heat exchanger, or both. A **two-stage heat exchanger** is basically composed of two separate units with separate cooling streams, but a common wort stream. Wort goes through the city water section first and then it goes through the glycol section or cold liquor section and emerges at fermentation temperature. A thermometer is always fitted to the heat exchanger outlet. The brewer controls the cooling by adjusting the flow rates of one or more of the fluids. Generally the goal is to have the city water do most of the work, dropping the wort to within 10 degrees of the water's temperature, so as to minimize the requirement for cold liquor, or avoid putting a heavier load on the glycol chiller.

The alternative is to go with a single-stage heat exchanger and use cold liquor to do all the cooling. This takes a good-sized cold liquor back, and the heat exchanger will cost nearly as much as a two-stage that will do the same job — that is, cool the same volume of wort in the same time. But it will require less water in total, and the water will come out hotter — so from the standpoint of energy costs, this can be a net savings if the brewery is running multiple brews per day. The cooling water from one batch is used for the mash and sparge of the next.

Brewpubs often recover hot water from the heat exchanger to fill their hot liquor back, but because of the intermittent brew schedule the energy savings are less. The economy is mostly in water consumption.

In addition to a thermometer, brewery heat exchangers are fitted with an *aerating stone,* which is used to diffuse oxygen or air into the cooled wort as it flows to the fermenter. This is the most convenient point to introduce oxygen into the wort to promote yeast growth. The stone is actually stainless steel as a rule, with tiny pores to break up the airstream into bubbles and promote dissolution in the wort.

In most pubs, as in larger breweries, the **fermentation tanks** are made of stainless steel and consist of four layers. First is the inner tank, which is the tank proper; if it is a closed tank, which is the most common and arguably the best design, it is fitted with a **manway** for inspection and entry. It also will have a valve fitted to the bottom for pumping in wort and drawing out the beer, and other fittings in the top for a pressure relief safety valve and a CIP (clean-in-place) pipe and sprayball.

To the outside of the tank wall is welded one or more **cooling jackets**, which permit thermostatic cooling of the tank by way of the

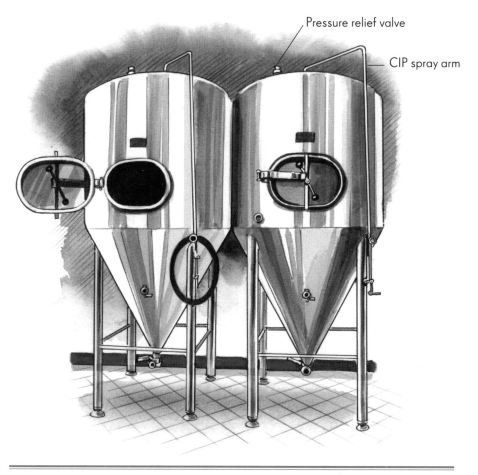

Pressure relief valve

CIP spray arm

Pub fermenters. Cylindroconical fermenting tanks, insulated and fitted with cooling jackets. The tank on the left is open for drying.

glycol chiller. Next comes a layer of insulation, and finally, the outer skin, or ***cladding***, which is usually made of thinner stainless steel.

Normally, the top of the vessel is a single piece of stainless formed in the shape of a dish. It is not insulated. The bottom, which is always insulated, is either a dish or a cone. A conical-bottomed cylindrical fermenter is sometimes called a unitank because it is possible to conduct the entire fermentation and any required cold maturation (lagering) in the same vessel; yeast removal is facilitated by the conical shape of the bottom.

The most critical specification of a fermenter, or any beer tank, is the smoothness of the interior, especially the weld seams. These must be ground and polished to exacting standards because they must be capable of being cleaned. A rough surface is a sure harbor for soil deposits and, sooner or later, bacteria.

Some breweries have secondary fermenters, also called *lager tanks*. These are either horizontal cylinders or dish-bottomed vertical tanks. They are used for maturation and also for clarification of the fermented beer. Often fining agents are added to these tanks to help yeast and other haze-forming matter settle out.

Almost every brewpub *filter* is of one of two designs: a pressure leaf filter or a sheet filter. Both work by pumping the beer through a layer of material that removes particulate matter, either by attaching them

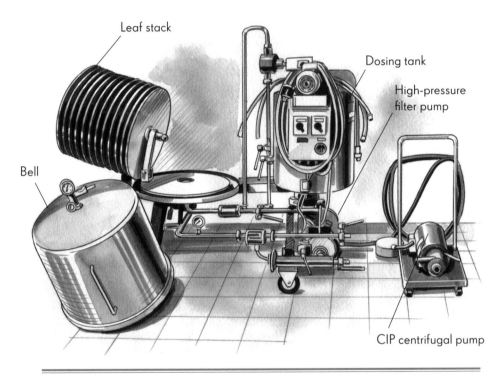

Filter/CIP pump. The type of pressure leaf filter typically used in small breweries. During operation, the bell (left) is clamped to the base of the filter leaf stack, and a layer of powdered filter media is formed on the leaves. The dosing tank (right) is the reservoir that holds the media slurry for injection into the beer stream. Alongside is a small sanitary centrifugal pump, used for CIP of tanks and sometimes for the transfer of unfiltered beer.

(*adsorption*) or physically obstructing them. Filtration has been called "instant aging" because it does the same job in removing all the hazy and often harsh-tasting colloidal particles suspended in the young beer. It is the key to the 10- to 14-day production cycle that most pubs follow.

The filter is listed as optional because not all pub breweries filter their beer. They rely on settling, aided usually by fining agents, to achieve acceptable clarity and flavor. This is perfectly acceptable, but it introduces an element of uncertainty, as different beers will "drop bright" at different rates. It usually requires more time from brew kettle to glass.

Serving tanks, also sometimes called bright beer tanks, serve as a substitute for kegs in some pubs. They are a great time-saver — it is far easier and faster to clean, sanitize, and fill one 10-barrel server than 20 half-barrel kegs. Physically, serving tanks resemble dish-bottomed fermenters. They may be built like fermenters, individually jacketed and glycol cooled, or they may be built as simple single-wall vessels like kegs, in which case they are kept in a walk-in cooler, just as kegs would be.

The ***walk-in cooler*** is just a large, built-in refrigerator for keeping tanks cold, including, sometimes, the cold liquor back. It is listed as optional because you can do without it if you have all your bright tanks jacketed and piped into the glycol system. This is how Blackstone is set up. It is not the cheapest way to go, but the owners wanted the tanks out in the restaurant/bar area, where they make a strong visual impression.

The ***draft beer system*** can be regarded as including the servers and walk-in, but it also includes the carbon dioxide tank, beer lines, fittings, and faucets that convey and pour the beer at the bar. The whole system is the brewer's responsibility, because no matter how wonderful his beer may be going into the servers, it will taste awful if the draft system is not maintained. In fact, one of the most common complaints of shipping breweries is that their distributors do not do a good job of making sure the draft lines and taps at their accounts are cleaned regularly and properly. This results in returned kegs and lost money. Pub brewers are in the enviable position of keeping control of their beer's quality all the way to the glass.

I've already noted how the ***transfer pump*** and all the associated hoses and fittings are used, but there's another pump that comes into play: the ***CIP (clean in place) pump***. In a pub brewery, the usual method of cleaning tanks and other equipment is to circulate hot

Calibrated
sight glass

Manway arm

Carbonation tester

Serving tank. A bright beer tank, right, in a small shipping brewery. A calibrated sight glass is mounted on the right, and hanging from the manway arm is a Zahm and Nagel carbonation tester.

cleaning solution through them and let the chemicals and water pressure do the cleaning. Brewers try to avoid manual cleaning as much as possible — it requires entry into enclosed spaces and is dangerous, tedious, and exhausting.

For tank cleaning, CIP means making a hose loop from the tank bottom to the circulating pump to the CIP arm, which terminates in a *sprayball* mounted near the roof of the tank. The brewer puts some hot water in the bottom of the tank, makes up the loop, then adds the cleaning agent, closes the tank manway door, and starts the pump. The ball sprays detergent on the entire surface of the tank, cleaning the same way that your dishwasher does.

However, there are limits. Even though he will CIP everything he can, a pub brewer still does manual cleaning. The biggest job is shoveling or hoeing out the mash/lauter tuns. Most do not have motorized rakes, so the mash must be stirred with a big paddle, and the spent grain has to be pulled or pushed out after the kettle is full. In larger breweries the motorized rake assembly not only cuts the mash bed but also pushes the spent grain into a discharge chute located in the false bottom.

Well, that's the tour of what was my world for more than a decade and a half. Now that I am back in homebrewing, I find that it still permeates my thinking. I want to apply what I learned to the challenge of making beer on an even smaller scale.

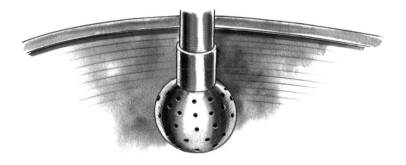

Kettle sprayball. A typical sprayball fitted to the CIP pipe (arm) of a brewery vessel — in this case, a kettle.

The modern, 30-barrel, four-vessel brewhouse at the Blackstone Brewing Company in Nashville. Left to right: mash kettle, lauter tun, wort kettle, hot liquor tank, cold liquor tank. The squat vessel on the near side of the work platform is the whirlpool.

Alternatively, the two-vessel pub brewery at the Blackstone Restaurant & Brewery. The third vessel, at the left, is the hot liquor tank and is considered a utility because it only supplies hot water for the process. Note the control panel mounted to the work platform: it has pump switches and thermostats for the kettle and hot liquor steam jackets.

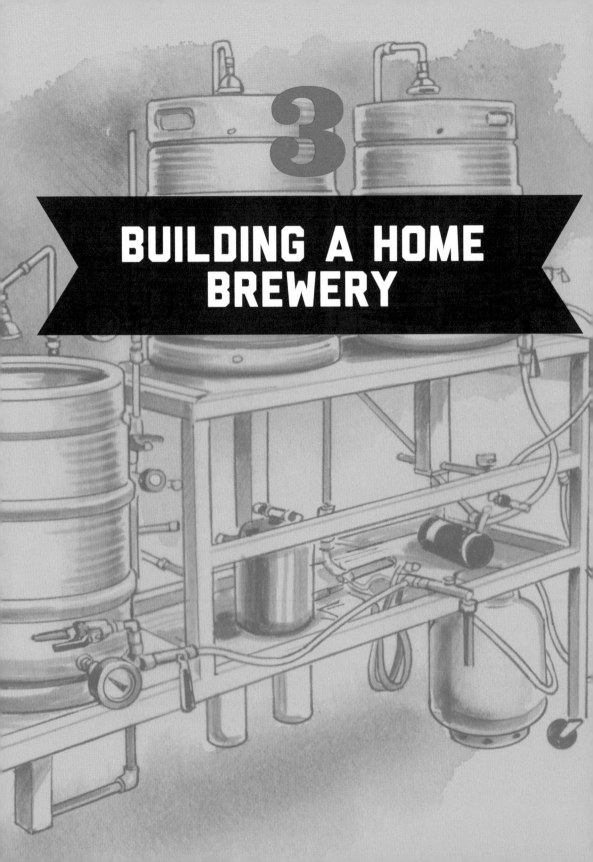

3

BUILDING A HOME BREWERY

Having taken a look at how brewpubs make beer and the equipment they use, it is time to explore the options in setting up a home brewery. There are many differences between even the smallest pub system and what is feasible in a private home. Size matters. Brewpubs typically make beer in batches ranging from 217 to 465 U.S. gallons (7 to 15 U.S. barrels). Their equipment usually is a mix of custom-built brewing vessels (e.g., the mash/lauter tun) and general industrial and commercial equipment sized and specified for its intended use (e.g., sanitary pumps, glycol chiller). Homebrewers make 5- to 15-gallon batches, mostly using equipment that has been built from scratch or modified to serve a role never foreseen by the manufacturer.

Sometimes you run across a pub or even a small micro that has been put together in this way. The common term for such operations is "Frankenbrewery." That may not sound kind, but — if the beer is good — it could be taken as a compliment. After all, the main point of the Frankenstein story is that the monster *lived*. Likewise, the (successful) Frankenbrewery *works*. For a homebrewer, the term is definitely a compliment. Engineering a system is quite an accomplishment, even if it is backyard, patchwork engineering. By contrast, the ready-made rack systems seem, to some homebrewers, to take half the fun out of it. For certain, they require that you adapt yourself to them, rather than the other way around.

Okay, let's break it down. If we're going to build a brewery, what do we need?

Space

For some homebrewers it's part of the garage, or the deck, or the cellar, or the kitchen, or some other room of the house. Some brave renters manage to make beer in studio apartments. Generally, where there's a will, there's a way.

The first decision to be made, assuming you have a choice, is whether to brew (that is, create and boil your wort) indoors or out. The primary benefits that come with brewing outdoors are flexibility in layout and getting the heat and smell out of the house. For indoor brewing, the main positives are comfort and consistency. Outdoor brewing means being hot in the summer and cold in the winter. The fluctuating ambient temperatures can also lead to process problems, especially in very cold weather. Insulation requirements for a mash/lauter tun, for example, are much different in 10°F weather than they are in 90°F weather. On the other hand, indoor brewing raises ventilation issues, and it imposes a significant load on the air conditioner in hot weather. All told, in a climate like my home state of Tennessee's, the best option is to brew outdoors most of the year but to move all or most of the brewing operation indoors in the winter.

The spousal dimension of this decision is outside the scope of this book.

HOW DOES YOUR SPACE STACK UP?

You can set up a home brewery practically anywhere, but not all spots are created equal.

- ▸ Having a cool cellar is an advantage.
- ▸ Having a garage is an advantage.
- ▸ Having a backyard, patio, or deck is an advantage.
- ▸ A floor drain in your brewery and/or kegging area is a big advantage.
- ▸ Tempered air (heating and cooling) in your fermenting area is a big advantage.
- ▸ Having a place indoors for a second refrigerator is a necessity.
- ▸ Lack of ventilation in your brewing space is an obstacle that must be overcome.

Utilities

Just like a pub brewer, the home brewer has to consider the available utilities in putting together a brewery. The time to do this is before you start spending money on equipment.

WATER AND SEWER

The quality of your water supply is obviously a major issue, and I discuss water treatment in a later chapter. When it comes to sewer, a city connection is preferable because yeast slurry and cleaning chemicals are major trouble for a septic tank. I'll give some general guidelines for dealing with septic tanks, but you should also consult your septic service company or other experienced homebrewers in your area. Remember, this comes from somebody who has never had to deal with a septic tank.

In practice, city treatment systems are a lot more resistant to shock simply because of their size. However, commercial breweries, even small brewpubs, are finding themselves under increasing scrutiny from environmental authorities.

One thing you need to consider when setting up your brewery is how you are going to get your spent cleaning solutions and sanitizers to the drain. These things cannot be dumped on your lawn. In my case, a fair amount of the lifting and carrying I do is hauling liquid waste to the kitchen sink. I wish my house had a drain cleanout or some other point of access closer to the deck where I do my brewing. In fact, the main reason I have not set up my brewery in the garage is that it has no floor drain, and neither does the driveway.

SUGGESTIONS FOR HOMEBREWERS WITH SEPTIC TANKS

▸ Minimize your use of chemicals. Don't mix up 5 gallons of sanitizer when 1 gallon will do.

▸ Keep wastewater temperatures and volumes reasonable.

▸ Don't send spent grains or trub (kettle residue) down the drain. Compost them or take them to the landfill.

▸ If possible, consider a miniature version of the most primitive sort of wastewater pretreatment, a holding tank. This could be a 55-gallon or smaller drum where all your liquid brewery waste goes. It offers a place where it can cool down and, if necessary, be neutralized with washing soda or citric acid (depending on its pH) before being sent down the drain.

▸ Yeast is a living thing and its biological oxygen demand (BOD) is so high that, even if you use a holding tank, it can play havoc in a septic system. You should kill it before sending it down the drain. However, killing yeast with a chemical sanitizer is problematic. Unless you have a microscope and some training, it is hard to check on whether you have given a sufficient dose for sufficient time. Heat is the better method. Mix the slurry with an equal volume of water in an appropriately sized nonstick pot, heat it to 180°F, and hold there for half an hour, stirring occasionally. Boiling is fine but may make cleanup harder.

▸ Clean your septic tank regularly.

ELECTRICITY

If you have 230-volt service to your home you have options. By adding a circuit or two you could go with electric heating for your brewery vessels. This is convenient and clean, with no carbon monoxide issues, making it possible to brew indoors year-round — although you still need to look at ventilation for the steam from your kettle. Ongoing electrical costs are higher than for natural gas but (depending on local rates) probably lower than propane. And up-front costs for new circuitry can be high, if you have to hire an electrician to do the work.

All this refers to making or buying a custom brew kettle and perhaps other vessels with a high-wattage, low-heat-density heating element. Electric kitchen stoves have a bad reputation for kettle boiling. However, a modern conventional electric range usually has at least one 8-inch element rated at 2,000 watts, and theoretically this is enough power to boil a 5-gallon batch of wort. For some ranges, a special "canning element" of even higher wattage is available. By comparison, many 10-gallon electric brew kettles are fitted with a 3,500-watt element, for a batch twice the size. The problem is heat transfer. In an electric kettle, the heater element is mounted directly in the wall and is surrounded by the wort, whereas the heat from a stove element must be carried by conduction through the kettle bottom.

Suffice it to say, electric stoves can work for 5-gallon batches, if you have the right sort of kettle. The best is a stockpot with a flat bottom, either all aluminum or stainless with a layer of aluminum encapsulated. My own brew kettle, while far from ideal, fits this description, and I have been able to boil 6 gallons of water in it on my kitchen stove. It takes quite a while to reach boiling point, though.

I have no direct experience with ceramic cooktops, but from the few stories I have heard, it seems that the key once again is good contact with the heating surface and good conduction. It may work, but you need a high-wattage element.

So far we have gone into the use of electricity, but we also need to look at it from the opposite viewpoint: is electricity really needed in a brewery? The answer is: not for heating. If you work by daylight, you can brew outdoors or in a shed without any electric service at hand. Whether you should is another matter. Before you commit yourself to such an arrangement, read the forthcoming discussion on pumps.

NATURAL GAS OR PROPANE

Propane is the usual source of heat for home breweries. No installation required. Just buy a burner — they usually come with a hose and regulator — and pick up a tank at the nearest home goods store. Propane burners are expensive to operate, however. If your home has natural gas, you should look into the possibility of retrofitting your burner with a natural gas orifice and tapping into your natural gas line. This is pretty straightforward if you brew in the garage and your water heater is located there or in an adjacent utility room.

The biggest problem with propane is the need for ventilation. Carbon monoxide poisoning is no joke, and it's hardly an exaggeration to suggest that propane burners can be safely used only outdoors. If you put your brewery in a garage or shed, then at a minimum the doors and windows need to be fully open when the burner is running. In some sheds this still might not be enough. A good-sized fan to pull air through the brewery space is a wise investment.

I have read stories of homebrewers who have managed to brew with propane indoors without killing themselves, but they all seem to have taken extraordinary measures to ensure adequate ventilation (and perhaps had some extraordinary luck as well). I strongly caution against such a setup.

Gas kitchen stoves are a reasonable alternative to propane for a 5-gallon brewery; in my view, if indoor brewing is feasible otherwise, then there is every reason to take advantage of your gas stove. It may be possible to set the kettle over two burners, which almost doubles the heat and makes for a vigorous boil.

Equipment for the Draft Beer System

As promised, I am starting with the thing most homebrewers think of last. Build your draft beer system first, and you will be happy you did.

YOUR SHOPPING LIST SHOULD READ:

- Refrigerator
- CO_2 cylinder
- 5-gallon stainless steel premix soda kegs, often called Cornelius kegs, or Cornies

- CO_2 gas pressure regulator, usually just called a regulator
- Gas fittings and hoses
- Beer fittings and hoses
- Beer faucet(s)

REFRIGERATOR

The usual choice for a refrigerator is a moderately sized, conventional design with the freezer mounted above the refrigerator section, which is better for beer because it gives more square feet of floor space. This type of refrigerator will hold at least four kegs, or two kegs plus a pail or carboy.

It is a good idea to remove the vegetable bins and make a sturdier floor with some lumber and plywood. The other modification you need to make is to drill a hole in one side or the other for the gas hose to pass through. Measure the gas hose diameter carefully and try to make the hole just big enough. The hole should be up fairly high on the wall, and toward the front. Drill a pilot hole first — ½ inch is good. Then drill the hole to size using a step bit on the outside (if it is sheet metal) and a Forstner bit on the inside (which is almost certainly plastic).

I think I can hear some objections, and, yes, there is peril here. If at all possible, you need to find service diagrams for your refrigerator and make sure that the refrigerant (Freon) lines do not run in the side wall of your appliance. If they do, be sure to figure out exactly where (the manufacturer's website should help). In most refrigerators the Freon runs in the back, but there are lots of exceptions. I was unable to find drawings for my secondhand Hotpoint, and, after a lot of fear and procrastination, I decided to give it a shot anyway. I just pierced the outer skin with the pilot bit and then poked around with it trying to feel for any obstacles. I lucked out, finding none, but obviously there are no guarantees. The alternative is to keep the gas cylinder inside the refrigerator, which is a waste of precious cold space.

Many homebrewers use a chest freezer with an auxiliary thermostat for their second, or even their first, refrigerator. These provide more bang for the buck (i.e., more keg capacity for the price).

For lager brewing, you need a dedicated second refrigerator fitted with an auxiliary thermostat. The built-in unit cannot be set much higher than 40°F, and primary fermentation temperatures for lager are normally 46 to 53°F. There are several types of thermostats available from homebrew supply shops, one of the cheapest being the classic Johnson Controls dial unit. The newer digital models, although more expensive, are much easier to work with, especially at the beginning.

CO_2 CYLINDER

The carbon dioxide cylinder is a straightforward item. You can get nice shiny aluminum ones from your local welding or homebrew supply shop, or you can save a little by getting a reconditioned steel model on the Internet. Aluminum is preferable because of the weight. A more important decision is the size. I think a 10-pounder is about as big as you will want to carry any distance.

CO_2 GAS PRESSURE REGULATOR

The regulator is an important piece of gear, so it is worth getting a decent one. Secondhand is fine, but make sure you get a model made for carbon dioxide. Every type of gas has its own cylinder with its own fittings, and while adapters are available, by the time you have bought an adapter and changed out the gauges for ones with a suitable pressure range, you will not be ahead in money.

TWO SAFETY TIPS:

1. Watch your feet and shins when you carry your cylinder.

2. Never leave a CO_2 cylinder in a car in the sun. Even in mild weather, it can get hot enough to elevate the internal pressure and blow the safety valve. You'll find out when you open the door. Don't ask me how I know this.

Be sure your regulator is fitted with a hose nipple, a shutoff valve, and a check valve. The latter is a one-way valve that serves as the last line of defense should beer back up into the gas line. It is possible to clean out and rebuild a soaked regulator, but it's a hassle and the parts are not widely available. Your draft beer system will be down while you wait for them. The best source I know of is Foxx Equipment in Kansas City, but they do not sell retail. You can find the right kit in their online catalog and have your local shop order it for you.

Speaking of gauges, I think dual-gauge regulators are worth the extra cost. The second gauge reads the primary side pressure, that is, the pressure in the cylinder, which gives you a warning when the gas is getting low. Be aware, though, that carbon dioxide is held in liquid form. Only when the cylinder is nearly empty does the last of the liquid evaporate, and only then does the pressure begin to drop. Bottom line: When you see the needle drop out of the green zone, don't procrastinate.

Get your cylinder down to the welders' supply or wherever you refill right away.

5-GALLON STAINLESS STEEL SODA KEGS

Soda kegs are widely available at a great variety of prices. Some Internet vendors offer them for half the price you will see in most home-brew supply stores. Generally the cheapest ones have no guarantee, or at most the seller may claim to have pressure-tested it. On the other hand, if you decide to pay more for a reconditioned unit, find out what that word means. The usual process is to replace the plug O-rings (the plugs are the fittings that the gas and liquid couplers fit on to) and the large O-ring that seals the lid. The more expensive pieces — the poppet valves in the plugs, and the pressure relief valve in the lid — usually are not replaced unless they leak. Short of buying new, which is very expensive, any choice you make is something of a gamble.

The two styles of kegs are pin-lock and ball-lock, so called for the way the coupler attaches to the plug. They are also called Coke and Pepsi kegs, because Coca-Cola uses the pin-lock style, while everybody else, including Pepsi-Cola, uses the ball-lock. I prefer the pin-lock, but they are much harder to find on the used market and often command higher prices. Ball-lock kegs are made by several companies, and the key working parts, including the plugs and poppet valves, are not interchangeable between different makers. So if you buy used kegs and find that one has a leak, be sure to take the defective part to the homebrew supply shop with you to match it.

Some beginning brewers worry about their beer being tainted by the "soda-pop smell" of the keg. In practice, a good overnight soak in a cleaning solution (I use Five Star PBW at 3 ounces per 5 gallons), followed by a thorough rinse, is all I have found necessary to deal with any slight residual odor. It's only the rubber parts that can absorb odors, and there is not much rubber in a keg. The biggest piece by far is the large lid O-ring, which in a worst-case scenario is not that expensive to replace.

GAS FITTINGS AND HOSES

Gas fittings, hoses, and couplers are fairly easy to find; the same places that sell cylinders and regulators carry them. They can get expensive, especially if you go in for brass or stainless quick-disconnects. I recommend the plastic disconnects for those places where you feel they would be helpful. The illustration on page 44 shows an example of one such setup.

I put it together so that I could disconnect my cylinder and use it in other locations without having to open the refrigerator and disconnect the gas line from the keg. Note that the gas line is clear, thick-walled vinyl. I prefer a clear gas line because, if I ever screw up and get beer in the line, I want to be able to see it. However, the thin-walled stuff usually found at hardware stores and homebrew supply places is not sturdy enough for gas. The hose at welding supply places is usually colored. If you want clear, you may have to have some ordered from Foxx or another beverage specialist.

BEER FAUCET AND HOSES

The beer faucet and dispense line is pretty simple also. You should attach 5 to 6 feet of $^3/_{16}$-inch-inside-diameter vinyl tubing to your liquid coupler. As with gas hose, you need the thick-walled stuff — $^7/_{16}$-inch outside-diameter in this case. This will give the correct flow rate and balance for dispensing your beer without foaming. Gas pressure on the keg should be 12 to 15 PSI. Less is not better.

One problem with $^3/_{16}$-inch line is that it is hard to push over the $^1/_4$-inch hose barbs found on many couplers. The easiest way to get it to fit is to (1) soak the end of the vinyl tubing in very hot water — at least 140°F; and (2) wipe the hose barb with a thin coating of Petrol-Gel, which is a sanitary food-grade petroleum jelly. Then just push them together. You probably won't need a hose clamp, but I suggest one for peace of mind. For other hose-barb connections, including all gas ones, hose clamps are definitely required.

For a start, you can just use a "cobra head" faucet attached to the end of your beer line. This means you have to open the fridge every time you want to pull a beer, so many people go for a more elaborate setup by drilling a hole through the refrigerator door and then fitting a shank and a regular draft beer tap. If you do this, be sure to install a drip tray as well.

There are lots of kits for sale through homebrew supply houses and other outlets that offer most or all of the components necessary to build a home draft system, including the shank and beer faucet. The best ones include nearly everything except the refrigerator. They are worth investigating and may prove to be a bargain compared with buying every component individually.

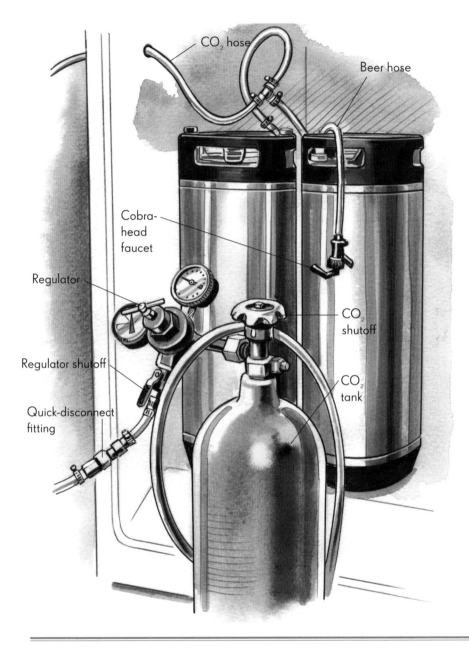

Draft system. A refrigerator with two Cornelius kegs, a carbon dioxide tank, a regulator, and hoses. The keg on the left is hooked up to dispense. Note the cobra-head faucet on the end of the dispense hose and the gas hose (fitted with a tee) coming into the refrigerator through a hole in the wall. Also note the quick-disconnect fitting on the gas hose.

A final bit of advice: before you start buying, get a look at a working draft system if you can. The equipment is simple and low-tech, but you need to understand a little about the fittings and how it all works before you start laying down your money.

Now, back to making beer.

Water Filter

Water treatment is discussed elsewhere in some detail; here I'll just briefly state the practicalities. First off, every home brewery needs a chlorine/sediment filter. The least expensive option is a marine/RV unit such as the Culligan RV-500 or RV-600. For outdoor use you will also need a potable-water hose. These are always white in color. You can find them at any hardware or home improvement store. A nice accessory is a shutoff valve for the hose end; it saves a lot of steps on brew day.

If your water has problems, then a reverse osmosis filter system is required. This will be a significant expenditure.

Malt Mill *(Optional)*

Milling is a balancing act. If the crush is too fine, it can cause problems with the wort runoff. If it's too coarse, lautering will go smoothly but you will not get as much sugar from the malt as you should. Thin beer is better than no beer, but every brewer I know dislikes both options.

There is no space in a general introductory book for a detailed write-up of my tests on homebrew mills, and the test equipment necessary to quantify the crush, while simple (a set of 8-inch test sieves with matching cover and bottom pan), is too dear to be cost effective for the individual homebrewer. Your best test equipment is your own set of eyes.

The photos on the inside front cover show properly and improperly crushed grain. The properly crushed sample was milled in a commercial unit that is similar in basic design to most homebrew mills: it crushes the malt between two steel rolls. The improperly crushed sample is too coarse. It was done at factory settings on a very popular homebrew mill, which I am not naming because my tests with other mills have shown comparable results. I have not tested every brand of mill out there, but I have done enough to say that most homebrew mills, at their stock setting, yield a crush that runs the gamut from coarse to extremely coarse. You can expect less-than-optimum yields from them.

Therefore, my first recommendation is: If you're going to buy a mill, get one with an adjustable gap. Then get a set of feeler gauges and start experimenting with the settings. Be sure that the gap is uniform from end to end. Mill setting is tedious but worth it.

As to particulars, if you look in the recipes chapter (page 226) you can see what I get in terms of extract efficiency: about 90 percent with my setup. The only "cheat" I have is access to the pub mill pictured in chapter 2. I have no doubt that I could do as well with a good, *properly adjusted* homebrew roller mill.

The alternative to roller mills is the old-style corn mill that crushes the grain between two serrated plates, one fixed and the other rotating. The crush is adjustable by means of a setscrew and locking wing nut, which fixes the gap between the plates. I use the term "fix" loosely; usually the outer plate wobbles quite a bit. Some homebrewers have modified the mill in order to eliminate the play and get a uniform gap. Others think that is a bad idea and that you want the plate to "float"

Rebel mill. A prototype two-roller homebrew mill. To the right is a sample of milled malt and behind it a set of test sieves used for analyzing the crush.

because this actually gives a better crush than the modification will. My own tests of a stock Corona mill yielded a satisfactory crush, so I tend to agree with the second group.

My research indicates that the main disadvantages of a corn mill, compared to a roller mill, are: first, it is much slower (though easier to crank by hand); second, adjustment is rather touchy — a quarter turn on the screw makes a big difference; and third, it requires some backyard engineering to devise a suitable mounting frame/platform and a shroud or hood to contain the dust and direct the flow into your grain bucket.

Then there is the option of having your malt milled at the home-brew store. This is the cheapest way to go, but chances are the grain will be very coarsely milled. Mill a cupful and examine the crush carefully. If it is too coarse, ask the shop owner to adjust the mill. If that gets a "no," the next-best remedy is to run the grist through the mill twice.

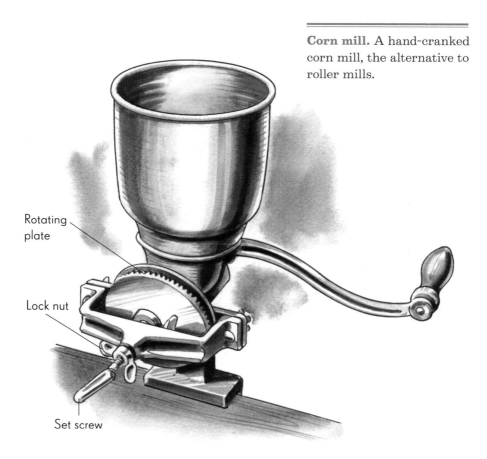

Corn mill. A hand-cranked corn mill, the alternative to roller mills.

Rotating plate

Lock nut

Set screw

For homebrew volumes, an elaborate grist case is unnecessary. Most homebrewers who do their own milling just use a 5- or 6-gallon plastic bucket to catch and hold the grist.

Mash Mixer *(Optional)*

I have yet to see a homebrew version of a grist hydrator, probably because it would be quite expensive, not to mention difficult to build and use. Nonetheless, the equipment serves a real purpose. Getting a smooth, evenly mixed mash is not that easy, and hitting the target temperature is vital when you are doing single infusion. Too hot and the enzymes will be destroyed; too cold and the enzymes won't work. And it does not take very long to destroy the enzymes, particularly the beta amylase, if the mash comes in too high. Fact is, the most critical time for a single-infusion mash is the first 5 minutes. If the temperature is too high at the beginning, the ratio of sugars in the final wort will be altered. This is especially true when working with British or continental malts, which have fewer enzymes to begin with. The best option is to mix the mash to the right temperature as it goes in, and a grist hydrator makes it fairly easy to do this.

Without a hydrator and water mixing manifold, the homebrewer who is doing single infusion in a mash/lauter tun faces a challenge. You'll find more on mash mixing in the chapter on homebrewing procedures (page 128), but to put it simply, employing a mash mixer makes your life easier.

Mash mixer. A 5-gallon porcelain kettle, shown here with a paddle on the kitchen stove, makes for a fine mash mixer.

The overshooting point begs for a bit of explanation. When you mix the mash, you have to keep stirring until all the balls of dough are broken up. Only when this is accomplished — and it can take 5 minutes, even with a 5-gallon batch — can you turn your attention to the thermometer.

The best way to sum all this up: a mash mixer is simpler to use because it allows you to separate stirring-in from setting the temperature. Brewpubs can do without a mash mixer because the hydrator takes care of the mixing, which leaves the brewer free to manage the temperature. In a home brewery, that same degree of precision is most easily achieved by taking the two tasks in sequence rather than attempting to combine them.

Any 5-gallon stockpot or canner can be used for a mash mixer. You may already have one in your kitchen, or you may have bought a 5-gallon kettle for making extract beer. If not, it is one of the cheapest upgrades you can make.

If you are building a 10-gallon brewery, adding a mash mixer will cost you more. If possible it also should be fitted with a big ball valve (1½ inches or larger) and set above the lauter tun, so that you can drop the mash in by gravity. The alternative is scooping the mash in by hand. A 10-gallon stockpot is too big to lift. If you are going to this much trouble, you should try to work out a system in which the mash mixer does double duty as the hot liquor back, as I used to do it. You will also need a second propane burner for heating the mash.

THE ADVANTAGES OF A MASH MIXER:

▸ No preheating

▸ No need for precise water volume measurements

▸ No "fudge factor" required to account for cooling during stirring

▸ Tempering requires only cold water; no need to have boiling water on hand

▸ Mixing is more thorough and faster, as there is no need for caution

▸ In case of an overshoot, it is noted and corrected almost immediately

▸ Ability to do step mashing (described in the next section)

Mash/Lauter Tun and Hot Liquor Back

In most home breweries, these two pieces of equipment are similar in appearance and size, and almost identical in their construction. In a high-end 10-gallon brewery they are both modified kettles — in fact, the hot liquor back in a rack system is often identical to the brew kettle, except for the hop strainer that may be fitted in the latter. The mash/lauter tun is also a kettle, but it is fitted with a false bottom screen to hold back the spent grains and allow the liquid wort to be strained off after mashing is complete.

The cheaper alternative is to fabricate these vessels out of a plastic picnic cooler, which can make the cost a fraction of what it would be for a stainless steel kettle. There are a number of alternative designs, but the most important difference is the type of strainer fitted, which has great implications for the lautering method and efficiency.

To define this term: efficiency compares how much sugar you extract from the mash with how much sugar could be extracted if every last bit of starch were broken down by the malt enzymes and rinsed out of the spent grains. Needless to say, 100 percent is the maximum and is never seen. However, the big commercial breweries regularly get 95 to 98 percent. Pub breweries and small micros can get more than 90 percent. Homebrewers can reach similar figures depending on their technique and the design of their lauter tun.

Efficiency, however, is not the sole consideration. Consistency is also important, and wort quality even more so. Cost also has to be a factor. All experts agree that the false bottom design offers the best potential efficiency and excellent wort quality. It is the only design currently used in commercial equipment. However, in my experience in both the pub brewery and home brewery, it can be prone to inconsistency, basically caused by uneven drainage, or "channeling" as it is often called. It is also the most expensive and difficult design to build; it is so difficult, in fact, that if I ever decide to switch to a false bottom I will undoubtedly buy a ready-made one from one of the homebrew specialty manufacturers.

If you want to go with a false bottom, I suggest stainless steel. I also prefer a slotted screen to perforated, but both work. If you go for plastic, try to work out a way to weight the rim down and/or seat it tightly against the edge of the vessel, because they are prone to floating. The easiest option is to buy a cooler already fitted with a matched false bottom and spigot.

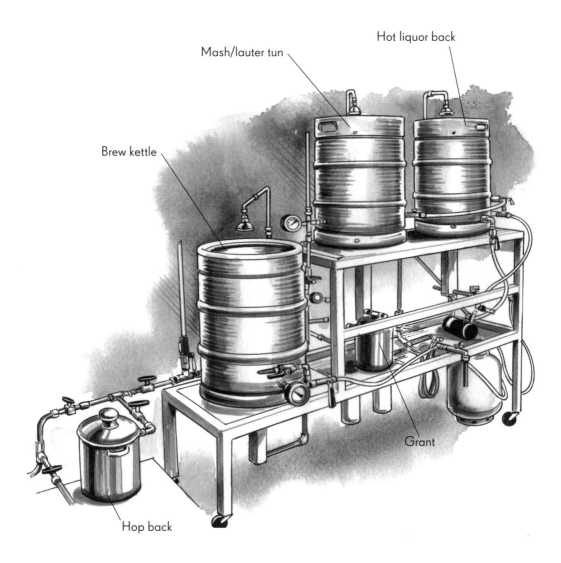

Mash/lauter tun

Hot liquor back

Brew kettle

Grant

Hop back

Rack system. A three-vessel, 10-gallon home brewery with (left to right) brew kettle and mash/lauter tun. The small pot below the mash/lauter tun is a grant; the one to the left of the kettle is a hop back.

By its nature, a false bottom is most easily made round and fitted in a round cooler or other vessel. By serendipity, the round beverage coolers are among the best. They cost more, but they have better insulation than most rectangular coolers and are actually designed for hot liquids.

If you want to save money, the most cost-effective design is to base your lauter tun on a square or rectangular picnic cooler. These are a natural match for a pipe manifold, which is easier to home build than a false bottom and, if properly executed, can offer good drainage and efficiency. They are less prone to channeling and the dreaded "stuck mash" than a false bottom. This is the design I chose, and I detail the process later in the Projects chapter (page 194).

Whatever type you decide on, the lauter tun and hot liquor back need to be approximately the same size as your batch, or slightly larger. A warning about picnic coolers: sometimes the capacity is less than advertised. This is one item you should look at closely before you buy.

The third option for lauter-tun drainage is a stainless steel braid, as used for reinforcement on many toilet tank and washing machine hoses. It is a good strainer and can serve as a replacement for slotted pipe in a manifold. The main disadvantage is its flexibility, which makes it hard to keep the arrangement in place, as is required for even drainage. Braids are most often used as a simple single-strand "pigtail" collector in mash/lauter tuns, designed for infusion rinsing, which is often called batch sparging. This is an alternative lautering scheme that eliminates the need for even drainage by forgoing a certain percentage of the potential extract. The method is discussed in the appendix (page 252); I have experimented with it, but I prefer conventional lautering.

In the section on mash mixers I mentioned the possibility of step mashing — that is, mixing the mash at a lower temperature and putting it through a series of rests at progressively higher temperatures. This has some advantages, explained in depth further along in the book. Precise, simple temperature control is also desirable. Step mashing can be done by normal hands-on methods, but easy automatic temperature control requires more elaborate measures. This is the rationale of the recirculating infusion mash system (RIMS) and its younger sibling, the heat exchanger recirculating mash system (HERMS). Basically, the systems start with a simple mash/lauter tun and then add a pump and some other hardware, so that the wort can be circulated through a heating device that is controlled by a thermostat before being returned to the tun. RIMS uses a heat chamber, usually made from large-diameter copper pipe, in which is fitted a water heating element that heats the wort as it passes through the chamber. The HERMS passes the wort through a copper coil that is immersed in hot water to accomplish the heating — a simple heat exchanger, hence the name.

RIMS and HERMS are the ultimate in ease and sophisticated control. They make brew day much simpler and even save time, because the recirculation clarifies the wort during conversion, eliminating the need for a separate clarifying step. On the other hand, putting one of these items together takes time, money, and/or skill — though the more time and skill you have, the less money it will take.

One nice thing about RIMS and HERMS is that they are upgrades: you do not have to scrap your lauter tun or anything else; you just have to add a few pieces of equipment to what you already have. Two of those pieces, though — the pump and the electronic controller — are high-ticket items, so the overall cost for retrofitting a RIMS is at least a few hundred dollars.

The hot liquor back is often matched to the lauter tun, though it need not be. During my early days of homebrewing, I would heat my sparge liquor in the brew kettle and then, as soon as the mash went into the lauter tun, I would move the hot water to the mash mixer and leave it there on top of the stove, on very low heat, to hold the temperature until it was time to sparge. This worked fine, though it meant ladling the sparge liquor onto the grain bed a cupful at a time.

Having been spoiled by the amenities of a pub system, and also doing most of my brewing outdoors, I find it safer and easier to use an insulated hot liquor back. I built mine from a picnic cooler, as described in the Projects chapter (page 194). If you do the same, then try to select a cooler with insulation in the lid. Many coolers do not have this, and they lose heat quickly. This is also a consideration if you forgo a separate mash mixer and use your lauter tun for mashing.

Sparge Arm *(Optional)*
The sparge arm is composed of one or more perforated pipes that are suspended above the lauter tun. It distributes water over the surface of the grain bed during sparging. This can be done by hand with a Pyrex pitcher, and I did that for years. However, sparge arms are cheap and easy to build, and if you can set your hot liquor back on a higher level, so that the sparge water feeds by gravity, they make the operation less tedious. If you have a round lauter tun, there are some nice ready-made rotating designs available.

Recirculation Arm *(Optional)*

The recirculation arm is another convenience. Like the sparge arm, it eliminates the need to ladle hot liquid onto the surface of the grain bed by hand. Unlike the sparge arm, though, it requires you to have at least one pump, so you need to make a decision on this big-ticket item beforehand.

In the Projects chapter (page 194) I describe how I fitted my lauter tun lid with both a recirc arm and a sparge arm.

Grant

Some sort of grant is necessary in order to recirculate and clarify the wort before running it into the kettle. Any appropriately sized (1- to 2-gallon) bucket, stockpot, or even a large mixing bowl will serve the basic function. Recirculation can be done by ladling wort from the grant back to the top of the lauter tun. However, a grant is equally useful if you have a pump, because it serves as a buffer and a sampling point. The grant I built, described in the Projects chapter (page 194), is as simple as can be; it does not even have a valve.

Brew Kettle/Whirlpool

The first thing a homebrewer thinks of when deciding to move to all-grain is, "I need a mash/lauter tun." The next thought is, "I need a bigger brew kettle." However, the kettle is the bigger investment, so you need to put more thought into your decision and consider the size, the material, and the source.

HOW BIG?

The standard answer: About 1½ times your batch size is the smallest you should consider. That would translate into a 7.5-gallon (30-quart) kettle for 5-gallon batches. Unfortunately, depending on your circumstances, that may not be big enough. You need to think about the geometry of the kettle and how you will use it. If the kettle is short and squat (diameter equal to or greater than its height), then by the time you put 6.5 to 7 gallons of wort in it — which is typical, as most homebrewers boil off at least a gallon of liquid — the pot will be full to within a couple of inches of the brim. Even after boiling, you still may have only 3 or 4 inches of *freeboard*, as it is called. Ask yourself: How much, if any, lifting and moving of my kettle full of wort do I intend to do, before and after the boil? If you say "some," or "a lot," then how young and strong are you? Can you hold that kettle full of hot wort steady enough to avoid sloshing it on yourself? Every time you brew?

The kettle is the centerpiece of a brewery not because it is elaborate or exotic, but because it forces you to look at the big picture. Seven gallons of hot liquid should make anybody step back. It's dangerous. You need to come up with a plan for getting your wort from the lauter tun into the kettle, onto the burner, then to the heat exchanger, and finally into the fermenter without damaging either it or yourself. Depending on how you intend to do it, you may decide you need a bigger or deeper kettle. You may decide you need a helper. Or you may decide that a pump is not so much an amenity as a safety measure.

WHAT MATERIAL?

The two usual choices are aluminum and stainless steel. Stainless is far more popular, despite its higher cost; this is because it is the safe choice. Nobody argues that stainless will affect the flavor of the beer or give the drinkers Alzheimer's disease. I do not believe either of these claims about aluminum, but I am not going to defend my opinion here; there are references in the reading list in Resources to discussions on both these questions, and you can read them — and many more that they refer to — and make up your own mind. If you decide aluminum is safe, then the only case I make against it is that it is a soft metal, softer than brass or copper, and it should not be exposed to harsh acid or alkaline cleaners. You will have to be careful how you treat it. Scratching is not much of an issue with a kettle, because it needs only to be cleaned, not sanitized; but I would be reluctant to expose it regularly to even the milder types of brewery cleaners.

If you decide to go with stainless, then watch out. There is a huge range of prices and quality. Especially on Internet auction sites, it is easy to find stockpots whose true capacity is smaller than advertised, and which are made from inferior grades of stainless steel. Regarding the former: give a seller points for disclosing the true capacity. He is probably selling the same item another fellow offers for the same price.

Regarding the latter, here's a primer: stainless steel is an alloy of iron, chromium, and sometimes other metals. The chromium is what makes it stainless. It oxidizes to form a thin layer of chromium oxide on the surface, which is hard, smooth, and resists corrosion. (This layer can be scratched through, and if you do this, the metal may rust, especially in a damp environment. Chemicals can also attack the oxide layer.) Different grades contain various percentages of chromium and other metals. What is wanted for brewing purposes is a 300 series grade of stainless. The 300 series contains nickel as well as chromium, which improves resistance. The best grade for brewery hot liquor tanks and other highly corrosive environments is 316, but 304 is fine for kettles, fermenters, and kegs. Other 300 grades are also available. These may be optimized for different uses. For example, 303 is optimized for machining, whereas 304 is optimized for welding; but both are suitable for brewery equipment. On the other hand, the 200 series contains no nickel and is decidedly inferior. The 200 series has a lower nickel content and cannot be recommended. Even worse are grades which contain no nickel at all. These are often magnetic, and any stainless that will stick to a magnet should be rejected out of hand. In the cookware trade, American companies will usually name the grade according to the numeric system I have been using. Overseas manufacturers often use an older system that lists the alloys by approximate percentages. Thus, 18/0 means 18 percent chromium and no nickel. You want an 18/10 grade, which means 18 percent chromium and 10 nickel. That is roughly equivalent to grade 304 and should perform satisfactorily. Of course, manufacturing quality is a separate issue altogether, and it can be hard to evaluate based on Internet photos. It is always better to look at equipment close-up. In any case, if you see a stockpot advertised with *no* information about the grade of stainless, stay far away — and avoid other "deals" from this vendor as well.

One often-touted feature of many stockpots is a three-layer bottom, where a 5-millimeter-thick aluminum disc is encapsulated in the bottom of the pot between two layers of stainless steel. This helps to spread the heat more evenly, which is an advantage; stainless is a rotten conductor. However, it is probably more important for making soups or browning vegetables than for boiling wort. It is nothing to weigh against an inferior grade of stainless, but it is a plus if you want to boil your wort on an electric stove.

CONSIDER THE SOURCE

Here is an unhappy topic I cannot avoid. That is, the practice of converting brewery kegs into homebrewing vessels. Let's get one thing straight from the start — every keg is built for, and initially belongs to, a brewery. The owner's name is on the keg. Brewing companies lend their kegs to distributors, and distributors in turn lend them to the restaurants, clubs, and retail beer vendors who are their customers. Breweries sell beer, and their customers have the right to do with it as they see fit, within the bounds of law. They have no such right to the kegs. Rather, they have a duty to take care of them, and return them to the person or business they got them from, as soon as they can. The security deposit confers no property rights. It is simply a customary inducement, often agreed to among parties in a transaction where only one bears a risk. In this case, the risk is the loss of a valuable piece of equipment. Stainless kegs cost a lot, typically more than a brewer charges for the half barrel of beer inside.

Unfortunately, the inducement is often insufficient. Stainless steel prices have gone up in recent years, and deposits have not kept pace. As a result, the scrap value of a keg may be higher than the security deposit. A distributor would be money ahead by selling empty kegs to a salvage dealer rather than returning them to the brewery. Distributors do not do this, of course, because they value the goodwill of their suppliers. Their customers, on the other hand, who have no direct relationship with the brewery, are less likely to be careful to fulfill their obligations. If a liquor store sells a keg to an individual, it has no financial stake in whether that person returns it or not. It has his deposit; if he returns the keg, it is returned to him; if not, it is handed over to the distributor.

Regardless of whether the distributor or liquor store cares about getting the keg back, the facts are not changed. Anyone who buys a keg full of beer and, after disposing of the contents, retains the keg for his own use, is misappropriating another's property. If he saws off the top or otherwise alters it to turn it into a brew kettle or other equipment, he is destroying another's property. Once you understand that kegs are brewery property, these statements are not debatable.

Most people do not do obviously dishonest things, and I do not believe that great numbers of kegs are being taken by homebrewers under the impression, or pretext, that paying a security deposit confers ownership on them. (Though during my time at the pub, I did field a few calls from people with just this notion, who wanted me to fill "their" keg with Blackstone beer.) I am much more concerned about indirect participation in plain old theft — the "lifting" of kegs from unsecured areas by people who have no illusions about what they are doing. As I mentioned before, the rising price of stainless steel has made it an attractive target, just like copper and other valuable metals. The sad fact is, though, that it takes more than high prices to drive this trade. There are far too many scrap dealers who are willing to buy kegs, pipe, you name it, no questions asked. And those dealers are quite willing to sell kegs to you. It spares them the trouble of crushing them, and they can likely get a higher price to boot.

If you do not want to be a receiver of stolen property, then you have to ask the scrap dealer, or whoever is offering you kegs for sale, where he got them. The only acceptable answer is, from the brewery whose name is on the keg. Breweries do sometimes dispose of kegs that are damaged, or simply because they have surplus inventory. This is not common, but it does happen. Usually their first choice would be to sell the kegs to another brewery, or to a company such as Sabco that makes a business of refurbishing them. Still, there is always the possibility that a scrap keg was legally acquired. However, knowing how often this is not the case, you have a duty to assure yourself about the provenance of kegs you find for sale by third parties — that is, anyone but the brewery. I know there are some other possibilities I am not going into here — kegs from overseas that the brewery has authorized the importer to sell off because the cost of return shipment is so high, for example — but they do not change the principle. If you know the facts about the used keg trade and still choose to participate without asking pointed questions, you make yourself part of the problem.

My son the economist says that this is a matter of prices. Breweries should charge a deposit high enough to cover the replacement cost of their kegs. His father the humanist answers, that would reduce the economic impact, for sure, but it would not eliminate it, nor alter the facts of the situation. Even if they eventually are reimbursed, breweries still suffer financially when kegs are taken out of circulation. And the small breweries suffer most, because they can least afford to lose the use of their capital.

KETTLES FROM SCRAP?

So much for the ethical issue. As far as the practicalities of making brew kettles and other vessels from kegs goes, the only attraction really is the low cost, and that applies only if you are building a 10-gallon system. The metal is thin and the construction is not ideal. For example, "keggles," as they are often called, do not sit well on some burners, and they are harder to clean than a stockpot. If you are planning to keep cost low by doing the modifications yourself, you should know that stainless is the very devil to cut and weld. Weldless fittings are easier but more expensive than welded, so there is no obvious right choice here. Unless you want to learn welding anyway, you should consider hiring a competent person to install welded fittings.

I think a better way to save money on a 10-gallon system is to follow the method I chose for my 5-gallon setup: only two metal vessels at most, one a kettle/whirlpool fitted with a ball valve and the other the (optional) mash mixer; my other two — the lauter tun and the hot liquor back — are plastic. This system is more flexible and easier to operate than most of the three-vessel rack systems I have seen. It also requires only one pump.

KETTLE FITTINGS

As far as fittings go, the only truly necessary one for a brew kettle is a ball valve. This is vital because it makes it possible to drain the kettle without having to start a siphon, which is not something to be considered with boiling hot wort. Other fittings, such as thermowells, are in my view best avoided. Thermowells stick out into the middle of the kettle and disrupt the rotation of the wort during whirlpool, and they present an obstruction at cleaning time. It's not that hard to take a temperature reading by hand.

A few homebrewers fit their kettles with a simple whirlpool arm, but this means using a pump to circulate wort in the kettle. For the reasons explained in the previous chapter, this is best avoided. Fifteen seconds or so of stirring with a paddle will set the wort spinning. Likewise, there is no need for a separate whirlpool tank in a homebrewing operation.

There are a number of "weldless" valve kits on the market. These are fairly easy to install on a standard stockpot: all you need is to drill a hole of the right diameter with a step bit. The lowest prices I have seen for these bits are at Harbor Freight. Make sure you get one that will make a hole big enough for your valve. Follow the directions in the kit regarding placement and other precautions, oil the bit frequently, and stop after every step. (You'll soon understand why I said stainless is the very devil.) Most of the bits have the hole diameters marked right on each step, so you can quickly check the diameter. Do it twice. If the bit is not marked, consult the packaging and work out in advance which step on the drill is the diameter you are looking for. Then mark

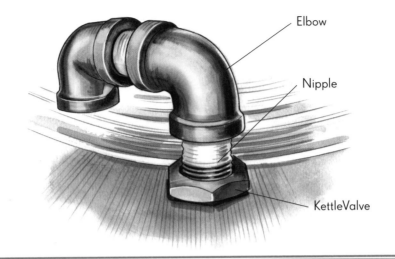

Labels: Elbow, Nipple, KettleValve

Kettle draw-off. Pipe elbows and nipples (³⁄₈-inch threading), fitted together and threaded into the KettleValve to bring the wort draw-off closer to the bottom. In practice, the kettle must still be tipped to draw off the last gallon or so of hot wort or water.

it yourself. Remember if you go too big, you will at a minimum face an expensive and time-consuming reclamation project.

The ball valve kit I chose is called the KettleValve. It is quite simple and one of the least expensive options. The instructions are very good. It does not protrude into the kettle as far as some other weldless fittings. Another nice feature is that the inside end of the valve has ³⁄₈-inch female pipe threading. I took advantage of this feature to install a U-shaped piping assembly — two elbows and two close nipples — that places the pickup point very close to the bottom. It greatly simplifies drawing off the maximum amount of wort while leaving the trub pile in the kettle.

Burner *(Optional)*

I call this piece of equipment optional, but if you are going to brew outside your kitchen, then a propane burner is mandatory. My own is the Bayou Classic SQ-14, and I think its large square base is its best feature. I find it hard to control the flame precisely, which would make it problematic for use with a mash mixer, where temperature overshoots are a serious issue. Despite being rated at 55,000 BTUs, its previous owner says that it did not produce a vigorous boil for a 10-gallon batch (approximately 12 gallons of wort); all I can say is that, with my 8-gallon kettle, it will boil off 1.25 gallons in an hour.

For heating a mash mixer, a smaller tabletop propane burner offers better control. You can find several models in outdoor stores and on the web. To lessen the expense you can get a gas tee and a few clamps so you can share one tank and regulator between two burners.

Heat Exchangers

For all-grain brewing, some sort of forced wort cooling is necessary. It just takes too long if you don't help the process along. If you have ever brewed with extract, you already know how long it can take, even when you are trying to cool only a couple of gallons.

The simplest wort-cooling device is an immersion cooler, which is a metal coil, usually of copper. It is immersed in the brew kettle at the end of the boil, and cold water is circulated through it. Thermodynamics dictate that heat will be exchanged between the hot wort and the cooler water, and there is no question that immersion coolers work.

Standard immersion wort chillers, which come in 25- and 50-foot coils, are widely used.

When I went back to homebrewing I used an immersion cooler for my first couple of batches. It did what I expected, but its limitations were obvious. Like most of its breed, it was too small for the job. Twenty-five feet of ⅜-inch copper tube just does not have enough area for the inefficient heat exchange mechanism it relies on (technically, it is known as crossflow cooling). Also, to get the fastest possible cooling, the wort had to be stirred constantly, exposing it to air and possible infection. Still, it took more than 20 minutes to get the wort to 90°F. The weather was warm, my city water was 80 degrees, and that was as far as I went. No heat exchanger, whatever its design, can possibly get wort down below the coolant temperature, and all of them become less effective as the temperature of the wort approaches that of the cooling water.

Thankfully, I was ready for this. I switched to a keg of water I had chilled in my refrigerator, and by pushing this slowly through the coil and stirring constantly, I was able to get the wort to 70°F — acceptable for pitching. However, I was by this time dripping with sweat and worried about my wort. Twenty minutes of exposure to air while the temperature slowly dropped through prime bacteria-growing territory had me thinking bad thoughts. After the transfer to the fermenter, an examination of the cool wort was not reassuring. It was muddy looking, even though I had carefully whirlpooled, settled, and siphoned. Slow cooling produces less cold break, and smaller cold-break particles, which stay in suspension. Sixteen years of commercial brewing taught me what cooled wort should look like, and this was not it.

I hope this explains why I cannot regard immersion coolers as anything more than a stopgap. There are many things you can do to improve their performance — doubling the length of copper from the customary 25 feet to 50 being the most obvious. You can also install a whirlpool arm in the kettle, in order to automate the tedious stirring that is part of using immersion coolers. Unfortunately, this means pumping wort that is full of break material, which, as I explained in the previous chapter, is not a good idea. Commercial breweries long ago settled on the closed counterflow design because it is simply the best tool for the job.

The argument in favor of immersion, and against counterflow, basically comes down to ease of cleaning and sanitation. The point is valid. Homebrew-sized counterflow heat exchangers, whether hand built or manufactured, cannot be taken apart for inspection, as bigger units can. This means that you have to be scrupulous about cleaning. The only reliable method is to use a circulating pump in a CIP loop. And suffice it to say the time required pretty well rules out hand pumps, drill pumps, and other makeshift measures.

Clean wort requires a counterflow heat exchanger, and the heat exchanger requires a pump, at least for CIP. This is an example of why equipment cannot be chosen in isolation. It also explains how I found myself, barely back into homebrewing, undertaking a major "capital improvement project." It was either that or compromise my results, plain and simple. I hate to spend money. But life is too short to make — or drink — second-rate beer.

If you accept my findings, then you have a choice to make, the same one as for a lauter tun: buy or build. The build option means making a pair of tube-in-shell heat exchangers. (The full details are in the Projects chapter on page 194.)

It is also possible to buy such a unit, but frankly, paying somebody else to build one almost wipes out the cost savings, compared to something smaller and more efficient.

If you can afford to buy, you should consider the all-copper tube-in-shell unit that is sold under the name of Convolutus. It used to be called the Chillzilla. No matter the name, it is well-engineered and highly effective. It has some advantages that come from its design. The wort is carried through a ½-inch copper coil, which is big enough that gravity can be used — no pump required. Clogging, which can be a real problem with plate heat exchangers, is usually not a factor with this design. However, you will still need to use a pump for cleaning. And while its cooling power is close to the biggest plate units, so is its price.

The two-plate heat exchangers sold by most homebrew shops are the Shirron and the Blichmann Therminator. They are similar in basic design to each other, and both have the same drawback. They need to be fed by a pump that can keep the wort flowing even if some trub partially clogs the passages. They are, however, sized and priced quite differently. The Therminator is bigger and more expensive, and it has greater cooling capacity. The manufacturer claims — accurately, I've found — that using 58°F water at a rate of 5 gallons per minute, it will cool 10 gallons of boiling wort to 68°F in 5 minutes.

The limitation of all three of these ready-made units is that they are single stage. This means that for summertime brewing, in most parts of the United States, you will have to use chilled water as your coolant. If you are doing 5-gallon batches, the Therminator has enough power to cool 5 gallons of wort to 70°F in less than 5 minutes, using 5 gallons of 40°F water. If you want 50°F wort — that is, you want to make lager — then the Therminator will still do the job, with the same amount of cold water, but you will have to slow down the cooling process drastically. Count on 15 minutes. The Chillzilla is not quite as powerful, but with chilled water it will cool boiling wort to 70°F at a rate of less than 2 minutes per gallon. I have not been able to either test or get hard data about the Shirron, so I cannot say how well it would perform, but judging by its size I would not expect it to be as efficient.

The problem with chilled water from a cold liquor back is that the supply is limited. This means you have to test your system in advance, or risk running out. However, if you can assure yourself that you have enough cold liquor to do the job — with a properly sized heat exchanger, the quantity is slightly less than the volume of wort being cooled — then a single-stage arrangement is in some ways simpler than two-stage cooling.

One way to get colder tap water is to use a *prechiller*, which is basically an immersion chiller that sits in a bucket of ice water. The city water goes through the prechiller on its way to the heat exchanger, so that it is cooled down to 60°F or less and can cool the wort. Still, I prefer working with a fixed supply of chilled water and a single-stage heat exchanger that is powerful enough to do the job.

The alternative to a high-powered single-stage heat exchanger is a two-stage unit. This is a less expensive, although bulkier, option that works very well. It uses more water, but that can be an advantage if you have to send the water onto your lawn. When cooling wort with a small volume of very cold water, the water comes out very hot. This is part of efficiency. You have to think about what you will do with it. If you don't mind the extra water consumption, then you will find that the 2-stage homemade tube-in-shell unit will cool 5 gallons of wort to 70°F using about 15 gallons of 80°F tap water, plus about 4 gallons of 40°F chilled water. The limitation here is that to get the wort down to 50°F, as required for lager, will require much longer. My advice, if you know going in that you want to brew lager in summer, would be to get a pair of small plate heat exchangers.

There are a number of companies that sell small stainless "generic" plate heat exchangers, which have many uses besides wort cooling. They usually market them for use in wood-fired home heating systems, or in home manufacturing of biodiesel. You can buy two of these for less than the price of a Therminator. For ales, the combination of a 20-plate

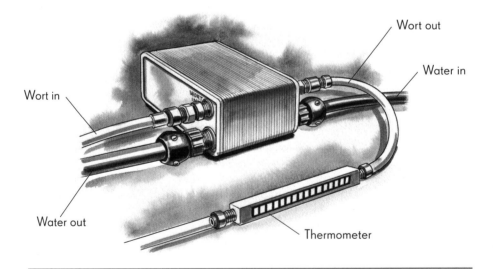

Heat exchanger. The Blichmann Therminator heat exchanger is an expensive yet effective option for cooling wort.

unit (tap water at 80 to 82°F) with a 10-plate (cold liquor at 40°F) will cool 5 gallons of wort to 70°F in 10 minutes. However, for summer lager brewing, you would need to pair the same 20-plate unit with a 30-plate for the cold liquor section. That would allow you to knock out 5 gallons of 50°F wort in 10 minutes.

Besides the heat exchangers and connecting hoses, there is one other thing you need to make the wort cooling operation go: a thermometer in the outflow stream. As I've said, I am not a big fan of thermowells in kettles and other brewery vessels, but this case is different. Without real-time monitoring there is no way to operate a heat exchanger effectively. Fortunately this is not a large expense, but it is a necessary one. The Projects chapter has details on a CPVC thermowell I built for my tube-in-shell (page 221). It can be adapted to a plate unit, or you can choose to spend more for a stainless steel equivalent.

Cold Liquor Back

If you have been following along carefully, then you know that if you have a draft system, you already have a cold liquor back. Just fill one of your kegs with water and put it in the refrigerator for a couple of days. The reason I set up my carbon dioxide regulator with a quick-disconnect on the gas hose was that I knew I would be hauling the cylinder, as well as the keg, out onto the deck for wort cooling. The gas cylinder is my cold liquor pump.

You need some way to control the flow of cold liquor out of the keg. Mine is fitted with a nylon ball valve in the outlet line. This is optional; I would suggest trying to control the water flow using the gas shutoff valve first. If you find it hard to do this you might consider the ball valve. I got mine from McMaster-Carr. The shutoff valves you find in the homebrew supply stores are not suitable for this. They will leak under just a few PSI of pressure.

A good alternative to using a keg is to fill an insulated cooler with ice water, which has the added advantage of freeing up a keg and making for less lugging on brew day. If you are running a system like mine, the hot liquor back can do double duty for cold liquor, feeding the cold liquor through the heat exchanger by gravity. Obviously you would need to test your setup in advance to be sure the flow rate is adequate. (A tip: Try filling the heat exchanger and hoses with water in advance.) You then need to work out a means of controlling the flow, probably by installing a valve on the heat exchanger output. If gravity cannot be used, then you will need some sort of small pump to move the cold liquor.

Pump

I have already touched on how desirable a pump is, even for a 5-gallon brewery. Probably the biggest advantage is safety, as I mentioned in the section on kettles. It is true that operating a pump in a wet environment carries some risk, and I discuss pump safety issues in the projects chapter (page 194). But I do not know of a single brewer who has been injured in an electrical accident. I know several who have been burned badly by hot wort or other liquid, including me.

The almost universal choice for homebrewers is the March Pump Company model 809-PL-HS or its sibling, the 809-PL-HS-C. Both of these pumps have a 1/25 horsepower motor, a magnetic coupled drive (this means there is no mechanical seal to wear out and leak), and a Polysulfil plastic body that is rated for 225°F. The plastic pump body keeps the price down, although it is still quite a hit to the brewery budget.

The difference between the two models is the pump intake. The C model has a central intake similar to the centrifugal pumps I worked with in the pub. I think it would be easier to mount this one on a carrier for portable use. The other model has the input on one side. This is a better layout for inline permanent installation in a rack system.

If you are looking for bargains on this pump, be careful. March sells this same pump body with a smaller, 1/100 horsepower motor. This is too wimpy for service in homebrewing. Make sure you are getting an HS model. Also check to see whether the motor has a mounting bracket. You need one for brewery use. On the other hand, a finished power cord, suitable for plugging into an outlet, is not worthwhile. You will almost certainly be wiring the pump to a switch, or a fan speed control. Speed controllers are, in most ways, superior to ball valves for controlling the pump output, and I make the case for using one in the Projects chapter (page 194).

My own pump is not an 809. It's an oddball model, not listed in the March catalog. I found it at an amazing price from an Internet surplus dealer. The pump is appropriately sized and actually has a motor superior to the 809 HS, the problem being that the body is glass-filled polypropylene, which is rated for only 190°F and is not FDA-approved for food contact. I consulted a plastics expert, who explained the problem. It is neither the polypropylene nor the glass fiber, but the "coupling agent" (silane) used to bind the polymer and the glass together, which is questionable. He advised that it would be better to select a pump made from FDA-approved materials. He offered his opinion that the risk was low, especially if I cleaned the pump well before use. However, "low" is not "none."

Because I already have the pump, I use it. It is slated for replacement as the budget allows. I suggest studying the March catalog. You may find a suitable pump at a bargain price, but most of the surplus pumps out there are made of the same stuff mine is. If you only need a pump for cleaning your heat exchanger, one of these is perfectly adequate. If you want to exploit your pump as much as possible, which means pump wort, get an 809 HS.

Aeration Stone and Air Pump

If you plan to use dried yeast exclusively, you may be able to do without an aerating stone (more on this in the next chapter on page 108). However, if you ever plan to try any form of liquid yeast, whether slurry from a local brewery or a strain from one of the yeast laboratories, you will need one.

Back in the days before I turned pro, and before stainless steel aeration stones were readily available, I tried most of the "low-tech" aeration methods that I had seen in homebrewing books, such as splashing the cooled wort into the fermenter or whipping it with a wire whisk. Finally, I improvised an aeration system using an aquarium stone, which was actually made of sand particles or some such material. The first time I used it was the first time I ever saw a fermentation take off the way it should. Some homebrewers say they get satisfactory results from other methods of aeration, and I have no reason to doubt them. All I can say is that I could not make them work. I think an aeration stone is as necessary as a brew kettle. It is a universal fixture in commercial breweries, whatever their size.

The illustration on page 68 shows the aeration kit that I use. It includes the stone, tubing, a small air pump, and a sterile filter, which is basically a small sheet of plastic perforated with holes about 0.1 micron in diameter. This is smaller than any bacterium, so the air coming out of the filter is sterile — obviously a very important feature. One of the only problems is that the tubing is curved and does not want to hang straight down so that the stone is on the bottom of the fermenter. Another problem is that it lacks any sort of bracket or clip to hold it snug

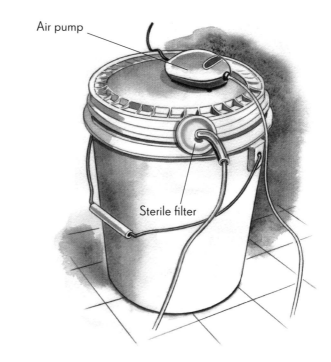

Air pump

Sterile filter

against the side of a fermenting bucket. So far I have been limping along by using the fermenter lid, weighted with my sanitizer spray bottle to hold the apparatus more or less in place during aeration, but sooner or later I will have to devise some more permanent way of doing this.

There are also kits available that are designed to inject pure oxygen, rather than air, into the wort. This is a common practice in commercial breweries, though far from universal. Lots of authors, from both the homebrewing and professional worlds, have weighed in on this issue. Several of the works in Resources mention it. Please note, though, that this is a rather mild controversy. Those who favor air do not deny that oxygen works, and those who favor oxygen do not deny that air works. The argument is over whether oxygen works better, is worth the trouble, and so forth.

Fermenting Vessels

The default fermenter for homebrewing is a 6.5-gallon HDPE (high-density polyethylene) bucket and matching, tight-fitting lid. You can find them in every homebrew shop, often sold under the name Ale Pail. They are cheap, light, and easy to clean. Many homebrewers have made excellent beer in them over the years. However, some homebrewers object to plastic fermenters, buckets or otherwise.

The objections to plastic have to do with one or another property of the material. As far as its chemical makeup goes, polyethylene and its cousin, polypropylene, are some of the most inert materials you can find. They don't react with much of anything, which makes them difficult to glue, for instance. The only serious objection from a chemical point of view is to the release agent that is sprayed onto the surfaces of the mold before the bucket is formed. You can remove this satisfactorily by giving the bucket a quick wash with PBW solution.

One fact that deserves to be more widely known is that almost all HDPE stock is made to food-container standards, even though most buckets are used for other things. This is just a convenience for the chemical companies who make the raw material. They never know whom their next shipment of HDPE pellets will be going to. They provide a "food safe" certificate, though, only if the bucket manufacturer requests it — which explains why most of the plastic buckets you see for sale are not listed as "food safe," even though, in fact, they are. Would I buy a plastic bucket from Home Depot for homebrewing? Sure, except that I object to the color. I prefer white buckets. But otherwise I would have no concern. Used buckets can be picked up for next to nothing from bakeries; the only problem is that they are almost always 5 gallons. That is why you may have to get your fermenter from a homebrew supply store.

The other objection to plastic is that it is soft. It can get scratched, and a scratch is a lodging place for soil and, sooner or later, bacteria. I think this is a better objection than the first one. When you clean a fermenting bucket, you should not use anything harder than a dish sponge. And of course, if you notice that the surface is scratched, replace the bucket. This goes for plastic carboys too. A bucket fermenter is cheap enough that replacing it every year or two is a fiscally sound way to run a clean home brewery.

If you want a hard, impermeable surface, then your fermenter will have to be made of either glass or stainless steel. Stainless is ideal if you can afford it. It is the universal choice for commercial breweries because it can stand up to the harsh acid and alkaline cleaners that are required for hands-off cleaning (CIP). Few if any homebrewers clean their fermenters in this way, but given an unlimited budget, I am sure most would still prefer to ferment in stainless. The only thing I would insist on is an opening big enough to not only look but also reach into, so that I could scrub the interior surface by hand if I felt it was necessary.

One feature of many stainless tanks is their ability to hold pressure. A conical-bottomed, pressure-rated unitank makes it possible not only to do the entire fermentation in one vessel, and to harvest yeast at will, but also to naturally carbonate the beer in the same tank. I feel this is a bigger advantage for a microbrewery, but if the tank can be cooled either in a refrigerator or with a professional-style jacket, it is a very nice capability to have.

Glass is another story. Five- or six-gallon glass carboys are heavy, fragile, and slippery when wet. They cannot hold pressure. They are also very hard to clean through that narrow opening. There was a time when I preferred carboys to plastic buckets, but years of experience with a carboy brush, as well as one breakage due to thermal stress during cleaning, killed my enthusiasm. These days I prefer a bucket. I'll accept the soft surface in exchange for easy access.

Every fermenter needs some sort of one-way device to allow carbon dioxide gas to escape from the fermenter while preventing the ingress of air. The common inexpensive plastic airlock is perfectly adequate for this. One reason for buying your fermenting bucket from a homebrew supply shop is that the lid will be drilled and fitted with the required neoprene (buna) grommet. I recommend against using a bucket with a loose-fitting or improvised lid.

PRIMARY AND SECONDARY FERMENTERS

It used to be common to divide fermenting vessels into "primary" and "secondary" and recommend a different type of vessel for each. The old default was a bucket or oversize carboy for the primary (or active) fermentation. Then, when yeast activity subsided, one would transfer to another carboy whose size matched the batch volume. The rationale was twofold: First, with little gas evolving, you need to minimize the headspace above the beer. Second, you want to get the beer off the spent yeast and cold trub so as to avoid autolysis.

This all makes sense, given that the homebrew is at room temperature. However, if you have a refrigerator, then you can crash cool the beer when fermentation ends. "Secondary fermentation" hardly happens with ales — lagers are a different matter and one that I go into in the discussion of lager brewing in the chapter on advanced techniques (page 180) — so there is little to be gained by leaving the beer warm once the yeast is finished. Rapid chilling also allows you to leave the beer in the same vessel, because the cold will forestall autolysis and also encourage precipitation of the remaining suspended yeast. Altogether this is a much better system and one of the many reasons why a homebrewer needs a refrigerator right from the start.

All that being said, is there any reason to buy a carboy as a "secondary fermenter" or, as I prefer to call it, a settling tank? It depends on what is coming next. If you intend to filter your beer, then you can rack (siphon) the beer straight out of your fermenting bucket into a soda keg and from there push it through the filter into its final destination, the serving keg. If, on the other hand, you intend to fine the beer (treat it with isinglass or other

A LESSON ON GASES

As the homebrewing legend Gary Bauer once said, in a mixture of gases, each gas behaves as if the other is not there. Think of a bottle of beer. It has a lot of carbon dioxide dissolved in it. The carbon dioxide pressure inside the bottle is far higher than it is in the atmosphere surrounding it. Gases want to diffuse — that is, spread out to an even pressure level. Therefore, if there is a way out, such as a permeable bottle wall or plastic cap liner, carbon dioxide will take that path out of the bottle and into the surrounding atmosphere.

Now, while it has a lot of dissolved carbon dioxide, beer has basically no dissolved oxygen. The oxygen pressure in the surrounding air is higher than in the beer. Therefore, while the carbon dioxide is pushing its way out through the permeable barrier, atmospheric oxygen is pushing its way in.

agents that will help it to "fall bright" without filtration), then you will be better off with a carboy as a settling tank. It is possible to use a soda keg or a plastic bucket for this job instead, but a carboy allows you to observe the yeast dropout, which is a great advantage.

If you decide to get a carboy for clarification, I recommend a plastic one, for safety's sake. There has been some discussion about this over the years, the main points against plastic being first, the cleanability factor, and second, oxygen permeability. Oxygen can migrate through most plasticsto some extent, which means that over a period of weeks or months beer in a plastic container can, in theory, be oxidized to some extent.

The question is, how much? It depends on the permeability of the plastic and also on the temperature of the beer. It does *not* depend on whether the beer is carbonated (as in a bottle). Oxidation reactions take place more slowly at cold temperatures. Some plastics are more gas permeable than others, and HDPE is one of the least permeable.

Polycarbonate (Lexan), which is used for most water carboys, is middling in its properties. PET, as used for soda bottles and also in the BetterBottle carboys, has about one-tenth the permeability of polycarbonate, but about three times the permeability of HDPE.

The bottom line: While not as good as glass, PET is good enough for any reasonable storage time. In fact, if you are not interested in long-term aging (lagering), polycarbonate is good enough. Yeast is an excellent oxygen scavenger, so any threat from oxygen ingress is greatly mitigated by the presence of live yeast in the beer. If you use your carboy as a short-term settling tank, oxidation is not a threat.

Cleaning is another question. You cannot use a bottle brush on a plastic carboy. That leads me to rule out using one as a primary fermenter, based on the quantity of sticky residue one would face. Nonetheless, many homebrewers have reported success with the BetterBottle, following the cleaning instructions on the manufacturer's website. In any case, the soil load in a settling tank is far lighter, and as long as you don't let the carboy dry out in a dirty state, cleaning is not a problem.

I chose to buy a settling tank because I wanted the option of filtering beer or not. I chose a BetterBottle because I like the wide mouth, light weight, and clarity of the PET material. This was a splurge. I feel it has been worthwhile, but in putting together your brewery, its importance depends on your decision about filtration.

Racking Arm, Transfer Hoses, and Fittings

The racking arm is simply a piece of plastic or stainless tubing with a hook bent into one end for siphoning beer from one vessel to another. I spent a few extra dollars for the Auto-Siphon, which has a hand pump built into it. It makes it easy to start the siphon flow without sucking on the end of the beer hose or resorting to other cleaner but more difficult methods. So far it has served me well.

Every brewery needs hoses to carry water, wort, and beer around. For pumping hot liquids, I suggest silicone rubber hose; it is the only type commonly available that is actually rated for boiling temperatures. It is also soft enough to pinch shut, yet seldom needs to be clamped down to form a leak-tight seal over a hose barb. It is dimensionally stable, meaning that when you pull it off the hose barb it returns to its original diameter and shape. It is altogether wonderful stuff, the only drawback being the price; ½-inch silicone tubing is pretty expensive. You need this for at least the input hose of your pump; ⅜-inch hose can be used for output and is a little cheaper, but I prefer the large diameter on both sides, especially because my pump has a ½-inch output with the hose barb molded into the pump body. I bought 10 feet of silicone hose when setting up my new home brewery, which was more than enough. All other hoses are vinyl, mostly the standard, thin-wall clear material available everywhere. This is fine for transfer applications. As noted in the discussion of the draft system, stronger stuff is needed for gas, or for beer under pressure.

Probably the largest cost for transfer is all the fittings and adapters needed. Number one on my list is hose clamps — I figure I use about 30 of them to hold everything together. I recommend the stainless steel band clamps with a stainless screw. The SAE #8 (½ inch to $^{29}/_{32}$ inch) is good for ½-inch hose, the SAE #4 ($^{7}/_{32}$ inch to $^{5}/_{8}$ inch) is best for thin-wall $^{3}/_{8}$-inch and smaller hoses, while the SAE #6 ($^{7}/_{16}$ inch to $^{25}/_{32}$ inch) will do for most everything. The $^{5}/_{16}$-inch band width is best for most applications. You can get band clamps at auto parts stores, hardware stores, and many other places, though not all stores will have the exact size and band width you want. Lowe's, for instance, carries mostly clamps with a ½-inch-wide band. McMaster-Carr has reasonable prices and the widest selection. They also spell everything out. (Sometimes a retail package does not tell you whether the screw is stainless or not.)

Many homebrewers like to use quick-disconnects wherever hoses have to be attached. This can get expensive in a hurry. I find that it is no hardship to keep a nut driver in my pocket while I brew, and making or breaking connections with band clamps takes no longer than the stainless tri-clamps I used in the pub. I do make an exception for some gas connections, where the auto shutoff fittings can be helpful.

Barbed hose couplers are another item that can add up as you assemble your brewery. One reason to settle on a single tubing size is to keep the number and type of couplers to a minimum. It is hard to do this because some equipment, such as a racking arm or a tube-in-shell heat exchanger, dictates a certain hose size for the initial connection. Other equipment such as a pump or plate heat exchanger may require NPT-to-hose barb adapters. This is inevitable. For kegs there is more flexibility. If you get the compression type couplers, they can be fitted with a range of hose barbs to match the tubing size you want. However, because they require a separate hose barb, the working coupler costs double what the simpler piece with its built-in ¼-inch barb does. One way or another, you are going to spend money.

It is usually cheaper to get plastic barbed fittings for wort, water, and gas, although they are often bulkier and harder to push the hose on or off. I feel that stainless is worth the money for draft beer lines. Also, any connections of hot water or wort lines will require either stainless or a suitable type of plastic. The McMaster catalog has a wealth of information on the heat specifications of various plastics.

Filters

Filtration is a hot topic among homebrewers. The majority do not do it, and many are strongly opposed to the practice, claiming that it is unnecessary and detrimental. On the other hand, the majority of microbrewers filter most if not all of their output, regarding it as the best way consistently to produce clean-tasting beer. A minority of homebrewers agree, and I am on their side.

THE BENEFITS OF FILTRATION

It is quite true that filtration always removes a certain amount of color, body, and flavor from the finished beer, as well as reducing its foam retention. So a filtered beer will always taste and look different from the same beer unfiltered. Whether it will look or taste *worse* is another matter. Filtration removes colloids and yeast cells that add harsh and sometimes astringent notes to the flavor. A clear beer will almost always taste smoother than the same beer, prior to clarification. Only a few mildly hopped styles of beer, such as Belgian Witbier, benefit from the presence of hazy material.

This, however, is not really the question. The question is how to remove the yeast and other haze components and how thorough that removal needs to be. Many homebrewers feel that a slightly hazy unfiltered beer is fine, as long as it does not have a distinct "yeast bite." They also contend that it is possible to clarify the beer adequately without resorting to a filter. I would agree, in the majority of cases. Given a low enough temperature and a long enough settling time, many beers will drop remarkably bright without any help. Once you pull out the sediment from the bottom with the first pint or two, the remainder of the keg will pour clear. Perhaps not as clear as filtered beer that is, but surprisingly close.

In my experience, the hands-off method of beer clarification requires (1) a cooperative yeast and (2) at least six weeks. It also requires that you leave the keg in one place from start to finish, because any movement will disturb the sediment on the bottom and recloud the beer. The yeast issue is big: few homebrewers want to limit their choices in this way. Time is an issue too. How many refrigerators do you have?

Practically speaking, if you only have one refrigerator, the choice comes down to filtration versus fining and settling. Both of these methods will allow you to make a clean-tasting ale in two to three weeks. I use both, and I used both when I was brewing professionally. I found that filtration is more consistent and usually faster. Settling works, but the effectiveness of finings depends on proper handling, which may not be easy. It also depends very much on wort quality. The cleaner the wort that went into your kettle, and then into your fermenter, the clearer and faster the beer will drop. In other words, if you are looking to avoid filtration, you'd better do everything right on brew day.

THE DRAWBACKS OF FILTRATION

As far as the drawbacks of filtration go, this is in large measure a matter of design — in other words, recipe formulation. If filtration is a regular part of your process, then as you develop your beers you will automatically compensate for the color, body, and flavor changes. You'll use a bit more colored malt in the darker beers, perhaps a touch more hops in some of the aggressively bitter beers, maybe an extra ounce of flaked barley or Cara-Pils in a heavy beer. Filtration does not take away that much. It certainly will not turn a pale ale into a light lager. Blackstone St. Charles Porter has been winning awards for 15 years, and for 15 years it has also been garnering criticism from the judging panels. From the judges who think it is not medal-worthy, one charge is consistently laid against it: it is too heavy, too malty, and too hoppy for the style. Its foam retention has never been criticized. St. Charles Porter is a filtered beer and always has been.

That is all I have to say about this question. I believe that filtration is something every brewer, sooner or later, should learn; it is a powerful tool and, in my view, a requirement in some situations. On the other hand, it is possible to brew great beer without ever coming near a filter. You just have to accept the limitations that come along with that decision.

SHEET FILTERS AND CARTRIDGE FILTERS

There are two types of filters that are widely used for homebrew: one is the plate-and-frame sheet filter, and the other is the ordinary household water-filter housing with a cartridge. Both work, and both, as you would expect, have their advantages.

The advantage of the sheet filter is that the material is specifically designed to filter yeast and colloidal matter out of fermented beverages. The sheets are strictly single use, but the cost is reasonable, and the frame is easy to take apart and clean.

There are three disadvantages of sheet filters. First, the small units sold for homebrew will not take pressure, so it is impossible to filter carbonated beer through them. Most homebrewers filter their beer flat, so this is usually not a concern. Second, by their design the units inevitably leak a little. Losses are small, but you have to place the unit in a shallow pan to avoid making a mess. Again, this is easy to deal with. Third — the most serious drawback — is that the base material of the sheets is cellulose. It is an excellent filter medium, but it needs to be flushed with water prior to use, in order to remove loose fibers and avoid a papery taste in the filtered beer. Again, this can be dealt with. Best practice in any case is to sanitize the filter before the run, and flushing can be incorporated into the sanitizing routine.

Cartridge filters do not leak if properly assembled, and the housings will take pressures well above what is encountered in handling carbonated beer. The filter media come in a broad range of types, but many are based on inert materials that impart no taste to the finished beer. Cleanup of the housing is quite simple. Cartridges can be cleaned by back-flushing and reused, potentially for dozens of batches, which cuts down on cost.

The problem is finding a filter cartridge that actually works. Many types of cartridges are available, and I have tried several. In my experience, micron numbers mean very little. The word "absolute" should mean something, but unfortunately, even among absolute rated filters there are large differences in performance. My experience with filters designed for water has been uniformly unsatisfactory. I have tried several types that failed to deliver bright beer. I finally shelled out for a pleated unit from The Filter Store, and I am happy to report that the one I chose works as advertised. Manufactured by Graver Technologies, it is designed for filtering beverages. As of this writing, the 0.5-micron unit costs $45 plus shipping. The 1-micron unit, which I have not tried, is a few dollars cheaper. I am sure there are other filters out there that also work, but if you want to filter beer on the cheap, you may have to search long and hard.

FILTER HOUSINGS

Filter housings are available from many sources. Clear bodies often cost more, but I feel they are worth it because they let you observe the flow of beer through the filter. You can find them online at a reasonable cost. A pressure release valve is not absolutely necessary but can be helpful to deal with foaming, especially if you want to try to filter carbonated beer. You will also need two keg couplers, some tubing, and barbed adapters for the housing.

A word of advice on filter housings: buy a new one for your beer filter and use it only for beer filtration. Take care of it. Never forget that what makes the seal between the "dirty" and "clean" (input and output) sides of the unit is a pair of simple knife-edges cast into the housing pieces, and the neoprene washers on either end of the cartridge. The seal depends entirely on compression. The knife edge therefore must be perfectly smooth. Take care how you store it. Also, to extend the life of the cartridge washers, I suggest that you assemble the unit and tighten it down only for filter runs, and otherwise store it covered but open.

Instruments

You basically need three measuring instruments for homebrewing. One is a small kitchen-type thermometer; I bought an inexpensive digital model from Harbor Freight. Then you need a hydrometer with case/ sample jar, available from homebrew supply shops. Finally, you need a pH meter. You can find cheap ones online, but I recommend the Hanna Checker 1 because it has two-point calibration and a replaceable electrode. You also need pouches of the 4.01 and 7.0 calibration solutions. You can spend a lot more on each of these items, and you may eventually want to upgrade, but for starting out, these bottom-of-the-line models are adequate.

You will also need everyday items like a small scale and a set of measuring pitchers, cups, and spoons. One of my splurges was a conical kitchen graduated cylinder, along with an electronic kitchen scale.

Recommended Setups

Now we've arrived at the practical matter of setting up a brewery. I assume that you will not be building a rack or framework to permanently mount your equipment, at least not at first. In fact, even if you think you would like to do this, I suggest you hold off until you have made a few brews. Your ideas about placement will likely change, and you may even decide you need to upgrade or replace equipment.

For a starter brewery, the equipment falls into three categories: the core, the contingent, and the optional.

WHAT WILL THIS COST ME?

You've likely been wondering about the expense of homebrewing while reading the previous chapter. How much you pay for your brewery depends on what kind of bargains you are able to find, how much you are willing to build rather than buy, and how much you already have on hand. I hope I have given you enough information to make up your own shopping list. If you want to keep costs down, building some items can save a significant amount of money, however, if you are not sure you will stick with the hobby for more than a few years, then you may want to look at things differently. Homemade equipment is hard to sell.

For the true neophyte, starting from scratch, I repeat my advice to shop for your draft system first. Take a look at different homebrew setups online, decide what you would like, then decide what you would accept to start out. Be sure to get at least two kegs — that way you can always have one full. Once you have a basic draft system in place, start pricing other big-ticket items. You should expect that the cost of your draft system will be about 25 to 30 percent of your entire home brewery. I use this as a benchmark because, in my acquaintance with many homebrewers, the elaborateness of the draft system generally mirrors the sophistication of the home brewery — what a particular hobbyist is able and willing to spend.

THIS *CORE* EQUIPMENT IS REQUIRED FOR ALL SETUPS:

- Draft beer system
- Water filter
- Mash/lauter tun
- Grant
- Brew kettle
- Hot liquor back
- Counterflow heat exchanger

- Wort aeration kit
- Fermenter
- Pump
- Racking arm and transfer equipment
- Measuring instruments
- Filter OR settling tank (one, not both, is required)

CONTINGENT EQUIPMENT DEPENDS ON YOUR CIRCUMSTANCES:

- Bulk grain or grist problems: malt mill
- Problem water: reverse osmosis filter set

- Warm summer water: second stage for heat exchanger or a high-power heat exchanger
- Outdoor brewing: propane burner and tank

OPTIONAL EQUIPMENT:

- Mash mixer
- Recirc arm

- Sparge arm
- Rack or "sculpture"

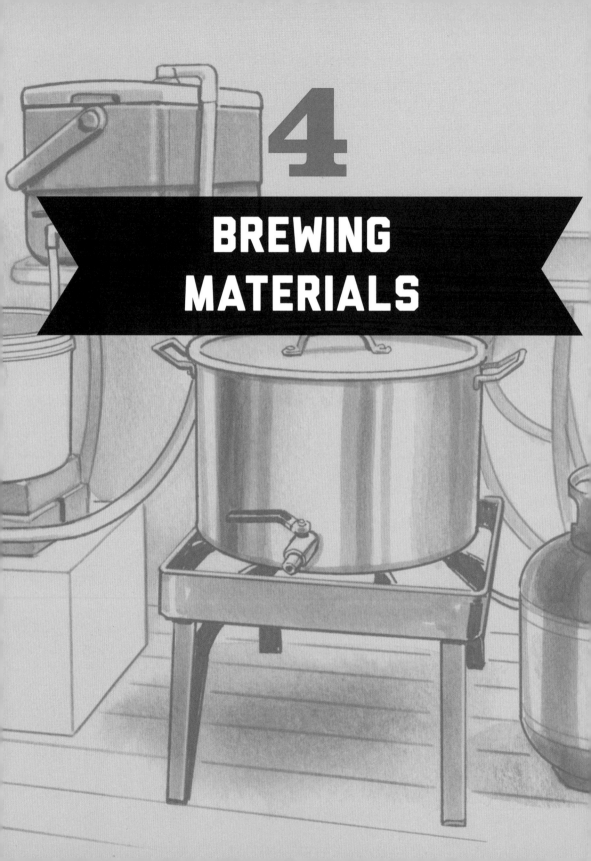

4

BREWING MATERIALS

The last chapter was all about equipment — the "durable goods" of brewing. The equipment represents the up-front cost of getting into the hobby, and all the pieces you acquire need to be carefully considered. But now that we've looked at the things we make beer *with*, it's time to turn our attention to the things we make beer *from*.

I have said on several occasions that homebrewers pay too much attention to recipes and too little to their technique. That does not mean your choice of brewing materials is unimportant. It only means that technique is the foundation. Sloppy brewing methods will nullify any amount of care and money you spend on your ingredients. On the other hand, if you are putting forth the effort — and it is considerable — to do things right, then it makes no sense to be haphazard about choosing your hops or grain. Or, for that matter, to ignore your water, which is the base on which all beers are made. We'll start with that.

Water

Water chemistry is not the sort of thing that excites most people for its own sake. I am no different. If I had not wanted to brew good beer, I would never have delved into this branch of applied science.

Simply put, if you want to make good beer, you have to find out about your water supply and work out a plan for treating it. Depending on the composition of your local water, the cost of turning it into suitable brewing "liquor" can be either negligible or significant. You need to know which while you are still in the planning stages.

The usual way of classifying water is to describe it as "hard" or "soft." That may be appropriate if you run a commercial laundry, but I think a better pair of terms for brewers is "hard" or "easy." Some water supplies require only simple, inexpensive measures to make them suitable for brewing. Others require fairly elaborate treatment. We are going to look at both possibilities here.

First, I have to say that if you are determined to completely avoid the technicalities of water chemistry, you can do that. You have the option of putting yourself in the hands of a professional. Water treatment companies seem to be flourishing these days, and you can easily get as many bids as you like from them. But I would urge you not to do this. Some water salespeople understand brewing, but most do not.

Instead, you should do the initial research yourself. That means getting hold of a quality report for your water supply. You can usually do this on the Internet. Just Google your water company. Poke around the website and find the complete water quality report (WQR). Print it out.

If you can't find the information online, you'll have to make a phone call and get a report sent to you. Don't hesitate to do this. It's public health information, and you have a right to it.

If you are not served by a public utility (in other words, you get your water from a well or spring on your property), then you need to get an analysis done. This is one situation where calling in a treatment company makes sense. They will do the analysis as the first step in working up their proposal. If this is the spot you find yourself in, do yourself a favor and study some of the more technical brewing books listed in Resources. You want to be able to understand what you are hearing. Or if, as is likely in this circumstance, you already have a treatment system installed, you need to learn about it and find out what kind of water it puts out. Then you will know what, if anything, needs to be changed before you can start brewing.

The same goes for anyone who has a water softener or other treatment system already installed in his or her house. You need to find out what that thing is putting out. If it's a typical water softener, it's giving you bad brewing water, loaded with sodium or potassium, and you will need to bypass it.

AN EASY CASE
We are going to start with a look at some easy water — in fact, mine. I found the most recent report on Davidson County, Tennessee's municipal water supply online.

The first thing you need to know, especially if you find multipage tables intimidating, is that most of the data is of no interest to you as a brewer. The report has two columns of numbers. The first is the average analysis for Nashville water. Unless otherwise specified, this will be in parts per million (ppm), or milligrams per liter (same thing). The second column is the MCL, or maximum contaminant level, — that's the standard.

As I scan my WQR, the first section I see is Inorganic Parameters. That sounds important; but in fact, only a couple of items are of

(continued on page 87)

Nashville, Tennessee Water Report 2010

Inorganic Parameters

Results in mg/L unless noted

Parameter	Metro Water Services	MCL
Antimony - total **	<0.001	0.006
Arsenic **	<0.001	0.05
Asbestos *	not detected	7 million fibers / L
Barium **	0.027	2
Beryllium — total **	<0.0002	0.004
Cadmium **	<0.0001	0.005
Chromium **	<0.0004	0.1
Cyanide	<0.005	0.2
Fluoride	0.97	4
Lead	0.001	0.015 (action level)
Mercury **	<0.0001	0.002
Nickel **	<0.0007	0.1
Nitrate	0.20	10
Nitrite	<0.02	1
Selenium **	<0.0006	0.05
Thallium — total **	<0.0006	0.002

* Analyzed 2002
** Analyzed 2009

Secondary Standards

Results in mg/L unless noted

Parameter	Metro Water Services	MCL
Chloride	7.8	250
Color	2	15 (Color Units)
Copper	0.380	1.3 (action level)
MBAS	<0.1	0.5
Iron **	0.017	0.3
Manganese **	0.004	0.05
Sulfate	38.4	250
Total Dissolved Solids	149	500
Zinc **	0.006	5
Odor (Threshold odor #)	1.1	3 (TON)
pH	7.0	6.5 to 8.5 (Std Units)
Silver **	<0.0004	0.1
Aluminum **	0.015	0.2

** Analyzed 2009

Nashville, Tennessee Water Report, 2010 (continued)

Trihalomethane

Results in micrograms per liter

Parameter	Metro Water Services	MCL
Trichloromethane	26.7	N/A
Bromodichloromethane	5.5	N/A
Dibromochloromethane	0.5	N/A
Tribromomethane	0.1	N/A
Total Trihalomethanes (THMs)	32.8	80

Haloacetic Acids

Results in micrograms per liter

Parameter	Metro Water Services	MCL
Monochloroacetic Acid	<2	N/A
Dichloroacetic Acid	14.2	N/A
Trichloroacetic Acid	13.6	N/A
Monobromoacetic Acid	<1	N/A
Dibromoacetic Acid	<1	N/A
Total Haloacetic Acids (HAAs)	27.8	60

Organic Parameters

Results in mg/L unless noted Regulated Pesticides

Parameter	Metro Water Services	MCL
Atrazine (Analyzed April 2008)	not detected	0.003

Organic Parameters

Results in mg/L unless noted Regulated Herbicides

Parameter	Metro Water Services	MCL
Simazine (Analyzed June, Aug., Nov., 2010)	<0.00009	0.004

Radiochemical Parameters   Analyzed November 2006

Parameter	Metro Water Services	MCL
Gross Alpha	<3.0 pci/L	15 pci / L
Radium - 226 / 228	<0.46 / 1.01 pci/L	3 / 5 pci / L

Miscellaneous
Results in mg/L unless noted

Parameter	Metro Water Services	MCL
Sodium	4.8	not established
Hardness (Calcium)	74	not established
Alkalinity	56	not established
Temperature	19	not established
Langlier Index	-1.2	not established
Aggressive Index	10.6	not established

Secondary Standards
Results in mg/L unless noted

Parameter	Metro Water Services	MCL
Benzene	not detected	0.005
Carbon Tetrachloride	not detected	0.005
Para - Dichlorobenzene	not detected	0.075
1,2 - Dichloroethane	not detected	0.005
1,1 - Dichloroethylene	not detected	0.007
1,1,1 - Trichloroethane	not detected	0.20
Trichloroethylene	not detected	0.005
Vinyl Chloride	not detected	0.002
cis - 1,2 - Dichloroethylene	not detected	0.07
Dichloromethane	not detected	0.005
1,2 - Dichloropropane	not detected	0.005
Ethylbenzene	not detected	0.7
Monochlorobenzene	not detected	0.1
o - Dichlorobenzene	not detected	0.6
Styrene	not detected	0.1
Tetrachloroethylene	not detected	0.005
Toluene	not detected	1
trans - 1,2 - Dichloroethylene	not detected	0.1
Xylenes (total)	not detected	10
1,2,4 - Trichlorobenzene	not detected	0.07
1,1,2 - Trichloroethane	not detected	0.005

Nashville, Tennessee Water Report, 2010 (continued)

Volatile Organic Chemicals

(Analyzed November 2010)

Unregulated Results in mg/L unless noted

Parameter	Metro Water Services	MCL
Bromobenzene	not detected	none
Bromodichloromethane	0.0028	none
Bromoform	not detected	none
Bromomethane	not detected	none
Chlorodibromomethane	not detected	none
Chloroethane	not detected	none
Chloroform	0.0084	none
Chloromethane	not detected	none
o-Chlorotoluene	not detected	none
p-Chlorotoluene	not detected	none
Dibromomethane	not detected	none
m-Dichlorobenzene	not detected	none
1,1-Dichloroethane	not detected	none
1.3-Dichloropropane	not detected	none
2,2-Dichloropropane	not detected	none
1,1-Dichloropropene	not detected	none
1,3-Dichloropropene	not detected	none
1,1,1,2-Tetrachloroethane	not detected	none
1,1,2,2-Tetrachloroethane	not detected	none
1,2,3-Trichloropropane	not detected	none

interest, and both of those are well within spec (nitrate and nitrite). As long as those meet the standards, we're okay.

We go down to the next section — Secondary Standards. Those sound less important, but in fact they aren't! Almost every one of them is critical. Take iron, for instance. In this case, it's okay, but if that number were close to the MCL, we would be in trouble. Same goes for manganese.

The usual suspects in the group are chloride and sulfate, and total dissolved solids. If any of those is near the maximum, your water is iffy. Water of that type is used to make beer in some places, but as a general rule you should expect that it will compromise your results, and you had better start thinking about reverse osmosis (RO) filtration.

The one meaningless number in this group is pH. That may come as a surprise. If you have heard anything technical about brewing, you have probably heard about the importance of pH. It sounds complicated and tricky, and it may be one of the things that has made you hesitant about jumping into brewing. Trust me — it's not that tricky. It *is* important for the mash and the wort, as I've noted previously. We'll get back to that. But the *water* pH does not matter at all.

We can ignore the next five sections of the report (Trihalomethanes, Haloacetic Acids, Organic Parameters, Unregulated Contaminant Monitoring Results, Radiochemical Parameters). All those are important for other purposes, but for brewing they are irrelevant. On the other hand, the Miscellaneous section — for which MCLs are not even established — is significant. At the top we see three of the most important lines to homebrewers in the entire report. Sodium is a make-or-break parameter. George Fix, the great brewing researcher, thought that anything over 75 ppm of this ion would damage the flavor of your beer. Well, some breweries use water with levels higher than that, but in general I agree with him. I might allow a little leeway, but if my sheet showed anything over 100 I would definitely be shopping for an RO system. Hardness — basically, total calcium and magnesium — is more questionable. A high figure here could be okay as long as sodium was not very high. Then comes the big one: alkalinity, sometimes called total alkalinity. This is another make-or-break number, and we need to examine it a bit.

Basically, there are several strategies for adjusting the pH of your mash. This is often necessary, especially with pale and amber beers, because the pH of a pale malt mash tends to come in a little too high —

around 5.8 pH. Many experienced brewers prefer to see it around 5.2, and 5.5 is widely regarded as the maximum acceptable pH. Now the usual ways of adjusting mash pH have definite limits. High alkalinity will defeat them. This means that high-alkaline water is hard to work with. Fortunately for me, my water has only moderate alkalinity; 56 ppm is within the range that can be corrected.

There are no other numbers of interest on this sheet. However, there is one more thing we need to know. Chlorine and related compounds, such as iodine, are bad for the flavor of beer. So I need to know how this water is disinfected. All drinking water has to be treated in some way to kill bacteria so that it is safe. Most communities still use chlorine, but chloramine is becoming more popular. Fortunately, the Nashville metro website has a document that explains its water treatment process; this says that the last step of treatment is to add chlorine.

That's the last bit of information I need. Chlorine is easy to remove. The alkalinity is moderate. No problems with mineral content either. The answer to my question — what do I need to do with this water? — is, thank heavens, pretty much nothing. However, there is always some grit in tap water, so a sediment filter would help. A combination sediment-odor filter would be even better. These filters are fairly cheap and easily available, and the carbon component removes the chlorine. I have listed one as part of the basic brewing equipment kit.

One problem I have with this report is that it gives a single number for every item. That means these are averages. To find out how much the numbers vary, I have to call the water company and ask a few questions. As it turns out, they are very cooperative. They even provide monthly reports to customers on request. Looking at a few of those, I get a picture of how the water changes throughout the year. Fortunately, this information is good news. The swings in key parameters are modest, and my assessment is confirmed.

The next question is, what if your water is "hard" — as in difficult? That depends on what is hard about it. The simplest, and one of the most common cases, is chloramine.

A KEY TO "EASY" WATER

- ▸ Disinfection with chlorine, as opposed to chloramine
- ▸ Total alkalinity under 75 ppm
- ▸ Sodium under 100 ppm
- ▸ Sulfate under 150 ppm (can be a little higher if sodium is low)
- ▸ Nitrite under 1 ppm
- ▸ Iron under 0.03 ppm

THE CHLORAMINE PROBLEM

There are many web pages that explain why water companies have moved to chloramination. In fact, if your water company has done this, it probably has such a page on its site. Chloramine is in many ways an improvement over chlorine, but it comes with some hazards, all of which stem from its main advantage, its stability. That means it is harder to remove than chlorine.

The most practical way to deal with chloramine is to run the water through either a carbon block or granular-activated carbon bed filter. These filters are special-purpose items and are not usually sold at the average home improvement store. You can find them at garden supply stores and aquarium shops. Two-stage filtration is best (i.e., two cartridges). Contact time is important. You need to know the maximum flow rate for your filter. If you run water through a 1 gallon-per-minute (gpm) filter at 5 gallons per minute, it won't work. Only a tiny fraction of the chloramine will be removed. Better to get a 5 gpm filter and run the water at 1 gpm — though this is probably overkill. The store should be able to give you full performance data on the filters it sells.

CHLORINE VERSUS CHLORAMINE

Chloramination is a little more complicated than chlorination. It involves injecting a second gas, ammonia, into the water stream along with chlorine. The two combine to form chloramine, which is less volatile than simple chlorine. Especially in warm weather, chlorine tends to "gas out" of solution as water travels through the piping system; chloramine does not.

Chloramination is trickier because the proportions of the two gases must be kept within a narrow range. One water chemist described it to me as "keeping in your lane" on a winding road. But the rewards for the water company are lower costs and more consistent water quality.

A HARD CASE

Now we are going to take a look at truly "hard" water. I could have chosen a lot of places as an example, but I've always liked the name of Lubbock, in west Texas. I don't like their water though.

The first thing I notice is that Lubbock's report does not give the same information as Nashville's does. The reports are organized differently and list different items. That's to be expected. Both of them include enough information for our purposes. You'll notice there's a line in the first section for chloramines. That answers one question.

Lubbock, Texas Water Report

Contaminant	Year	MCL	Highest Level Detected	
Alpha emitters	2005	15 pCi/L	5 pCi/L	
Arsenic	2004–2005	10 ppb	4 ppb	
Barium	2004–2005	2 ppm	0.15 ppm	
Beta/photon emitters	2005	50 pCi/L*	6.5 pCi/L	
Chloramines	2010	MRDL = 4.0 ppm	3.9 ppm	
Chromium	2004–2005	100 ppb	6.7 ppb	
Cyanide	2009	200 ppb	70 ppb	
Fluoride	2008–2010	4 ppm	1.46 ppm	
Nitrate	2010	10 ppm	1.65 ppm	
Nitrite	2005	1 ppm	0.13 ppm	
Radium 226 & 228 combined	2005	5 pCi/L	0.7 pCi/L	
Total organic carbon	2010	TT	3.29 ppm	
Turbidity	2010	TT = 5 NTU (TT = % of samples <0.3 NTU)	0.13 NTU (100%)	
Additional Monitoring				
Aluminum	2010	0.05–0.2 ppm	0.144 ppm	
Ammonia	2010	Unregulated	0.386 ppm	
Calcium	2004–2005	Unregulated	62 ppm	
Chloride	2010	300 ppm	378 ppm	
Conductance	2010	Unregulated	2144 micromhos/cm	
Hardness	2010	Unregulated	343 ppm	
Magnesium	2004–2005	Unregulated	35 ppm	
Nickel	2004–2005	Unregulated	0.002 ppm	
Sodium	2010	Unregulated	290 ppm	
Sulfate	2010	300 ppm	237 ppm	
Total alkalinity	2010	Unregulated	179 ppm	

MCLG	Range	Contamination Source	Compliant Regulated at Treatment Plant
0	N/A	Erosion of natural deposits	Yes
0	2–4 ppb	Erosion of natural deposits, runoff from orchards	Yes
2 ppm	0.10–0.15 ppm	Erosion of natural deposits	Yes
0	N/A	Decay of natural and man-made deposits	Yes
MRDLG = 4 ppm	0.5–3.9 ppm	Disinfectant used to control microbes	Yes
100 ppb	0–6.7 ppb	Erosion of natural deposits	Yes
200 ppb	30–70 ppb	Erosion of natural deposits	Yes
4 ppm	0.71–1.46 ppm	Erosion of natural deposits	Yes
10 ppm	0.86–1.65 ppm	Runoff from fertilizer use, leaching from septic tanks, sewage, erosion	Yes
1 ppm	0.01–0.13 ppm	Runoff from fertilizer use, leaching from septic tanks, sewage, erosion	Yes
0	N/A	Erosion of natural deposits	Yes
TT	2.22–3.29 ppm	Naturally present in environment	Yes
0	0.03–0.13 NTU	Soil runoff	Yes
N/A	N/A	Water treatment chemical	Yes
N/A	N/A	Water treatment chemical	Yes
N/A	59–62 ppm	Naturally occurring	Yes
N/A	N/A	Naturally occurring	Yes
N/A	N/A	Naturally occurring	Yes
N/A	218–259 ppm	Naturally occurring	Yes
N/A	14.1–35 ppm	Naturally occurring	Yes
N/A	N/A	Erosion of natural deposits	Yes
N/A	N/A	Naturally occurring	Yes
N/A	N/A	Naturally occurring	Yes
N/A	N/A	Naturally occurring	Yes

Lubbock, Texas Water Report (continued)

Additional Monitoring, continued

Total dissolved solids	2010	1000 ppm	1180 ppm	
Zinc	2004–2005	5 ppm	0.004 ppm	
Regulated at the Customers' Taps				
Copper	2009	1.3 ppm AL	0.103 ppm	
Lead	2009	15 ppb AL	1.72 ppb	
Unregulated Initial Distribution System Evaluation for Disinfection Byproducts				
Total haloacetic acids	2008	N/A	15.4 ppb	
Total trihalomethanes	2008	N/A	31.9 ppb	
Regulated in the Distribution System				
Haloacetic acids (5)	2010	60 ppb	8.2 ppb	
Total coliform	2010	Coliform bacteria present in 5% or more of the monthly samples	2.86%	
Total trihalomethanes	2010	80 ppb	22.8 ppb	
Unregulated Contaminants				
Bromodichloromethane	2010	N/A	5.1 ppb	
Bromoform	2010	N/A	3.3 ppb	
Chloroform	2010	N/A	1.7 ppb	
Dibromochloromethane	2010	N/A	8.6 ppb	
Unregulated Contaminant Monitoring Rule 2 Data Collection				
N-Nitrosodimethlamine	2010	N/A	0.0046 ppb	

N/A	N/A	Naturally occurring	Yes
N/A	N/A	Naturally occurring	Yes
1.103 ppm	0.018–0.243 ppm	Erosion of natural deposits, corrosion of household plumbing systems	Yes
0	0–6.91 ppb	Erosion of natural deposits, corrosion of household plumbing systems	Yes
N/A	0–21.8 ppb	By-product of drinking water disinfection	Yes
N/A	0–45.6 ppb	By-product of drinking water disinfection	Yes
N/A	4.1–10.6 ppb	By-product of drinking water chlorination	Yes
0 0	2.86%	Naturally present in the environment	Yes
N/A	13.4–26.2	ppb	By-product of drinking water chlorination
N/A	N/A	By-product of drinking water disinfection	Yes
N/A	N/A	By-product of drinking water disinfection	Yes
N/A	N/A	By-product of drinking water disinfection	Yes
N/A	N/A	By-product of drinking water disinfection	Yes
N/A	0–0.0046 ppb	By-product of drinking water disinfection, industrial solvent, rocket fuel production	Yes

However, you also can see that this report quotes a range of figures for some items. It acknowledges the fact — which is true everywhere — that water supplies vary throughout the year. This is better than presenting an average. For other parameters, it lists the highest level detected. This also is helpful. If you think you might have hard water for brewing, you are better off taking the worst-case scenario as your guideline.

And boy, is this water difficult. In 2010, sodium ran as high as 290 ppm, sulfate as high as 237 ppm, and chloride as high as 378 ppm. These numbers are all way out of bounds for any style of beer. Reverse-osmosis (RO) filtration is the only remedy.

This example shows why you have to look at your water before you make up an equipment budget. An RO system is expensive, especially if you get it installed by a treatment company. If you choose to install it yourself, it can cost quite a bit less, but of course this requires more time and work from you. Besides the initial installation, such a system requires regular monitoring and maintenance.

My suggestion, if you have to go the RO route, is to define your objectives first. If you want to treat all your drinking water, then installing the system will be a plumbing project, and you need to think about whether you can or want to take it on. If you only want to "fix" your brewing water, then you can find small, well-designed systems online. They are meant to be used with a storage tank or an aquarium. These systems will always include a sediment filter, two stages of carbon filtration, and an RO membrane filter. Output typically will be rated at around 50 to 75 gallons per day, which is only 4 to 6 gallons per hour. No problem for homebrewing, but it does mean that you cannot just pull your brewing liquor from a tap when you are ready to begin.

RO filtration systems are easy to price shop online. They represent a significant hit to the brewery budget. On the other hand, compare them to what 5-gallon carboys of RO-treated water cost, and you'll find that the payback is pretty quick. Note also, this is the only water filter you will need, because it incorporates sediment and chlorine/chloramine filters.

WATER-TREATMENT CHEMICALS

Most breweries do some water treatment in addition to the removal of sediment and chlorine compounds. This treatment usually amounts to mineral or acid additions to adjust the pH of the water or mash.

Obviously you need to have a calibrated pH meter to do this. The chemicals usually employed by commercial breweries are:

▸ **CALCIUM CHLORIDE:** added to mash to lower the pH. I prefer it to calcium sulfate because the chloride imparts a softer, smoother taste.

▸ **CALCIUM SULFATE (GYPSUM):** added to mash to lower the pH. Some brewers prefer it for dry, hoppy beers.

▸ **CALCIUM CARBONATE (CHALK):** raises the pH of the mash. It is soluble only in an acid environment, so it must be added to the mash after the grain is stirred in.

▸ **PHOSPHORIC ACID 10%:** added to sparge liquor to lower the pH. It may be added to the mash, but some brewers regard this as bad practice, like using a pair of pliers to tighten a nut on a bolt.

▸ **OTHER MINERAL SALTS SOMETIMES CALLED FOR IN BREWING:** magnesium sulfate (Epsom salts), canning salt (pure sodium chloride, without the silicates and other additives in table salt), and sodium bicarbonate (baking soda). Note: I would consider adding them only to RO water; they are seldom needed when dealing with an "easy" water supply.

There is a blend of phosphate buffers made by Five Star that is intended to do away with the need for pH meters and water treatment regimens. It is called "5.2," and the company claims that it will produce a pH of 5.2 in any mash, regardless of the malt bill or the mash liquor. This sounds like the answer to a maiden's prayer, and I actually tried it in one of my first batches. According to my pH meter, the recommended dose (1 tablespoon) did bring the mash down somewhat, but not all the way to 5.2. I thought maybe I had not calibrated correctly, but before I made another brew, I learned that the phosphates in "5.2" are sodium compounds. A tablespoonful of mineral salts is a huge dose in a 5-gallon batch. Because I believe that, except in the case of RO water, no one should add sodium to brewing liquor, in any quantity, this information put an end to my experimentation with the product.

Some homebrewers try to adjust the mineral content of their water to the exact beer style that they are making. For example, when making a stout, they will attempt to match the water of London or Dublin, by various additions of mineral salts. This is not always possible unless you first strip the water so that you can start with a blank slate, so if you ever decide to pursue this, you may have to get an RO filter.

Most brewers, including me, take a conservative approach to water treatment. The only goal is to remove chlorine and other undesirables, and correct the pH of the mash and wort. I believe in doing to the water no more than is necessary to meet those parameters. Pale ale, for example, can be and is made in a great many places, with quite different water supplies. Thus, I see no need to duplicate the water of Burton-upon-Trent, the English city where the style originated. Not everyone agrees with me, and I have no problem with that. What concerns me is brewers with only limited experience devoting their time and attention to such a secondary objective.

I strongly recommend that you hold off on experiments with water replication until you first have mastered the brewing process and are getting repeatable results from your recipes. The effects of water are rather subtle, so you first need to be sure of your basic technique. Only then will you be in a position to make comparisons.

Specifics on using water treatment chemicals are covered in the Operations chapter (page 128). The only thing I need to add here is that, if you are working with RO water and/or trying for precise adjustments of various minerals, you will need to get a small digital scale. The ideal tool for this would be one with a maximum capacity of 100 grams, and a display that shows hundredths of a gram — two numbers to the right of the decimal. Fortunately in this digital age such scales are common and reasonably priced. A calibration weight is a very useful accessory.

Malt and Other Grains

Malt is barley or other grain that has been steeped in water, drained, and then allowed to germinate. When germination reaches the proper point, which is before the embryonic plant actually emerges from the end of the grain, it is halted by drying the wet malt with warm or hot air in a kiln. The reason for this exercise is that during germination, enzymes are formed that soften the barley starches and break down the cell walls. These enzymes are preserved during kilning (usually), and are then activated by hot water when you mix the mash. There, they degrade the malt starch into soluble sugars — the nutrients that yeast ferments into alcohol. Other malt enzymes break down barley proteins, during malting and sometimes during mashing as well, which is important for yeast nutrition and beer clarity.

In practical terms, malts can be divided into four classes:

Pale malts. The base ingredient in most beer. Kilned at low temperatures to preserve enzymes. Used alone in a mash, they produce a pale (yellow) beer. Some examples are pilsner malt, pale malt, Vienna malt, pale ale malt. One designation unique to North America is two-row versus six-row. Elsewhere all pale malts are made from two-row barley varieties, and these are often named, such as Maris Otter or Golden Promise. Two-row barley is generally superior and is used almost exclusively by American craft brewers.

There is one pale malt that deserves a separate mention: acid malt (in German, *Sauermalz*). The malting process for it is unique in that it includes a low-temperature steep to allow lactic acid bacteria, which are found in all types of malt, to multiply and do their thing. The process is monitored and halted when a specified concentration of lactic acid is reached. Acid malt can be used as a natural method of lowering mash pH, making it as much a water treatment as a beer ingredient. In small amounts, it contributes no flavor other than that of pale malt. If used in large quantities it imparts a flavor note similar to what you would find in a Berliner Weisse style wheat beer, which is soured deliberately by fermenting with a mixed culture that includes lactic acid bacteria and brewer's yeast.

High-kilned malts. Like pale malt except kilned at a higher temperature. The dividing line between pale malts and high-kilned malts is blurry. The paler types, like Munich malt, preserve some enzymes and can be used as base malt. Used alone they will produce a deep-yellow-to-amber-colored beer. Some examples are light Munich malt, dark Munich malt, Victory malt.

Caramel malts. These are made by heating the green malt while it is still wet. This is called stewing, and it fosters the development of sugars in the kernel. Drying temperature determines the color. Most caramel malts are darker than the typical high-kilned malt and will give beer a red-orange "sunset" color. They have no enzymes and can only be used as flavor and color modifiers in conjunction with paler malts. Some examples are light crystal, dark crystal, caramel 10, caramel 40, Cara-Munich, Special B. One special variant of caramel malt is dextrin malt, often called Cara-Pils. It is high in complex carbohydrates, which are not fermentable. This makes it useful for "building the body" of heartier beer styles.

Roasted malts. These are made by roasting pale malt in a drum similar to coffee beans. This destroys the enzymes and gives a deep brown to black color and an intense coffee-like flavor. Very little of this material is needed to darken a beer — only a few percent. Some examples are chocolate malt and Black Patent malt.

Other malted grains. The most common of these are malted wheat and malted rye. They are usually pale malts, but some darker or kilned types have appeared. The flavor is different from barley malt and in the case of rye, quite distinctive.

UNMALTED INGREDIENTS

These fall into three classes — **adjuncts**, **roasted grains**, and **sugars**.

Adjuncts are unmalted cereals that substitute for some portion of the malt in certain styles of beer. The big "macrobreweries" in North America most often use corn or rice, which have little protein or color, and therefore make a beer with a lighter body and hue. They normally process these grains through a separate mill and a "cereal cooker" vessel, which is similar to a brew kettle. The raw cereal starches have to be cooked to soften them up before they can be added to the mash. I still remember the first time I hosted a group of professional brewers at the Tap Room in St. Louis, where I worked for several years before I moved to Nashville. They had a lot of questions, but the first was, "Where's your cereal cooker?" I explained that because most of our beer was all-malt, this would not be a good investment. We did the same thing I did and still do as a homebrewer: we bought our adjuncts as steamed, hot-rolled brewer's flakes. They cost more that way, but they can be added straight into the grist for an infusion mash. I have nothing against adjuncts as such. Oatmeal stout is one of my favorite styles of beer. Adjuncts have gotten a bad reputation among homebrewers based on their use as "lighteners," which is unfortunate.

If you would like to try your hand at cooking raw adjuncts, consult my *Homebrewing Guide* and some of the other advanced brewing books in the resources section.

Roasted grains are unmalted grains that have been roasted in a drum like roasted malt. The taste is different because the grain has no sugar. Roasted barley is by far the most common representative of this group. The difference between roasted grains and adjuncts comes down

The Tap Room. The author (left) cut his teeth brewing for Tom Schlafly (right) at the Tap Room in St. Louis.

to two factors: adjuncts contribute sugar to the wort, and they are generally used in a relatively large proportion. Like roasted malts, roasted grains are used in small amounts, for their flavor and color contribution.

Brewing sugars and syrups are more commonplace and versatile than you might expect. Most homebrewers know that some of the big, flavorful Belgian ales are made with a significant proportion of crystal sugar (often called Kandi Sugar) or sugar syrups. These have some flavoring properties, but they also serve to lighten the body of high-alcohol beers so that they do not feel so thick on the tongue.

A more common form of brewing sugar is high-maltose corn syrup, which is often used as a more convenient and cheaper substitute for adjunct grain. The result is always different, though, because the syrups do not have exactly the same assortment of sugars as would be created by adding corn or rice to the mash tun. I have not seen brewing corn syrup in homebrew supply shops, which is probably just as well. The only corn sugar product I commonly see is straight dextrose, and its use is mostly confined to priming bottled beer and casks. Kandi Sugars are available in both crystal and syrup form for making Belgian-style ales at home.

MALT SPECIFICATIONS

Malting companies always test their products for some basic parameters and publish the results as a set of rather esoteric-sounding specifications. The basic properties they are testing for are:

Color. This is pretty obvious. Make a mash, strain off the liquid, and check its color. However, two different standards are used — EBC (European Brewing Convention) and SRM (Standard Reference Method) — and you have to know which is being used. European malts are of course measured by the EBC method, but almost always an approximate equivalent SRM value is also noted. You'll find that most recipe software uses SRM (also called Lovibond).

Modification. This is the softening of starches and proteins that takes place during germination. For single-infusion mashing you need a well-modified malt. Most pale and high-kilned malts made today are well modified and suitable. The best measure of modification is "fine/coarse difference" — I guess I'd better explain that. Grind one malt sample fine. Make a mash with it. Measure the yield of sugars. Then grind the other sample coarse, make an identical mash (same temperature, water, and so on), and measure the yield. Then compare the yield numbers. The smaller the fine/coarse difference, the better the modification. For infusion mashes, you want to see a percentage number under 1.8.

Enzyme content. Also called *diastatic power*, this is measured in degrees Lintner or W-K (Windisch-Kolbach) units. These scales translate pretty well. For a base malt you need at least a 40 to 50 degrees Lintner malt, and if you are using adjuncts 60 to 75 is better. American malts almost always have excellent diastatic power; the finer British and continental malts have less.

Protein content. Measured as total nitrogen, this quantifies the "haze potential" of malt. Most beer haze comes from malt proteins and husk tannins. Because enzymes are proteins, it is no surprise that haze-prone malts are also the ones with the highest diastatic power.

Starch content (yield). Brewers need enzymes, but what they really want is sugar. This comes from malt starch, as explained earlier, so the higher the starch content, the higher the yield will be. I have already mentioned yield measurements in connection with modification. The best real-world predictor of yield is the "coarse ground, as-is" number. However, the malting companies usually publish a "coarse ground, dry basis" figure, which factors out the moisture content of the malt (usually 2 to 4 percent). As long as they also give the moisture content, you can easily calculate the as-is yield.

You can see how some of these numbers are related. The best malting barleys have the highest percentage of starch, or yield; that means a lower proportion of their weight is made of husks and proteins. Husks are the source of tannins, so high-yield malts, with less husk and protein, have a lower haze potential, but also less diastatic power. Because heat destroys enzymes, higher-kilned malts, with more color, also have less diastatic power.

There are other useful numbers that malting companies provide, but these are the ones with the greatest practical implications. If you understand why they are important, you are well on your way toward being able to make intelligent choices when you try your hand at creating your own recipes.

SELECTING MALTS

If you are trying to follow someone else's recipe, then you need to be precise about it. At least for all the caramel and roasted malts, stick to the brands listed by the author. Different maltsters have different ideas about what is "chocolate malt" or "roasted barley." For the base malts, I would say the same rule should be applied, though you can be a little looser. The Rahr company's pale two-row malt should substitute for, say, Cargill's reasonably well, because most of the big American and Canadian companies like those use the same barley varieties for their standard malts. However, the special lines can be different. If the company says that they are making a pilsner malt, for example, using a new barley variety, it may be significantly different from anyone else's product. Similarly, one brand of Maris Otter pale malt may be significantly different from another.

Any brewer who aims to make great beer needs to learn a lot about malt. Fortunately, you can gather quite a bit from manufacturers' and importers' websites. Some of the advanced books that are listed in Resources (see page 255) have excellent chapters on malt and malting. More exact information is often found on the tags of individual sacks of malt. If your homebrew supply shop gets its pale and high-kilned malts in sacks, they should be happy to show the tags and spec sheets to you.

I would advise against purchasing precrushed malt if possible. Buy whole kernel and mill it, or have it milled at the store. If precrushed is the only form available for a malt you want, use your eyes and your nose to evaluate it. The slightest hint of mustiness in the aroma is reason enough to change your brewing plans.

THE BULK MALT OPTION

If you brew regularly, you can save money by buying 50- or 55-pound sacks of your base malt(s). Obviously you will need to invest in a tight, sturdy storage container, in addition to a malt mill. Most people get a malt mill primarily for the sake of convenience and, if they are unhappy with their yields, for a better crush. The savings on bulk malt is a bonus. One factor that should be considered, though, is storage life. Crushed malt will pick up moisture and begin to go stale relatively quickly, especially in an opened bag or other container. This means that if you are far from the nearest shop and you often buy several batches' worth of malt at a time, you might have another reason to consider buying whole-kernel malt in bulk.

The drawback, of course, is that you lose some flexibility. You may find your choice of pale malt determines your recipes. Small brewpubs do not face this problem so much, but slightly larger breweries do. Most have only one or two grain silos and therefore have to base all or most of their product line on a single malt. My advice is always to use the malt that matches the beer: Crisp Maris Otter or other high-grade British pale malt for a Best Bitter or an ESB, for example, or Weyermann or other fine Munich malts for a dunkel or Märzen. However, for some styles the base malt matters less. For example, Irish stout has such a strong specialty-grain presence that you may as well go with a standard North American two-row pale malt.

Hops

If there is one brewing material that has star status these days, it is the hop. Hop bines loaded with ripe cones are shown in commercials, and while even committed beer drinkers often ask rudimentary questions about malt (such as, "What is it?"), they clearly understand what hops are. Sierra Nevada Pale Ale and other well-hopped brews deserve a lot of credit for that. This is one area where craft beer has made a huge impact.

Hops, which grow on bines that climb trellises, have become especially popular with today's beer drinkers, thanks to the slew of pale ales and IPAs flowing out of craft breweries.

Craft beer also lives on the margins of the hop industry. If you look at the total acreage of hop farms in the United States, the overwhelming majority is given over to what are called high-alpha and super-alpha varieties. *Alpha* refers to alpha acid, or humulone, which is the substance responsible for the bittering quality in hops. Over the years hop breeding programs have focused mainly on developing hops with higher and higher percentages of alpha acids. Aromatic and flavor components are not ignored, but they are a secondary consideration. The price of these hops is pretty much tied to their alpha acid content.

Craft brewers use high-alpha and super-alpha hops, but they also use — in a much larger proportion, relative to most of the big industrial breweries — hops with a more modest alpha content, but with outstanding flavor and aroma properties. The varieties that I base most of my beers on, such as Willamette, are planted in much smaller acreage than the alpha varieties such as Columbus and Tomahawk. Willamette is an interesting case. A few years ago, Anheuser-Busch decided to reduce the company's traditional commitment to low-alpha, aromatic hops, and in particular, to Willamettes. As a result, Willamette production has decreased drastically. The ongoing movement toward super-alphas is one of several reasons small brewers more and more are contracting for hops in advance. Increasingly this is the only way they can ensure that they will have the varieties that the character of their beers depends on.

One fortunate fact for homebrewers and craft brewers is that in Europe, things are not quite so far along, and they may never be. Breweries everywhere try to economize on their materials costs, but there is still more of a market for the traditional low-alpha or aromatic hops across the pond. As a result, it does not appear that the traditional "noble hops" of central Europe — such as Tettnang, Saaz, or Hallertauer Mittelfrüh — are in danger of disappearing. The same goes for the great English varieties, including Kent Golding and Fuggles. Still, on a recent trip to England, I was surprised and a little disturbed to see how enthusiastically British craft brewers have taken to American hops. Granted, these are usually the fine-aroma varieties, such as Liberty and Cascade, but still, it's a little jarring to discover a floral and even citrusy "signature" in a real ale brewed in the West Midlands. I hope they don't forget their roots (pun intended).

PELLETS OR WHOLE?

I have already stated that my brewery plan, like that of most pubs, is based on a kettle/whirlpool combination vessel. This is the simplest and most practical arrangement, but, as acknowledged, it demands that you use pelletized hops. The whole cone (sometimes called leaf or whole leaf) natural form is from many points of view less desirable: it requires more storage space and is more prone to oxidation and alpha loss as time passes. On the other hand, there is no question that pelletizing is an instance of the changes wrought on brewing by modern technology, and while some of these are universally welcomed (the counterflow heat exchanger, for example), others are more controversial. When hops are pelletized, that means they are pulverized in a hammer mill. Then the shredded particles that were once a hop cone are formed under heat and pressure into pellets that resemble rabbit food. There is no question that this change is not all for the better.

One of my most vivid brewing memories is of the time, early on in my tenure at the Tap Room, when I was having lunch with two good friends and great brewers, both, alas, now departed: Roger Bergen and George Fix. We were talking about my new job, and I mentioned that in my former life as a homebrewer, I almost always had used whole hops, but now that I was compelled to use pellets, I had found them to be "just fine." Roger brought his fist down on the table. "Have you seen it?" he demanded (meaning pelletizing). George looked over at me and shook his head solemnly. "Aw, Dave, it's brutal," he lamented.

Well, since then I have seen it, and George was right: it is brutal. Watching lovely hop cones being reduced to powder in a hammer mill, then pressed into pellets, is a sad sight, and the oxidation that hop oils endure during this ordeal is considerable. I hope they will forgive me for saying that I still believe that great beers can be made with pelletized hops, and that their advantages outweigh the small degradation that comes with the processing. Anheuser-Busch, the most traditional of the big American breweries, finally went over to pellets a few years before it was sold to InBev; it took a long time, but years of trial brews and tastings finally convinced them that Budweiser tasted no different whether it was made with pellets or whole hops. Some craft brewers have yet to be convinced. Because the hop profile of their beers is so prominent, it may well be that a change over to pellets would perceptibly alter their beer. But, if you formulate a recipe with pellets from the start, this is not an issue.

I would not discourage any homebrewer from experimenting with whole hops, or for that matter, from opting to use them exclusively. But I would suggest that this is another complication that is best deferred until you have become proficient in your basic technique. At that point, you can fit your kettle with a hop screen or strainer such as the Kettle-Screen and work with whole hops exclusively, or in combination with pellets. The two things you have to be prepared for are higher wort losses, owing to the greater bulk of the hop material, and lower hop utilization, meaning that you will need to use more hops to get the same level of bitterness in the finished beer. Most beer recipe calculator programs include algorithms that adjust for the difference in utilization, which should help with matching the bitterness when you change from one hop type to the other.

Buying hops used to be fraught with difficulty for the homebrewer. Fortunately, most vendors now understand the importance of refrigerated storage for all hops, including pellets. The odds of getting old, cheesy-smelling hops are not nearly as bad as they once were. One of the advantages of pellets for the homebrewer is that they are not as susceptible to deterioration as whole hops are. Nonetheless, I recommend that you store all your hops in the freezer once you get them home. And if possible, you should do a "rub test" on whole hops (this means rubbing a few cones between your palms to release the humulone and hop oils, and sniffing) before purchase. Pellets need to be smashed back to powder, which is harder to do.

As for selecting varieties: as with malt, I think the best course is to follow tradition. For example, if you want to make an American Pale Ale, Cascades and similar floral varieties almost define the beer. The same goes for the traditional English varieties in an ESB. For pilsner, I can think of only a handful of noble hops that I would consider in lieu of the classic Zatec Red (Saaz); Polish Lublin and German Spalt are two that come to mind offhand. Once again, as with pale malt, beers that are defined by a big specialty grain character have more leeway. As Dave Line observed long ago, there's no need to insist on Fuggles or East Kent Goldings in an Irish Stout.

The best source of detailed information about specific hop varieties are the websites of major hop suppliers, such as Hopsteiner and Hopunion. Time spent looking over their online pamphlets and data sheets will be well rewarded.

Yeast

Far from being simply a microscopic alcohol factory, yeast plays just as big a role in beer flavor as malt or hops do. Indeed, the number of aromatic compounds produced by yeast during fermentation is amazing.

This means, obviously, that the choice of a yeast strain is just as important a recipe decision as the choice of hops or malts. And in fact, one of the biggest limitations facing the pub brewer is that practical necessity usually dictates the selection of a single "production yeast" for all, or at least most, of his beers.

The normal method of handling yeast in a pub is to draw the slurry off from the bottom of one unitank and pitch it into the next. Because in most pubs brewing is only done twice a week or so, the next batch is most likely a different beer from the last one. Furthermore, there is no yeast brink or other permanent dedicated vessel available for yeast storage or washing. If the yeast needs to be stored for a few days because there is no empty tank available for the next batch, it is put in a keg and kept in a refrigerator. Propagation of a new yeast culture is normally done in the cone of an empty fermenter. It requires "stealing" a barrel or so of pale wort from a normal batch to provide the growth medium. This is a nuisance, and it requires having two tanks empty at the same time — something that is not always possible.

All told, it is not hard to understand why pub brewers do not want to handle multiple yeast strains. Typically, each yeast needs to be repitched every 14 days at most (for ales, this is stretching it) or if not, it will need to be "roused," which is basically the same as a repropagation. The facts of yeast life also explain why pub brewers put a premium on stability and practical performance characteristics, especially attenuation and flocculence.

Attenuation is the reduction of sugars to alcohol, and therefore the drop in specific gravity that occurs during fermentation. A sugar solution is denser than pure water, which means it will weigh more, pint for pint. Alcohol is lighter than water, pint for pint. As fermentation goes along, the volume in the fermenter stays the same but the weight drops. This is attenuation. Some yeasts ferment more completely than others; this is another way of saying they are more attenuative. Both strong and weak attenuating yeasts can make good beer. What matters most is that attenuation is consistent from batch to batch. Some yeasts tend to become less attenuative over time, which is undesirable.

Flocculence is the tendency of yeast cells to clump together and drop out of suspension in the fermenter. Some ale yeasts are early floccers: they start forming clumps while fermentation is still very active, so the flocs are carried to the surface by the evolving carbon dioxide where, in an open fermenter, they form a "pancake" that can be skimmed off for repitching. This phenomenon of early flocculation is what is referred to by the old phrase "top fermentation." The phrase is a misnomer, because only the yeast cells that remain suspended in the beer actually engage in the intake of sugars and output of alcohol and carbon dioxide. Once a cell flocs, it has gone into retirement.

Early floccing, or "top-cropping," yeast strains are a difficult match for closed fermenters. Unless a blowoff hose and bucket are attached, they can make a mess on the brewery floor. Even if the blowoff is controlled, the yeast is out in open air or stuck to the top and sides of the tank, and is not suitable for repitching. There are special fermenter designs that can accommodate a top-cropping yeast, such as the Yorkshire Stone Square system, but standard closed fermenters — which are much preferable for the sake of maintaining sanitary conditions — pretty much dictate a bottom-cropping yeast strain.

One other problem with top-cropping yeast is that paradoxically, it can make beer difficult to clarify. If the pancake is not skimmed, it will eventually fall back into the beer as fermentation comes to an end, and it may well not drop through to the bottom. The result is stubbornly yeasty beer.

All this is a long way of explaining why bottom-cropping ale yeasts are preferable in modern breweries, and the same thing is generally true for homebrewing. Even if you do not plan to harvest and repitch your yeast, a bottom cropper will prove easier to deal with. As far as propagation goes, you can imagine why pub brewers would prefer a stable strain, that is, one whose fermentation and flocculation performance do not change with multiple repitchings. At Blackstone I went as many as 60 generations before getting a fresh culture from the yeast lab.

Obviously, in homebrewing, yeast stability is not as much of an issue. Because most of us brew only once every two or three weeks, the best strategy is to start with fresh yeast every time. Of course, if you brew more frequently, then you will want to look carefully at Yeast Propagation and Culturing (page 181) in the chapter on advanced brewing methods.

For those just starting out in grain brewing, I recommend first settling on a single user-friendly ale yeast strain until you get your technique down. Second, as for sources, the first option would be to cadge yeast from the brewers at your local pub. They are probably using Wyeast Labs 1056 or another good all-purpose strain. If there is no local pub you can turn to, the next best source would be a dried yeast strain from the homebrew supply shop.

DRIED YEAST

You read that right. Dried yeast has come a long way. Brewpubs and small micros are making award-winning beers with dried yeast. While it is true that most will buy a liquid slurry of their standard yeast and propagate it up to a pitchable volume, then repitch it many times, for one-offs or special-run beers that are made less frequently, some are turning to dry yeast and using it with success. The purity of dried yeast has been improved to the point where it can even be repitched several times without fear of increasing bacteria counts. The flavor and fermentation properties of the dried yeast strains closely resemble the same strains as available in liquid or slurry form. This means that you no longer have to do propagation in order to make great beer at home. You can begin with a packet of dried yeast and expect it to ferment and flocculate in the same way a liquid yeast would.

Liquid yeasts still have the enormous advantage of offering great variety. No matter what kind of beer you want to brew, there are several strains available from White Labs, Wyeast, and the other liquid yeast suppliers that will give excellent results. Most of those strains are the same ones that are employed in the classic breweries that define the certain beer style. By contrast, the total number of dried yeasts available can almost be counted on two hands, and there is quite a bit of overlap among them. Most are classic British ale strains. There is a range of characteristics — some are top croppers, some bottom, some are more alcohol tolerant, some less, and so forth — but still, that is what they are. I know of only one dried American ale yeast strain, only two strains of lager yeast, and two wheat beer yeasts. There is no dried Kölsch yeast, to name one very popular style.

The reason there are so few dried yeasts available is what you might expect — economics. Producing a batch of dried yeast requires skilled operators, expensive equipment and materials, and time. Production is profitable only on a fairly large scale, and only if you can sell the quantity you make. By contrast, the process of making liquid slurry is far more flexible. You can grow up a batch to any size that the market requires. I am afraid this means that, although there may be more dried yeast strains available in the future as pub and homebrewing continues to grow in popularity, there will never be dried equivalents for more than a small fraction of the brewer's yeasts that are kept and sold in liquid form.

I am not here to tell you that you are likely to be content to use dried yeasts forever, or for everything. Sooner or later, you will want to branch out into liquid yeasts, for the sake of making the beers you want. I am saying that dried yeasts should not be regarded as a compromise, or a limiting factor, when used to ferment the types of beer that they are designed for. They are a great help especially for new brewers who have plenty of other things to learn. Personally, I go through a decision tree when I am planning a brew. First question: Will Wyeast Labs 1056 be a good match for this beer? If so, can I get a fresh slurry from my colleagues at Blackstone? If not, I'll use a comparable dried ale yeast. Second question: Is there another dried strain that looks like a good fit? If so, I'll get some and try it. I am still learning, and by no means have I tried all the dry yeasts out there. As a pro I used only about half a dozen liquid yeast strains, and most of them only for seasonal beers. Still, if none of the dried choices looks promising, I will go for a liquid yeast.

My suggestion for someone starting out in grain brewing would be to standardize on a good dried yeast strain that will suit a wide range of ales. Stick with it for at least a half dozen batches before you try to branch out. One yeast that I have personally used, which has good attenuation and flocs well, is the Danstar Nottingham strain made by Lallemand. It is suitable for pale, mild, and brown ales, as well as darker ales such as porters and stouts.

Also, you should to be aware that dried yeast is not necessarily cheaper than a liquid culture. This is particularly true for lagers, because you will need two packets for a 5-gallon batch.

LIQUID YEAST

I have already said something about liquid yeasts, both the advantages and the disadvantages. The obvious advantage is variety, and the obvious disadvantage is that they may have to be propagated, as my previous comments indicated.

I need to clarify that point, because the instructions on some liquid yeast packages state that, at least for ales, there is enough yeast to pitch directly into a 5-gallon batch of wort. This is a subject that can be argued back and forth. The White Labs tubes have 70 to 140 billion cells. Wyeast Activator packets are stated to contain about 100 billion. For 5 gallons, the high number of 140 billion is close to the pitching rate used by most ale brewers. (For the technically minded, a conservative recommendation is 0.75 million cells per milliliter per degree Plato. If you do the conversions and calculations, that works out to 171 billion cells for 5 gallons of 1.049 original gravity wort.) However, the yeast labs point out that their yeast is actually in much better shape than yeast that has gone through the stress of a beer fermentation, so that it will multiply and ferment more vigorously than a normal brewery slurry. All this is perfectly true when speaking about freshly packaged yeast as it leaves the lab. (See photographs on inside cover.)

What happens afterward is partly outside the lab's control, and this is where things can get dicey. The labs always ship yeast in an insulated package with an ice pack. So do most wholesalers. Nonetheless, the ice pack has only so much cooling capacity, and in warm weather a long shipment, especially if delayed, may allow the yeast to get too warm. If that happens viability will fall precipitously.

My recommendation, especially if you intend to do a "straight pitch" of a White Labs tube or a Wyeast Activator pack, is to buy from a local homebrew supply shop that gets its yeast air-freighted directly from the lab. This arrangement ensures that the yeast you get is in the best possible condition and will perform as expected.

I also recommend aerating the wort thoroughly when doing a "straight pitch" — this means using an air pump and diffusing stone, no halfway measures — as well as using a yeast nutrient. I have had good results with Servomyces, which is available from many homebrew supply shops. Do not exceed the recommended dosage as it can affect the beer flavor. When used as directed, it improves yeast growth and vitality.

Without a doubt, even if it takes a more circuitous route, most liquid yeast arrives at the homebrew shop in excellent condition and well within its "best before" date. If pitched directly into 5 gallons of well-aerated, normal-gravity wort, it will perform well. Still, this is not always the case, and then of course there are beers that require a higher pitch rate — high-gravity ales, and any lager. The pitch rate rule for lager is twice that for ales, 1.5 million cells per milliliter per degree Plato.

All the uncertainty and exceptions mean that homebrewers who get seriously involved with liquid yeast almost always get into propagation — making "starters," as it is known.

Propagation sounds complex, but it's really not. Reasonably priced stir plates are now available, which means it is possible for homebrewers to get excellent, repeatable results. I detail the process of creating a yeast starter in Advanced Techniques (page 180). While the process is simple, you'll see why I recommend sticking with normal gravity ales for your first six months or so of brewing.

Clarifying Agents

These are not beer ingredients, strictly speaking, but they can be added to wort or beer to aid clarity and flavor. Sometimes called *finings*, they fall into two classes according to where they are used: kettle coagulants and beer finings.

KETTLE COAGULANTS

This class of additives has several brand names, including Whirlfloc, Koppaclear, Super Moss, and the generic term "Irish Moss." They are added to the kettle to promote the formation of *hot break*, which is the protein material that comes out of solution and forms visible particles during the boil. They also help to promote the formation of *cold break* in the heat exchanger, and this action also has an impact on the clarity of the finished beer. Anyone who has boiled wort has probably seen hot break, but cold break is less familiar because many beginning home-brewers use slow and inefficient methods of wort cooling.

Suffice it to say the use of a kettle coagulant in combination with a counterflow heat exchanger will result in cold wort full of visible particles, even though the hot wort in the kettle was properly whirlpooled and run off clear. The effect is best seen with pale and amber worts. I consider kettle coagulant to be a required ingredient. Not all are equal in their effectiveness, but all will help if used properly. For beginners, I suggest a form that does not need lengthy preparation before being added to the kettle. Whirlfloc tablets are one example. However, those forms tend to cost more on a per-use basis. Whichever you choose, be sure to read and follow the preparation and dosing instructions carefully.

BEER FININGS

I have already mentioned this class of clarifiers in the equipment section, because they can be used as a substitute, or an aid, for beer filtration. Most are based on isinglass, which is made from the swim bladders of fish, or on gelatin. There are some non-animal-derived alternatives as well. You should keep in mind that isinglass, which I have found to be the most effective type of fining agent, can be problematic to work with. Small clear packets of premixed liquid finings are available and easier to use, but note that storage at temperatures much above 60°F will sooner or later make it go "slack." The substance's molecular structure is undone and the material will no longer attract and hold yeast cells together in flocs. On the other hand, simply keeping the mixture in the refrigerator does not work either: such cold temperatures prevent the solid fining particles from properly dissolving. For best results, powdered isinglass must be prepared and allowed to *cut* (liquefy) exactly according to the manufacturer's directions, with special attention to temperature.

Other types of finings have their own problems. Some may not settle out into a compact solid mass on the bottom of the keg or carboy; instead you may see a gelatinous-looking haze that hangs in the lower fourth of the vessel. Others just do not seem to clarify very well. It is possible to find people who have used almost every type of fining agent out there and swear they have achieved such excellent results that they would never bother to filter their beer. You can also find other people who will swear that same agent failed miserably, whereas another product was completely effective.

So much disagreement leaves me just as confused as you. My best advice is that if you want to use finings, follow the maker's instructions to the letter, and then see what results you get. Personally I use isinglass finings, a practical choice because my friends at Blackstone dose their casks of "real ale" with it and usually have some on hand. They also have a separate cask cooler that is set at 50°F, the perfect temperature for mixing and storing isinglass. I bring it straight home in a cooler with a small ice pack and add it directly to my carboy.

Cleaners and Sanitizers

The last "ingredients" in beer making are not exactly brewing materials, but they are just as important as water, malt, hops, or yeast to the success of your efforts.

Cleaning and sanitizing is the key to making good beer. It's as simple as that. All successful brewers I know have developed routines that they follow faithfully, knowing that their beer and their jobs depend on it. Unless you do the same, you are doomed to failure sooner or later.

Beer is made by the fermentation of a carefully selected strain of yeast. The only exceptions are the so-called wild or farmhouse beers, in which a mixture of different yeasts and bacteria do a sort of fermentation by committee. But even with these exotic beer styles, the brewer chooses the organisms that ferment the beer. The general rule is that beer is fermented by brewer's yeast, and any other microorganism that takes part in the fermentation is an invader — to borrow a medical term, an infection. You have to be ruthless with infectors. Deprive them of nutrients and places to hide, and when you have them in the open, kill them.

The two-part strategy that I have described covers cleaning and sanitation, respectively. The first thing to be clear about is that these are separate operations. Some products are marketed as being cleaner-sanitizers, which implies that they can be combined. This is not good brewing practice. A surface must always be cleaned before it is sanitized. They are different jobs that require separate steps using different products.

Consider what a sanitizer is. A sanitizer is a chemical, or blend of chemicals, that kills microorganisms (and in some cases, their spores) on contact. They have to touch their targets. Any bit of organic matter left on the surface of a fermenter or other piece of brewing equipment provides both food and cover for the enemy. Until it is cleaned away, there is no way for the sanitizer to do its job.

When a brewer has an infection problem, it is almost always related to cleaning, not sanitizing. Every case that I have seen personally, in breweries of all sizes from home operations to brewpubs to regional craft brewers putting out 30,000 barrels per year, was caused by a cleaning failure. This is not the place to take shortcuts or gamble on unproven products.

CLEANERS FOR HOMEBREWING

I have not tried every cleaning product out there. I cannot speak about the ones I do not use except in a general sense. I have used several different *types* of cleaners and that is the way I will discuss them here. However, do not assume that I am not familiar with a product if I do not mention it. I may not have heard of it, but also I may have gathered information from its manufacturer or elsewhere and decided it is not suitable for brewery cleaning.

Caustic. The best cleaning agent for common brewery soil is caustic, either sodium hydroxide (caustic soda) or potassium hydroxide (caustic potash). Caustic is the mainstay of large commercial breweries and many craft breweries. I used it for several years with excellent results. Nonetheless, I do not recommend it for homebrewing. Caustic is sticky as well as slimy, so it is hard to rinse clean. It requires a fairly strong neutralizing acid rinse. It is highly corrosive to soft metals — a category that includes brass and aluminum — and human skin. Even people who work for big commercial breweries, where safety is a byword, have suffered severe burns and eye injuries as a result of accidental contact. Fortunately, except for a few relatively mild draft beer line cleaners based on potassium hydroxide, it is pretty difficult for homebrewers to get hold of caustic products.

Chlorinated Cleaners, Including Chlorinated TSP. This class of strong, noncaustic cleaners includes some automatic dishwashing detergents. These products are safer than caustic, but you should still wear rubber gloves while using them. If misused, the chlorine component is corrosive to stainless steel and most other metals, so contact time must be limited and the detergent must be thoroughly rinsed from the surface. Some are effective, but I think there are better choices out there.

One thing to note is that chlorinated TSP and other chlorinated cleaners are *not cleaner-sanitizers*. The chlorine is used as an oxidizing agent to boost the cleaning power of these formulations.

Automatic Dishwasher Detergents. At one time, most automatic dishwasher detergents were similar to noncaustic oxygenated cleaners (covered in the next section) in their composition and could be recommended for cleaning brewery equipment, with stipulations. This is no longer the case. Most dishwasher detergents have been or are being reformulated to eliminate phosphates and also sodium metasilicate and chlorine- or oxygen-containing compounds, such as sodium percarbonate. Current dishwasher products rely instead on enzymes to do the heavy lifting of breaking down organic soils. I do not trust these products to work on brewing equipment. In the future, perhaps the reputable brewing chemical makers will reformulate their products with enzymes and the like, as the dishwasher detergent companies have done. If they do, then I will wait until the new formulas have been tested in the field before making the switch.

Noncaustic Oxygenated Cleaners. Noncaustic, oxygen-based cleaners were the mainstay of my cleaning regimen for most of my pub-brewing career. A number of companies make these products. They use different formulations depending on the intended market and also the price point. A product intended for breweries will be based on sodium percarbonate (not sodium perborate) and will also include sodium metasilicate, along with one or more surfactants, which reduce surface tension, and chelating agents, which remove metallic ions and prevent the formation of scale. The best of these products are powerful, environmentally friendly, and fairly safe to work with. Rubber gloves are still recommended, however.

Like chlorinated cleaners, none of these products are sanitizers. Claims to the contrary are, for want of a better word, bogus.

The particular product that I used professionally, and still use in my homebrewing, is PBW from Five Star. A similar product made by Eco-Logic called Straight-A is also very good. Both of these are more expensive than other types of cleaners, or generic oxygen-based cleaners, but they are specifically designed for cleaning brewing equipment. If cost is an issue, there are ways to cut down on your usage. However, you must also realize that PBW, like other noncaustics, is basically a one-shot cleaner. The oxygen released when you make up your solution will "gas out" in a relatively short time. Therefore, I do not recommend trying to save and reuse it.

Noncaustic Home Remedies. The price of PBW and Straight-A has prompted many homebrewers to try cheaper homemade alternatives. These are usually based upon OxiClean Free, which is marketed as a stain remover and nonchlorine bleach. There are other OxiClean formulations that have scents and dyes, but no one has ever suggested using those for brewery cleaning. From here on out, when I use the name, I mean the stuff that says "free of perfume/dyes/chlorine" on the package.

OxiClean is basically a mixture of sodium carbonate and sodium percarbonate, which is the oxygen source in the brand-name brewery cleaners. Some homebrewers say they get satisfactory results cleaning fermenters with straight OxiClean. Others, looking at the MSDS (material safety data sheet) for PBW, and finding that it also contains sodium metasilicate, have been mixing up what they think is a home-brewed equivalent by combining OxiClean with sodium metasilicate in various proportions.

I am not going to turn this into a chemistry book, but I must point out two facts. First, chemical companies do not list every ingredient in their formulas on the MSDS. They list those that they are required to list. PBW is more complicated than a simple mixture of sodium carbonate, percarbonate, and metasilicate. Its exact formulation is known only to some of the people at Five Star Chemicals.

Second, any practical alkaline cleaner will include a chelating compound of some kind in its formulation. This is true of caustic as well as noncaustic brewery cleaners. I won't get into the chemistry of chelation, but suffice it to say if you leave out the chelating agent, then natural water hardness will result in diminished performance, and the formation of precipitates and scale. I have seen brewery tanks whose interior surface was covered with a thick layer of rough, hard mineral deposits. Omitting the chelant from a metasilicate cleaner is especially bad because the scale formed will be very hard and inert (glass is made from silicates).

If you want to try OxiClean, go ahead; I think you will find, as I have, that it is not nearly as effective as PBW. Based on my trials in open vessels, where I could observe the results, I would not trust it in a CIP application where I was working blind (in other words, a counter-flow heat exchanger). I cannot be even that positive about homemade combinations. They may seem to work well, but I fear they will lead to grief for you later on.

Acid-Based Cleaners. Acid cleaners are widely used in commercial breweries for special purposes, such as de-scaling hot liquor tanks. Their most common use, though, is as an acid rinse to neutralize residual alkalinity in a tank after washing and rinsing. Most acid cleaners are a blend of nitric and phosphoric acids, with compatible detergents added. None of these products is being marketed to homebrewers, probably because of safety considerations.

If you want to acid-rinse your stainless, I suggest citric acid, which is readily available at homebrew supply stores. It can also be found in bulk quantities online. A solution of 30 grams (one ounce) per gallon works well.

It is also possible to purchase bulk quantities of phosphoric acid online. Straight 75 percent or 85 percent phosphoric is not as dangerous as other concentrated mineral acids, like nitric, though it still demands respect. Being a liquid, shipping is likely to be problematic and expensive. However, it is safe enough to consider using and the flavor is very neutral. I suggest a 1 percent solution for acid-rinsing stainless or copper — that is, 7 milliliters of 85 percent phosphoric acid per liter or 27 milliliters (a bit less than 2 tablespoons) per gallon of water.

There is an alternative strategy for CIP that is said to work better than the conventional water rinse → hot alkali → water rinse → acid rinse method. This method runs water rinse → hot acid → hot alkali (no rinse in between) → water rinse. The idea is that the acid cleaner softens up the soil deposits, which then can be more easily dissolved and removed by the alkaline cleaner. This strategy also works well and it is a good idea to use it periodically instead of the alkali-first plan. Note that the acid needs to be hot (120 to 140°F) for best results, and more acid is required, because it is actually involved in attacking the dirt deposits. I suggest a 2 percent solution of phosphoric acid for this cleaning method, run hot for 15 minutes before draining out, then followed up directly with hot PBW at the normal concentration and time. Then treat with an ambient temp water rinse. No acid rinse is needed.

SANITIZERS

Homebrewers tend to have strong opinions about sanitizers, and they like to make claims about the performance of their favorite product. The fact is that most of us are working blind. That goes for a lot of professionals as well. Most pub brewers, including me, did not have a lab on the premises. I did the same thing I do now. I cleaned, I sanitized, and I trusted. After a few dozen batches I was pretty sure that my chemicals and procedures were working. The beer was clean. After a few hundred, I was sure of it.

Any of the sanitizers discussed here, if used properly, will do its job. There are, however, reasons for choosing one over another.

Chlorine. This is the granddaddy, the original — sodium hypochlorite, most widely available as unscented 5 percent household bleach. Bleach mixed at the ratio of 1 tablespoon per gallon of water gives 200 parts per million of free chlorine. This was the mainstay for years, but it has several drawbacks.

The first is that chlorine is very corrosive even to most brewery materials, including stainless steel and glass. That is reason enough to use something else.

The second reason is that chlorine readily reacts with components of beer to form chlorophenols, which are nasty medicinal-tasting compounds. I did not learn this from a book. Long and bitter experience with glass washing machines in two different pubs has shown me that both iodine and chlorine sanitizers do exactly what the brewing chemists say they do. Therefore, chlorine-based sanitizers must always be rinsed out with clean water.

The third drawback relates to the chemistry of bleach. Its effectiveness is highly dependent on the pH (acidity or alkalinity) of the solution.

Because tap water varies so much, in some places a "normal" 200 ppm (parts per million) solution will not do the job. Furthermore, increasing the concentration can actually make things worse instead of better. These facts probably account for some of the sanitation failures that homebrewers have attributed to bleach. It also explains why other sanitizers have become popular. They work pretty much regardless of the water you mix them in.

Lately interest in bleach has somewhat revived, owing to a new and improved method of usage. Instead of a straight 200 ppm dilution, the new "recipe" calls for an 80 ppm solution, which is 1 fluid ounce, or 2 tablespoons, in 5 gallons of water. After mixing, you then add 2 tablespoons of white vinegar, which is a 5 percent acetic acid solution. The vinegar lowers the pH, which promotes formation of hypochlorous acid. This is the form of free chlorine that actually does the sanitizing, which is why you only need 80 ppm. Altogether this new recipe is a major improvement.

Nonetheless, I am not convinced that homebrewers should go back to using bleach. While dropping the pH with vinegar does make the solution a better sanitizer, it does not answer any of the other objections; 80 ppm is still a lot of chlorine. Also the recipe remains inexact, owing to the variations in local water supplies. For best results, you need to proceed empirically rather than follow a set formula. The vinegar should be added a little at a time while monitoring the pH of the solution, either with test papers or a meter. The goal is 5.0. At that point, almost 100 percent of the free chlorine is hypochlorous acid. If too much is added, and the pH gets down below 4.0, then some of the hypochlorite will become chlorine gas, which was the first modern chemical weapon. This stuff can cause serious damage to lungs and other soft tissues, including the eyes. So if you choose to acidify your hypochlorite solution, work in a well-ventilated area and proceed with caution.

Iodophor. Iodine-based sanitizers were the next wave in homebrewing. Because they are typically effective at 25 ppm, they do not pose as big a residue problem as chlorine sanitizers do. Because they are acid-based, they are fairly immune to the pH problem and will be effective no matter what the alkalinity of the mixing water is. They generally last for several days, and it is easy to tell when they have lost their killing power because the solution loses its brown color. One drawback is that they stain plastic badly, which is a serious problem if you use a white bucket for fermentation. The brown stain makes it hard to judge how clean the surface is. Altogether, though, iodophors are good sanitizers, and throughout my professional years I used them most of the time for sanitizing my fermenters. However, I always drained the tank and rinsed it well, and if you use iodophor you should do the same. While the residue problem is not as bad as it is with chlorine, it still exists.

The No-Rinse Ideal. At this point, you may be wondering why I have spent so much ink on the subject of residue. Everybody knows that after you clean a piece of equipment, you have to rinse the detergent off. Why not do the same with your sanitizer?

The problem is that brewers often do not quite trust their water. In most municipalities, at least once in a while, the water will not be totally germ-free. The bacteria count will always be so low that the water is safe to drink, but it may not always be zero. And nothing scares a brewer more than introducing bacteria into his system.

There is also the problem of airborne — actually dust-borne — bacteria, yeast, and spores. Any vessel that sits open to the air will eventually acquire a small collection of microbes. It will still be clean, but it will not be sanitary.

The way around these problems is largely a matter of timing. Always clean your equipment immediately after use. After the final rinse, let it drain and air-dry. Shortly before the next use, sanitize it, and leave it closed up until you use it. This is sound brewing practice. However, if your equipment cannot easily be kept closed, you have to sanitize *immediately* before use. And if you rinse out the sanitizer, there is always the worry about your water.

I hope this explains why most brewers, including me, would prefer a no-rinse sanitizer, at least for some applications.

That said, I think these concerns are often blown out of proportion. I have made hundreds and hundreds of batches of beer in fermenters that had been rinsed out after the sanitizer treatment. The tanks were left closed, most of the time, but the iodophor was always rinsed thoroughly. The beer was always clean. A few bacteria may have come in with the water once in a while, but as soon as the yeast got going, those bacteria died. The bacteria that can survive in beer are specialized organisms and not the ordinary coliforms that you might encounter in potable water. Given a good start to fermentation, the latter will have no impact on the beer. The same goes for airborne yeasts and other bugs. As long as they don't get a long head start, there won't be enough of them to make a difference.

So my advice is, don't worry too much about your rinse water. But also, don't trust your sanitizer to make up for sloppiness in your cleaning. Rinse or no rinse, there is no panacea.

Now for the sanitizers I actually use in my homebrewing.

Acid Anionics (Star San). Star San has made a huge, foamy splash since it was introduced on the homebrewing scene. It is now the standard, for some very good reasons. It is effective and easy to use, with excellent penetrating ability. It is mild in flavor and does not react with beer compounds. At Blackstone, we always kept a spray bottle of it on hand and used it to sanitize hose ends, draft beer fittings, and other small parts before connecting them. We used it to sanitize our filter, because it would not stain the plastic parts and foam was not an issue. Now, I always keep a freshly mixed spray bottle on hand, and I also keep a small bowl to dip my hands in before manipulating items that have been sanitized.

However . . .

Star San does have some drawbacks. It's a huge foamer, which makes it impossible to use in a CIP loop where the solutions are sprayed onto the walls of a tank. At Blackstone, we also found it does not have a great shelf life, at least when mixed with our tap water. The manufacturer says when the solution gets cloudy, it has lost its sanitizing ability. If that is the criterion, then 48 hours is about the limit. This may be different if you make it up with RO or distilled water, but I can't vouch for that.

An even bigger concern for me is the soapy residue. This is the reason, when we sanitized our filter, we always flushed it out with water afterward. We noticed that as Star San solution ages, it not only becomes cloudy, but it also becomes clingy — slippery sticky, if you will. Even when fresh it's a bit viscous and doesn't seem to drain very well. That is one reason I never considered using it as a no-rinse. A bit on a hose end is all right, but the amount that can cling to the walls of a fermenter seems excessive to me.

I am also concerned about its effect on yeast. I have a good friend, a pub brewer and also like me a big fan of Star San. As I do, he used 5-gallon soda kegs for short-term storage of yeast slurry. Once he made an unintended discovery. He gave a soda keg a short soak in Star San, drained it out, then filled the keg with yeast from the bottom of a fermenter. Unlike me, he had a microscope, and the next day, before pitching the yeast, he made a routine check on yeast viability. You can imagine his dismay when he found it was less than 50 percent. Based on prior experience he expected 95 to 98 percent. (Note to the knowledgeable: the count was done on a hemocytometer, methylene blue stain.)

Admittedly, this is not a controlled experiment. But in a brewery, you don't wait for scientific confirmation. My friend went back to his old sanitizing methods and the slurry cell counts returned to normal. He is quite sure that the only difference from his normal routine was to use Star San as a no-rinse. This experience certainly confirms that Star San is a stone killer. However, it also calls into question the claim that it only kills as long as the pH is less than 3.5. Yeast slurries, like beer, run between 4.0 and 4.5, yet he got a fairly significant kill from the residue in his keg.

Most homebrewers sanitize their fermenters with Star San before filling them with wort. Wort has a pH of 5.0 to 5.5 as a rule, which is a good deal higher than the pH of beer. (The pH scale is logarithmic.) This may account for the success many homebrewers seem to have with using Star San as a no-rinse. However, I think it is safer to rinse it out. As I said before, I am not concerned about a few stray enterobacteria in my water as long as my fermentation gets off to a quick start. Also, I think that there are better no-rinse sanitizers out there.

Saniclean. A companion product to Star San, Saniclean was created by Five Star specifically to address the foaming issues I mentioned above. Because of the expense of the certification process, it does not have "official papers" as a sanitizer, as Star San has. However, the manufacturer, whom I trust, says it is in fact just as effective as Star San when used at the recommended dosage.

Saniclean seems to drain a little better than Star San, but the flavor of the prescribed solution (3 fluid ounces per 5 gallons) is strong and unpleasant, and I would be much more hesitant about using it as a no-rinse than I would Star San. Because the foam issue is mostly a problem with commercial CIP procedures, I do not see much need for it in homebrewing.

Chlorine Dioxide. Chlorine dioxide has been proved to be highly effective against a wide range of microbes, and it has many uses outside the brewing industry. It is employed as an alternative to chlorine and chloramine for disinfecting water supplies, and it is also used in hospitals, veterinary clinics, and food processing plants. People keep finding new uses for it. In breweries, it is widely used as a no-rinse sanitizer for kegs, bottles, bottling lines, tanks, hoses, and other equipment.

It drains clean and has no impact on the flavor of beer, even at many times the recommended concentrations. Altogether it's as close as we are likely to come to a magic bullet.

Nonetheless, chlorine dioxide has been slow to gain a foothold in homebrewing for two reasons. First, it is not easy to get. However, if there were demand, homebrew supply shops would start selling it. The root cause is widespread confusion about what chlorine dioxide is and how it works. I'll spare you a chemistry lesson. If you want the full story, you can easily find it on online at the Bio-Cide website. (Bio-Cide makes Oxine, which was the first stabilized chlorine dioxide product.) The one point I want to make is that chlorine dioxide is not a chlorine sanitizer. Its mode of operation is totally different from, and much more selective than, hypochlorite/hypochlorous acid. In fact, when chlorine dioxide breaks down, chlorine is not formed. What you get is sodium chloride.

Of course, there is no such thing as a free lunch. There must be some drawbacks, surely? Well, yes there are.

First, chlorine dioxide is not cheap. It is more expensive than Star San on a per-use basis. And even more than Star San, it is strictly a one-shot product. The diluted working solution begins to lose potency in 6 to 8 hours. Also, as noted above, it is hard to find. The only brand that seems to be available to individual consumers is Oxine. However, the main drawback is that it requires activation, and this procedure must be done carefully.

I don't want to exaggerate here. Oxine is not nearly as dangerous as caustic. In fact, the stabilized 2 percent solution you buy in a gallon jug is quite safe and does not require hazmat shipping labels or protocols. The danger comes when you go to activate it. This must be done with a mild acid (usually citric acid, which also is quite safe), but if too much acid is added, and the pH goes too low, then instead of chlorine dioxide, chlorine gas will be generated — the same thing that can happen when mixing up the bleach-vinegar recipe, as I mentioned before.

Oxine is sold to and used by poultry ranchers and horse breeders, and I don't suppose many homebrewers consider themselves less competent than the people who follow those endeavors. Still, if you are the type who generally knocks back six pints of a previous batch every time you brew a new one, you'd better stay away from Oxine. Even if you don't gas yourself, you probably will not get it mixed correctly.

Working with Oxine. Oxine comes in different packaging for different markets. The stuff in the bottle is the same, but the labeling differs, and if you get Oxine AH (animal health, aimed at the veterinary/animal breeding segment) it may not have the information you need. You have to be careful and fairly precise in your measurements.

Basically, there are two ways to activate Oxine. The first method is to add a carefully measured quantity of citric acid crystals to the concentrate and stir for about 5 minutes. When done correctly, this will generate a concentrated solution of chlorine dioxide (20,000 ppm), which must then be immediately diluted in water to working strength — typically between 40 and 200 ppm. If you use this method, be sure to work in a well-ventilated area, and don't get your face too close to the mixing vessel. I usually go for 5 gallons at 40 ppm, so my basic recipe is to measure out 40 milliliters of the concentrate into a cylinder. Then add 10 percent by weight of citric acid to the cylinder — 4 grams. I usually do this by placing the cylinder with the Oxine concentrate on my scale and noting the reading. Then I use a plastic spoon to put citric acid crystals into the cylinder until the weight rises by 4 grams. You can tell the chlorine dioxide is forming because the mixture will turn a bright greenish-yellow. After 5 minutes of slow, gentle stirring with the spoon, I pour the activated Oxine into 5 gallons of tap water.

The advantage of this method is that once the chlorine dioxide is generated, the pH and mineral content of the diluted solution are unimportant. Chlorine dioxide is effective at pH values from 3.0 to 10.0, and it is unaffected by common water ions like calcium, or by organic material. You can soak your feet in it. In fact, that's exactly what horse breeders do with it. They soak the animals' hooves in activated Oxine solution as a treatment for thrush.

The second method is the way I did it when I was sanitizing serving tanks at Blackstone. It is not quite as touchy, but you do need a pH meter or strips, because the amount of acid required depends on your tap water. You can use citric or acetic acid (white vinegar). If you decide to go with citric acid, I suggest advance preparation of a stock solution — say, 20 grams in 500 milliliters of water — to make it easier to mix. We'll stay with the 5-gallon 40 ppm example. Fill the bucket or keg to the 5-gallon mark, measure out and add 40 milliliters of Oxine, and stir. Then add your acid in small increments, no more than 10 milliliters (2 teaspoons) at a time. Stir it in and check the pH. You are looking for a value between 5.0 and 6.0. When you get below 7.0, use smaller additions. Values as low as 4.0 are okay, but under no circumstances should you go to 3.0 — if you do, you'll know it before you use the pH meter.

There is no need to come close to that. As long as you get below 6.0, the solution will do its job.

The advantage of this method is that it is more flexible. With white vinegar or a dilute solution of citric acid, you can make up small volumes of very low concentration, which can be useful for a final rinse.

A final but very important note about safety: if you spill the Oxine concentrate, do not let it dry. Mop it up with a damp rag or wash it away. Although the danger is not great, the dry residue is potentially flammable.

Other Sanitizers. For the sake of thoroughness, I should mention two other sanitizers that are sometimes used in breweries. The first is peracetic acid, also known as peroxyacetic acid. This is very effective and is used no-rinse in many commercial breweries. I do not think it is suitable for homebrewing. While not as dangerous as caustic, in concentrated form it is corrosive and hazardous to skin and eyes. I have burned myself with it. It is also unstable, losing potency over a matter of weeks if it is stored at warm temperatures. Commercial brewers and their suppliers have carried on a lively debate over the years about the relative merits of chlorine dioxide and peracetic acid, which are generally acknowledged as the two best no-rinse sanitizers. As a commercial brewer I have used both. As a homebrewer, I would not consider peracetic, even if I could find a seller who was willing to ship it to me.

The other sanitizer is actually a whole separate class of chemicals known as quaternary ammonium compounds, or *quats*. One of the things every student at Siebel, the renowned brewing school, is taught is that quats should never be used in any vessel, pipe, hose, or other brewery equipment. Not because they don't work. They are stone killers. Their flavor impact is minimal. But they utterly destroy the foam retention of beer. Years after my Siebel training, when I was working at Blackstone, I had occasion to get involved in some contract brewing. We wanted to put out bottled beer for the local market, and we had neither capacity nor space in our pub.

Our first shipment of bottles was okay on flavor, but the beer had no head at all. I made a trip to the contract brewery and found a suspicious-looking gallon jug sitting next to the bottle rinser. I asked about it and was told it was an "acid sanitizer." Hmm. The label showed that it was not sold by one of the regular brewery chemical companies. I pulled out my pen and notepad and copied the active ingredients list from the label. As soon as I got to a computer, 30 seconds of Googling told me what I had already guessed. These guys were spraying quats into their bottles. Mindful of the bottom line, they had accepted the guidance of a salesman who was ignorant of brewing but carried a persuasive price list. Yet again, the lore of my teachers had been confirmed. In a brewery, quats are very helpful for controlling mold on wet floors and walls, but that is all they are good for.

USING CLEANERS AND SANITIZERS

There are very few secrets to cleaning and sanitizing equipment. The usual routine followed in small commercial breweries is fairly simple:

STEP 1. Immediately after use, rinse with tap water to remove as much loose soil as possible.

STEP 2. Hot-wash with alkaline detergent. Drain.

STEP 3. Rinse with tap water. Drain.

STEP 4. Acid-wash at ambient temperature to neutralize remaining alkali residue. Drain. Do not rinse.

STEP 5. If equipment is not to be reused/filled immediately, open tanks/ pots/buckets/carboys to air-dry. Hang hoses and other enclosed pieces to promote drainage and drying.

STEP 6. Before next use, rinse with tap water.

STEP 7. Wash with sanitizer at ambient temperature. Drain.

STEP 8. *(Optional, depending on sanitizer)* Rinse with tap water. Use or fill equipment immediately or leave closed until use.

Notes on some of the steps (relevent step numbers in parentheses):

(1) The more dirt you can get off by rinsing, the less detergent you need to use.

(2) Follow directions on cleaner package for temperature and concentration. With PBW, 1 ounce (2 tablespoons) per gallon is normal. PBW works best at 120 to 160°F with the higher end of the range preferred for heavy deposits. Note that water at temperatures over 140°F can burn skin almost instantly. Wear heavy rubber gloves and other appropriate protective gear. If the solution becomes dark, this is a sign that it is "used up." Dump it and inspect the vessel carefully; you may need to do a second wash.

Many homebrewers prefer to soak equipment rather than scrub. In my experience soaking is rarely effective with kettles; they need some hand scrubbing, so you may as well save your money and only make up 1 to 2 gallons of solution. Back-flush the counterflow wort cooler (heat exchanger) at the same time. After cleaning the kettle, I use the same solution to clean the mash/lauter tun.

Soaking is preferable for fermenters because scratching must be avoided. Carboys, if lightly soiled, can be cleaned by rolling around with 1 to 2 gallons of solution. The BetterBottle instructions have a nice hint for dealing with heavier deposits by rolling with a washcloth in the carboy. Plastic bucket primary fermenters can be capped and shaken to save on detergent, but this is one case in which I prefer to fill the fermenter and try to soak it clean. Usually an overnight soak will do the job. When stirring the cleaning solution, don't use a metal spoon and try not to touch the walls. I don't like to use even a sponge if I can avoid it.

Hoses, racking arms, aerators, and similar pieces need to have solution run through them (by siphon or pump) and then be left to soak full for at least 40 minutes.

Some equipment, in particular counterflow heat exchangers, require a professional-style back-flush using a pump. Bottle cleaning is covered on page 187.

(3) Thorough rinsing is important, but hot water is not necessary if using noncaustic cleaners.

(4) The acid wash is optional with noncaustics but is preferable for stainless. Ten minutes is enough. I use a separate sponge for the acid wash (no scrubby pads) on the kettle. I prefer to acid-wash everything.

(7) Equipment used on the "hot side" of the process — including the mash/lauter tun, kettle, and immersion cooler — does not need to be sanitized before use. They do need to be rinsed off, especially if they were acid-rinsed. However, any equipment used to move cold wort requires sanitizing.

Use Star San as instructed on the package, 1 ounce (2 tablespoons) per 5 gallons. More is not better. This translates to 1 teaspoon for 106 fluid ounces, which is about a pint less than 1 gallon. This amount is adequate for sanitizing carboys and fermenters using the "cover and shake" method. Contact time is 2 minutes. Never forget to sanitize all hoses and other small pieces as well. Anything that touches or carries cooled wort or beer falls under the rule. This includes counterflow chillers.

Oxine can be used at 100 ppm as the sole sanitizing agent. Ten minutes of contact time is enough.

(8) If you prefer to use Star San but want to rinse it out as I recommend, you can make up a 10 ppm solution of activated Oxine and use it as the final rinse. This is enough to kill any stray water or airborne microbes. Flush the equipment well with tap water before applying the final Oxine rinse. Ten ppm amounts to 10 milliliters, or 2 teaspoons, in 5 gallons of water. The rinse must be activated by adding acid to drop the pH below 6.0.

5

HOMEBREWING OPERATIONS

Okay. You are almost ready to make beer. If you have made it this far, you understand the process, the equipment, and materials required. What remains is (to me, at least) the real fun — putting your knowledge to use.

Before You Start

By now you should have gathered that you cannot just buy or build equipment without some plan for using it. If you have only one pump, for instance, you have to think about how you can make the most of it during lautering. Obviously it cannot pump hot sparge liquor and wort at the same time. You have to decide which job to give the pump, and which you will handle in some other way.

BREWERY LAYOUT

Until you make a few batches of beer, you should not commit yourself to a set layout. Many homebrewers enjoy putting together a custom-built framework, or "sculpture" as it is sometimes called, as a permanent housing for their brewery. Some enjoy it so much that they build a new one every few years. As your involvement with homebrewing increases — which it probably will — you are likely to find reasons for adding extra equipment that makes brew day go faster and easier for you. But at first, you should try to use outdoor or indoor tables, chairs, and fixtures for your equipment.

My recommendation for an outdoor brewery is to place the propane burner and kettle on the ground, deck, or patio floor. Set your lauter tun on a table. Your hot liquor back can sit alongside it on the same table, either at the same level (for manual sparging) or elevated, using a couple of milk crates or other boxes (for gravity feed to a sparge arm). The grant can either sit directly inside the kettle (manual recirculation) or alongside it. If you are using the pump for lautering, I recommend placing the bottom of the grant at approximately the same height from the ground/floor as the kettle bottom. This simplifies things because the same pump intake hose can be used for both lautering (attached to the grant) and knockout (attached to the kettle). This sort of layout also speeds up your brew because you can fire the burner under your kettle when it is half full, or whatever time it takes to get the wort to boil just as sparging ends

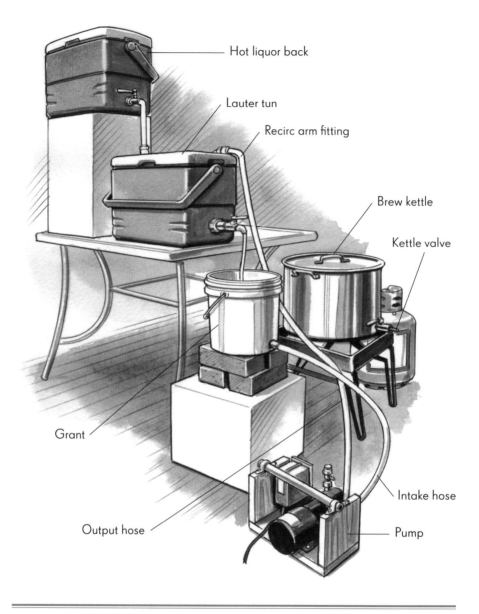

Hot liquor back

Lauter tun

Recirc arm fitting

Brew kettle

Kettle valve

Grant

Intake hose

Output hose

Pump

Brewery setup. The author's home brewery setup uses a single pump for lautering. The hot liquor back is to the left, set above the lauter tun so that sparge water flows by gravity. A grant is set below the draw-off of the lauter tun and feeds the input of the pump. A pump output hose is attached to the recirc arm fitting of the lauter tun. This setup is used for clarification; when the wort is clear, the output hose is moved to the kettle valve.

and your kettle is filled. For knockout, the heat exchanger can be placed at any height if you are using a pump, but it is simpler if the outlet is at least as high as the top of your fermenter.

When I first thought about how to incorporate a counterflow heat exchanger into my brewery, I realized that my deck would make it possible to knock out by gravity. The deck stands 6 to 8 feet above the yard below. I finally decided not to bother with this, because I would have to haul the fermenter back up the steps afterward, and I needed a pump to back-flush the heat exchanger anyway. Still, in some situations — say, for example, you brew in the kitchen but ferment in the basement — gravity may be a better way to do a transfer, even if you have a pump at your disposal. It is always the preferred option in commercial breweries.

The general rule is to keep your hose runs as short and as vertical as possible. This is especially important for the pump intake hose. Loops or even sags make it much harder to prime the pump and keep it primed during operation.

For brewing in a kitchen, the biggest difference is that the burner — the stove — is at counter height. For the sake of safety and efficiency, it is much better to use the pump to fill the kettle, even if it means you have to sparge by hand. However, if there is space above a countertop next to the stove, you can elevate the hot liquor back and make a layout roughly similar to the outdoor one I described earlier, the only difference being that the grant will have to sit lower than the kettle, which means more lengths of hose may be needed for the pump.

It is hard to suggest a general plan that will cover all types of kitchens. Outdoor breweries are easier to lay out. However, indoor brewing has some advantages and may be your only option; if so, there is always a way to make it work.

With any home brewery, you need to think about where the wastewater from your heat exchanger(s) is going. In a kitchen the sink is the obvious destination. Outdoors, either a floor drain or the lawn will do, unless the water is very hot. Just be sure you have enough tubing for the job.

One other aspect of layout that can be thorny is the problem of where to locate the draft beer refrigerator. A basement is usually all right, as long as the space is somewhat heated so that it stays at or above 50°F, even in winter. Refrigerators are designed to cool; the manufacturers expect them to be placed in an environment significantly warmer than their interior temperature (34 to 40°F). Refrigeration equipment that is installed outdoors and expected to run year-round requires special additional circuitry to keep it from damaging itself in cold weather. These circuits are not found in normal domestic refrigerators, and thus, placing one in a shed or unheated garage — even an attached garage — usually results in an early death. My friend and former assistant, Josh Garrett, lost a garage refrigerator after less than two years.

Of course, the opposite is also true: putting a refrigerator in a very hot environment will shorten its life because the compressor will have to cycle more to hold the set temperature. Still, hot is not as bad as cold. Usually, though, the worst spots — for example, my garage (110 to 120°F in summer and often 20 to 40°F in winter) — will be bad in different ways, according to the season. In short, put your refrigerator in the house, even if you have to spend some goodwill capital to do it.

GATHERING INFORMATION

Before you ever get to the point of buying your materials and planning out your first brew day, you need to get some information together. Some info — such as your water quality report — is necessary before you can even plan a brewery budget. You also need to know something about your electrical service and wiring to be sure your draft beer refrigerator will not overload the circuit.

Get as much information as possible on the specifics of the equipment you are thinking about buying or have already purchased. For example, once you have acquired some soda kegs, you need to take a careful look at them, find out who made them — Cornelius and Firestone are the biggest manufacturers — and to the extent possible, identify the models. If you don't have wrenches in the correct sizes, get the ones you need and unscrew the plugs, just so you know what a poppet valve looks like. You are probably going to be changing your Internet habits. For a while at least, you'll be spending more time on the websites of McMaster-Carr and Foxx Equipment than you will on the social networks.

GATHERING EQUIPMENT AND MATERIALS

In the prior chapters I described the equipment you need to brew beer, but aside from the actual brewery, a brewer needs a number of items to operate it.

For ongoing brewing, a simple set of hand tools is all you need: a utility knife, slot blade and Phillips screwdrivers, all-purpose pliers, and a couple of nut drivers are all you'll likely use on brew day. Don't omit the nut drivers: one for each size of band clamp nut will save you countless gouges.

Other safety items include pot holders and rubber gloves. But the most important safety item is also the most basic: appropriate clothing. At minimum, you should go with pretty much what you should wear to mow the lawn — long pants and leather shoes. After a couple of brews you'll probably put duck boots on your Christmas list. They should come up over the ankle. High boots can be problematic. The lace-up types are best because your pant legs will go over them. This can save you a cooked foot if you ever spill hot water or wort. If you are rinsing equipment in cool weather, you may want rainwear.

If your brewery floor does not have a drain, then you need to think about how to contain the inevitable drips and spills. This goes double if the brewery is your kitchen. A few widemouthed buckets or small tubs at least give you a chance when you are siphoning beer or filling a keg with cleaning solution. You can avoid some of the mess by working out-doors, but as I mentioned earlier, you can't just dump cleaning and sanitizing solutions out on the lawn, so even there, containment is going to be necessary. Furthermore, the kitchen or bathroom is often the only ready access to hot tap water. It is not ideal, but for many homebrewers, "cellar operations" — racking, filtration, kegging — are going to happen in one of those rooms. My rule is to never set a keg or fermenter directly on the floor. I still have to do some mopping up, but since I changed my habits, I am not going through paper towels nearly as fast as I used to.

What I am urging you to do here is to think about exactly what you are going to do on brew day and exactly how you are going to do it. Unless you are able to sit in on an all-grain session with an experienced brewer, you almost need to stage a "dress rehearsal" at which you set everything up and pantomime your way, so to speak, through the brewing process. In fact, I recommend that you do both. You will pick up a lot from observing a brew, but you will also get to talking and miss things. Experienced brewers work largely by rote. To the extent that you can, try to keep the talk on brewing, not beer, and ask as many questions as you can, even about things you think you understand. It's a good idea to take notes if you can.

CALIBRATIONS, CLEANING, AND MEASUREMENTS

Part of your dress rehearsal should be some calibrations and measurements. For a start, you need to calibrate your instruments. All pH meters come with calibration instructions, so I am not going to go into that here other than to say, practice with it, do it twice, and always use the two-point method, calibrating to pH values around 7.0 and 4.0.

Calibrating a thermometer seems pretty simple because you can make the "calibration solutions" yourself by filling up a glass with ice water and boiling some water on your stove. The only tricky part is getting the right mixture of ice and water. Ice is usually well below freezing temperature, so a predominance of ice may give a temperature below 32°F. Likewise, too much tap water may put the mixture above 32°F.

An alternative method of calibration is to check your thermometer at a single point, against a narrow-range, highly accurate instrument. I use an old-fashioned oral fever thermometer for this. The procedure is to draw hot water into a pint jar or glass while continuously stirring with your dial or digital thermometer. When the temperature reaches 100°F, turn off the tap, and continue to stir while you plunge in the shaken-down fever thermometer. Continue to stir for 1 minute or so, note the reading of your wide range at the end, then remove both thermometers and check the fever thermometer. Compare the reading with what you noted for your brewing thermometer.

I have four thermometers. One, an old Beseler darkroom model, can be adjusted by turning a nut on the back. I calibrated and adjusted it 30 years ago and it still reads spot on. My two cheap digitals read 1°F low and 0.5°F high respectively. Another dial thermometer, nonadjustable, reads 2°F low.

None of these errors is that big. Still, especially for mashing, you want as much accuracy as you can get, and you also want the fastest possible response. The Beseler beats out the digitals on both scores, so I still use it.

Another instrument that needs to be calibrated is the hydrometer. One way to explain how this is done is to ask, "At what temperature is this instrument accurate?" Almost all hydrometers come with a little slip of paper that gives the corrections to be applied depending on the temperature of the wort. They usually state that the hydrometer is accurate at 60°F. I like to check this by adjusting the temperature of the water until the instrument reads zero. Mine does this at 70. So I have made up a customized table that lists the correction factors for other temperatures. Everything is offset 10 degrees, so for example, the point where one must add one specific gravity point to the hydrometer reading is not 67°F, but 77 . . . and so forth.

You also should make a dipstick. I used a ½-inch square hardwood dowel from Home Depot. The best tool, if you do not have a 1-gallon measuring pitcher, is a milk jug. Wash it out, then fill it right to the ring at the neck: that is 1 gallon. Set your kettle on a level surface and measure water in, 1 gallon at a time. After each gallon, put the dipstick straight in and mark the level with a pencil, straight across. When finished, mark that side "K" for kettle and then move on. Repeat the procedure for the lauter tun, and the mash mixer if you have one. Finally, calibrate one of your 5-gallon buckets and also your primary fermenter bucket if it is not marked already. For the buckets, mark the levels on the outside of the kettle with a Sharpie. Putting a dipstick into a bucket of cooled wort is unsanitary.

HEAT EXCHANGER CIP

Before you can calibrate your wort knockout rate, you will need to run a full CIP (clean-in-place) on your heat exchanger. This will familiarize you with pump operation and will remove any oil, grit, or other residue from the interior wort passageways. The procedure is worth spelling out stepwise. However, before we get to specifics of CIP, we need to understand the basic principles that govern centrifugal pump operation.

▸ FIRST: The pump must always be placed below its supply or feed vessel. It relies on gravity to fill the pump body. Loops or dips in the intake hose must be eliminated.

▸ SECOND: The pump body must be flooded with liquid completely (primed) before the pump is started. This type of pump relies on the fluid for lubrication, and it cannot move air. Dry running will destroy it quickly. March Manufacturing says 30 seconds is the maximum safe time that an empty pump may run. That is a lot more leeway than I got with the sanitary stainless steel pumps I had at Blackstone. When the pump body is dry, the motor will "spin up" because it is not working against any resistance. You should keep your ears cocked for pump sounds that may indicate trouble. This is difficult when you are just starting out, but for experienced brewers it becomes a habit.

▸ THIRD: Never restrict the pump input. Make sure the intake hose is at least equal in size to the intake fitting. Any valves in the intake line must be wide open. To restrict flow either use a speed control, a smaller output hose, or a valve on the output side.

STEPS FOR INITIAL HEAT EXCHANGER CLEANING

STEP 1. Pump problems are best discovered when the worst you can get is a drenching. If at all possible, you should do your preliminary test run outdoors, even if you plan to brew in the kitchen. Set up your kettle and run in about 3 gallons of tap water. Then connect the intake hose between the pump and the kettle, and connect the output hose to the pump. Silicone tubing should be clamped only if this is necessary to hold the hose in place. To prime, first make sure the intake hose is straight but not taut, then open the kettle valve fully. Then, momentarily hold the output hose flat on the floor or ground until you see water flowing through the pump. At that point, lift the end of the output hose above the water level in the kettle. Check to see there are no air bubbles in the intake hose. If there are, drop the hose back down until water starts to flow again. Catch it in a small pitcher or bucket. When the intake hose and pump body are full, hold the hose over a bucket and start the pump. Again, observe the intake hose to make sure there are no bubbles. If there is a bubble in the line, you may be able to eliminate it by giving the intake hose a momentary pinch. Now, set the speed control about halfway. Lay the hose back in the kettle and let the pump run for a few minutes to make sure it is pumping steadily. Then play with the speed control, turning it to minimum and maximum. Depending on positioning, you may find that minimum speed does not deliver enough pressure to lift the water back into the kettle.

STEP 2. After you have a feel for the flow rates, get out your dipstick and reduce the kettle volume to 2 gallons by pumping the surplus into a bucket or onto the ground.

STEP 3. Put the heat exchanger(s) into the loop. Shut off the pump, attach the pump output hose to the wort output hose barb, and run another length of hose from the heat exchanger input back to the kettle. Circulate water as before. You may need to use a clamp at the heat exchanger output barb (here the cleaning solution enters the heat exchanger). If so, do not tighten it any more than necessary. Run the pump for a few minutes at a fairly high speed — the flow rate should be 1 gallon per minute or more.

At this point, indoor brewers will have to relocate to the kitchen, as the next step requires heat.

STEP 4. While continuing to circulate, fire your burner and add ¼ cup (2 ounces) of noncaustic cleaner. Stir to dissolve. Also adjust the burner if necessary (see page 138).

STEP 5. When the kettle solution reaches 140°F, check your watch. Circulate the solution for 40 minutes, keeping the temperature between 140 and 160°F by turning the burner on and off as necessary. Keep a close watch on the thermometer when you have the heat on. When the heat is off, just check it every 5 minutes or so. Don't worry if the temperature goes out of range a bit. While the CIP is going on, put on a pair of rubber gloves and use a blue pad to hand clean the interior of the kettle.

STEP 6. After 40 minutes, if you have other equipment to be cleaned, pump the solution into the next item. Otherwise, pump it into a bucket. Using pot holders or mitts, tip the kettle to get as much solution out as possible. When the pump is about to suck air, set the kettle flat and quickly shut off the pump. (You may want to practice this move ahead of time.) Disconnect the pump intake hose from the kettle and set it in a small bucket or bowl. Set the end of the heat exchanger output hose in a bucket. Pour out the kettle dregs by hand, but be careful — the stainless is hot.

STEP 7. Attach or hold your water hose to the pump intake hose and run a few gallons of water through the pump and heat exchanger. The faster the flow rate the better, but watch out for the hose popping off the intake of the heat exchanger. Then dump the rinse water bucket and rinse out the kettle by hand. Be sure to flow clean water through the kettle valve. Disconnect all hoses and drain the heat exchangers.

Congratulations! You have just done a pro-style CIP.

BURNER ADJUSTMENT

When you first fire the burner and begin heating water in the kettle, you may have to adjust your burner. Fire the burner only when a kettle of liquid (water or wort) is in place on it. Units like the Bayou Classic SQ-14 have an air gate on the gas intake. This can be rotated open or closed to control the amount of air being mixed with the gas. The adjustment is usually quite simple, just a matter of loosening a couple of screws and rotating the gate to the correct position, then tightening the screws down again. The correct adjustment is one where the flame is entirely blue and can be seen all the way down to the nozzles of the burner casting. If the flame is "elevated" — there is a gap between the nozzles and the blue flame — then too much air is being fed and the gate needs to be closed. On the other hand, if the flame is yellow at the tips, then too little air is being fed; open the gate. Gas pressure is controlled by the red knob on the regulator. With most burners, you do not need to screw the knob all the way down to get maximum heat. Changes to the gas pressure will require an adjustment of the air feed to compensate.

Over the course of a few brews you will be able to adjust your burner so that it gives a strong rolling boil with a nice blue flame. When you find the right settings, mark the gate and regulator so you can return to them.

Air gate burner. The Bayou Classic SQ-14 propane burner has an adjustable air gate.

Air gate

One tip on flame adjustment: always do this with the burner in the shade. It is almost impossible to see the flame in sunlight. If necessary, prop up a big umbrella or a sheet of plywood to block the sun while you are working with the burner.

FLOW RATE CALIBRATIONS

The other calibrations are for fluid flow. You need to find the speed setting for your pump, which will enable you to knock out at a reasonable rate: about 10 to 15 minutes for 5 gallons. The procedure is simple: if you haven't already, fill your kettle with cold water, then arrange your hoses and heat exchangers in knockout configuration. Be sure you have the bucket marked. Get the pump primed and the output connected to the heat exchanger intake. Now, get out your stopwatch and start it ticking as you turn on the pump. Set the speed controller to a middle position on the dial and collect 2 gallons of water. Then shut off the pump and stopwatch at the same time. If the time was less than 4 minutes — or much longer — dump the water back in the kettle and do another run with a higher or lower speed. Repeat as needed until you have nailed down your setting.

The other required calibration is for your cold liquor flow. This applies only if you are using chilled water. If so, then you need to fill a keg with tap water and connect it via a black "product" coupler and vinyl tubing to the water input of the cold liquor section. Position the

---

FOR THE NEOPHYTE: ADJUSTING THE CARBON DIOXIDE REGULATOR

If you have never used a regulator before, here is the lowdown: if a regulator has only one gauge, it is always the output gauge. It will read 0 to 30 or 0 to 60 PSIG, full scale. The second gauge, which reads to 2,000 or so, tells the pressure in the cylinder. It is there only for informational purposes. The cylinder gauge often will be marked with green and red zones to indicate when it is time to refill. As for setting the regulator, first the output valve must be shut or the gas hose must be connected to a keg or a fitting such as the gray keg coupler, which has a built-in automatic shutoff valve. Likewise, the valve at the top of the gas cylinder must be fully open. Now, to set the pressure, first zero the regulator by turning the adjuster nut or bar counterclockwise until you hear a puff of gas escape from the regulator body. The gauge should drop to zero. Then slowly turn the adjuster clockwise until the gauge starts to creep up. Stop a bit below your target, as the gauge typically lags a little. If you overshoot, go back to zero and try again.

water output over a calibrated bucket. Now get your carbon dioxide tank. Set the carbon dioxide pressure to 6 PSIG (pounds per square inch gauge) — probably the second hash mark on the output gauge.

At this point, all hoses should be connected — gas to gas plug, water to product plug — and heat exchangers should be in line, pressure set to 6 PSIG. Now all you need to do is get your stopwatch ready and start it as you slowly open the regulator gas valve. Run a gallon of water, stop, and note the time. It should be between 2 and 2½ minutes. If so, mark the regulator to indicate the valve setting. If not, dump the water and do another run with the valve more or less open as needed.

If you are using ice water and feeding cold liquor by gravity or by a pump, the same methods apply as for calibrating wort flow.

The importance of these flow rate calibrations will become apparent when you do your first knockout. If you want to do a trial run using a kettle full of hot water instead of wort, I would not discourage you. However, as long as you have done the calibrations and understand the operation of the heat exchanger, which is explained further down, your first knockout will go smoothly.

Another, optional calibration that you can do with your heat exchanger is tap water flow. This is not usually critical, but it may save some water. Calibrate a setting about three times your knockout rate. For a 5-gallon batch and 10-minute knockout, that would be 1.5 gallons per minute. With a properly sized heat exchanger, this should be fast enough to drop the wort to within 10°F of the water temperature.

Before You Brew

The initial tests and measurements only need to be done once, but there are other operations that need to be performed prior to every brew. The first time through will take longer because you will have to determine correct adjustments or quantities. But don't worry — you'll get faster with practice.

CHOOSING A RECIPE

This is an important decision, because you should stick with one recipe for your first four to six brews. The reasons for this should be clear by now: a newcomer to all-grain brewing first has to achieve consistent results, and the only way you can possibly know if your results are consistent is to make no changes to your recipe. Adjusting hop quantities to suit your taste is okay, as long as you keep them within bounds for the style of beer, but please, use the same yeast and grain bill. Of course, this means you should pick a beer style that you really like.

I suggest starting out with a light- to amber-colored beer for a couple of reasons. It is easier to assess the clarity of a pale wort, which helps when you are just learning how to handle the lautering operation. Also, light-colored worts give a bigger, more definite hot break in the kettle, making it easier to see the results of your boil and whirlpool.

Wheat beers are a bad choice for a first recipe because wheat malt, like rye malt, flaked oats, and certain other adjuncts, tends to gum up the mash and make lautering difficult. For this reason I think you should start with a recipe that calls only for barley malt, or barley malt and relatively unproblematic adjuncts, such as flaked maize or rice.

The reason for sticking to the same yeast is that one measure of consistency is attenuation. Because yeasts vary so much in this respect, you have to stay with the same strain. This means not just the "type" or brewery of origin, but the actual brand. There are lots of American ale yeasts. The Ballantine strain is available in liquid cultures from both Wyeast and White Labs. It is also available in dry form from Fermentis/Safale. Do not assume these are interchangeable. They have the same origin, but they have been handled differently afterward and may behave differently in your fermenter. Pick one and stay with it.

If you intend to use a dry yeast, there may be a rehydration procedure you need to plan for. Fermentis states that this is not necessary, but Danstar has detailed instructions on its package, so the makers clearly prefer it. You should do what the manufacturer recommends. Danstar's rehydration procedure requires boiling water and cooling it to around 85°F, so you need to think a little about where in the brewing process you need to start this operation. Boiling the water in your 1-cup Pyrex measure in a microwave is probably the easiest way.

If you want to devise your own recipe, I recommend Nelson's Beer Quick-Calculator online recipe software. I like Nelson's because it links directly to the BJCP (Beer Judge Certification Program) guidelines for whatever style you select to brew. It also compares your predicted results with the style parameters. Now, I do not care for all the defaults. For example, the extract efficiency is assumed to be 70 percent, which is very low. I routinely get 85 to 90 percent when making average-strength beers (4.5 to 5.5 percent alcohol by volume, original gravity 1.044 to 1.055). I also am not on board with some of the BJCP's specifications for some styles of beer. Nonetheless, they are extremely helpful, especially when you are just starting.

My own recipes are based on what I like and what I think a style should taste like, as well as the specifics of what I get out of my home brewery. Thus, for example, I set my recipe volume to 5.3 gallons, which is approximately the volume of cooled wort I collect in my fermenter. I set my boil volume to 6.2 gallons, which is the average kettle volume over the course of the boil: I typically collect 6.8 to 7 gallons of wort and boil it down to 5.5 gallons hot, which is about 5.3 cooled. Grain bills are based on the efficiency I get. Hops are the toughest thing to pin down. The Beer Quick-Calculator, like most others, assumes that zero minutes of boil time means zero bitterness contribution from the hops. In my experience, hops added to the kettle/whirlpool at flame off do contribute some bitterness. I also believe the hop calculators tend to underestimate bitterness for short boil times. For this reason, if my recipe calls for aroma hops near or at the end of the boil, I generally set my recipe bitterness (IBUs) a little lower than I really want. However, in any case, you must regard your first brews as a test and then adjust your hopping to taste.

Because of the broad range of bitterness and initial gravity that can fall under its various subcategories, British pale ale is an excellent choice for a first brew. Its original gravity can run anywhere from 1.032 to 1.060, and bitterness anywhere from 25 to 50 IBUs. If you aim for the center, you are pretty certain to hit the target somewhere.

Regarding water-to-grist ratio, most people will find that 1¼ quarts per pound is about as thick as they want to stir. This ratio is used in many pub breweries where the mash must be stirred by hand (actually, by back, shoulder, and elbow). However, you also need to consider the space under the false bottom, if your lauter tun has one, and the volume of wort in your grant. The hot liquor to cover the false bottom is called foundation water and is always run in separately; it does not factor into the water-grist ratio. As far as I know, the operating volume of the grant has no name, and in a pub brewery it is usually small enough that no provision is made for it. However, in a home brewery the grant may be larger relative to the mash volume; if its working volume is not accounted for, then when vorlauf begins, the wort level in the lauter tun will drop below the surface of the grain bed. This is bad: first because the grains contain hot wort, and hot wort aeration (hot-side aeration) causes rapid staling of the finished beer; and second because the bed is compressed by gravity, which makes it prone to *channeling* (uneven drainage) and getting stuck during sparging. For these reasons it is worthwhile to measure your grant's working volume in advance, and add that to the quantity of water you calculated by the 1¼ quarts per pound ratio. For example, my grant has a working capacity of 2 quarts, so if I am mashing 8 pounds of grain, which means 10 quarts of water, I actually use 12 quarts. Then I enter the new water volume into the calculator program to get the correct strike temperature.

GRAIN MILLING

As mentioned in the equipment chapter, a proper crush is essential for a good yield and an easy lauter. If you are having your local shop mill for you, ask if you can operate the mill yourself, or at least have the setting adjusted. If so, then you can follow the same procedure as you would if you were using your own mill. Start off at whatever the manufacturer recommends for an initial setting, run a cup of pale malt through, and examine it. If there are unbroken kernels, set the gap smaller and run another cup through. If on the other hand there are few or no large husk pieces, widen the gap and try again. The best advice I can give you is that the interior of the grain must be exposed so that the starches can be liquefied and broken down, but the husks must not be pulverized. This inevitably means that the starch pieces will be of varying size, and some will look like corn grits or other coarse-ground grains. (Think of bulgur wheat.) This is all right: if the malt is well modified, the starch does not need to be ground to flour in order to be broken down in the mash tun.

The photos on the inside cover show examples of properly crushed and overly coarse milled pale malt.

When you think you have found a good setting, the only way to test it is to mill a batch's worth of grain and brew with it. Once you have proved a setting, it needs to be marked. However, be aware that slowly over time mill rollers and plates wear down, so you should never stop examining your malt crush. One tip for milling very hard grains, such as Cara-Pils, is to mix them with the rest of your grist before you start. Also, never mill flaked adjuncts, as they have already been flattened during processing. Add them to the mash directly.

PLANNING AND IMPLEMENTING WATER TREATMENT

What you do with your water on brew day will depend not only on its properties but also on the beer you choose to brew. The overriding concern is to get the pH of the mash and wort right. A pH of 5.2 is considered ideal, although values from 5.0 to 5.5 are acceptable.

There are several brewing liquor treatment calculators available online. Most are aimed at duplicating famous brewing waters, but they also can be used for simpler jobs such as figuring out how much calcium chloride you need to add to a quantity of mash liquor to get the calcium ion number where you want it. The one I use is the Brewer's Friend Brewing Water Chemistry Calculator. It gives additions in teaspoons as well as grams, which is helpful. When working with natural water, you must first fill in the Source Minerals row with the figures from your water quality report. Be as accurate as you can in stipulating the water volume, and remember, you are treating your mash and sparge liquor separately. Don't pay too much attention to the program's recommendations. You don't need 150 ppm of alkalinity to make even a very dark beer, and you certainly don't need at least 50 to brew an amber beer.

You should already know whether your water is "hard" or "easy." Assuming your water is easy, you can anticipate to some extent how it will react with your grist in the mash tun. Rules of thumb: If you want to make a pale or amber beer, then you will want to add enough calcium chloride or gypsum to bring the calcium content of the mash water up to 100–125 parts per million. For 5-gallon batches (3 to 4 gallons of mash liquor) ½ teaspoon is almost always enough. This can be added directly to the mash. For dark beers, if the alkalinity is over 50 ppm, you can usually eschew any additions. However, it is wise to have some calcium carbonate on hand in case your mash pH turns out to be too low. For natural waters with low alkalinity (below 50 ppm), some calcium carbonate will probably be needed.

That is it for mash treatment. For sparge liquor, the rules are simpler.

For pale and amber beers, no mineral additions are needed. Adjust the sparge liquor pH to 5.7–6.0 with phosphoric acid 10%. With my water (66 ppm alkalinity) 1 tablespoon does the job on 6 gallons. You can work this out before your first brew. Just filter 6 gallons of your tap water into your fermenting bucket, then add phosphoric acid 1 teaspoon at a time, checking the pH after each addition. When you have hit the target, note the amount and the pH achieved. As long as you have not gone too far, you can save the water and use it, assuming you will be brewing within a few days.

With easy water, the rule for sparging dark beers is, leave it alone.

If you are working with RO water, your preliminary water treatment is a bit more complicated, and as mentioned, you really need a miniature scale for weighing out your mineral additions. Once again, assuming you do not want to duplicate a famous brewing water, here would be my recommendations for infusion mashes:

- **PALE BEER:** calcium 75–125 ppm, magnesium 5–15 ppm, sodium under 25 ppm, chloride under 100 ppm, sulfate under 50 ppm, alkalinity under 25 ppm
- **AMBER BEER:** same except alkalinity 25–50 ppm
- **DARK BEER:** calcium 50–100 ppm, magnesium 5–15 ppm, sodium 25–50 ppm, chloride under 100 ppm, sulfate under 75 ppm, alkalinity 50–100 ppm. Alkalinity depends on how much dark roasted grain there is in the recipe. Stouts can take, and may need, more than brown ales, for example.

With RO water, you may be able to treat the whole lot at the same time, if you have a bucket big enough. The only exception is alkalinity. Calcium carbonate is only soluble in an acid solution, so it needs to be added straight into the mash. Therefore, your strategy for dark beers should be to use calcium carbonate in the mash, and use sodium bicarbonate (baking soda) to alkalize your sparge liquor. For example, we're making a stout with RO water and we want around 100 ppm alkalinity. We will be using 3.5 gallons of mash liquor and 6 gallons of sparge liquor. We'll do the sparge liquor first. We assume our RO water has zero level for all minerals. (This is not exactly true, but with a good RO filter, it's close enough for our purposes. The people who supplied your RO system can give you specific information.) What we find, keying some numbers into the calculator program, is that if we add 2 grams of Epsom salt, 4 grams of calcium chloride, and 3 grams of sodium bicarbonate, then our sparge liquor will come in at: calcium 48 ppm, magnesium 9 ppm, sodium 38 ppm, sulfate 34 ppm, chloride 85 ppm, and alkalinity 79 ppm.

For the mash liquor, if we add 1 gram of calcium chloride, 1 gram of Epsom salt, plus 3 grams of calcium carbonate, then we will have: calcium 111 ppm, magnesium 7 ppm, sulfate 29 ppm, chloride 36 ppm, and alkalinity 111 ppm. Actually, for the mash, I would start with 2 grams of calcium carbonate, and add more if required.

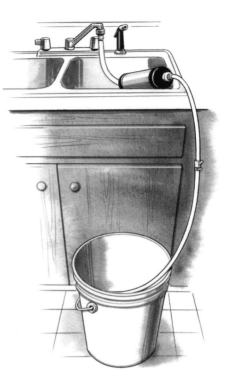

Water filter. Filtering sparge liquor the night before a brew.

We did not add any sodium to the mash liquor, but with 38 ppm in the sparge liquor there will be around 28 ppm in the collected wort. This is acceptable. As you know by now, I try to keep both sodium and sulfate levels low. On the other hand, a little magnesium is good in brewing liquor, and Epsom salt is the only readily available source.

Once again, never forget that pH is the overriding criterion here. You should take and save samples of your mash and wort, especially during your first few brews. Samples must be cooled to room temperature before they can be checked, and what with everything else you are doing, you may not get to all of them during your first brew. The most critical one is mash pH, so plan on having a small jar or cup of ice water on hand so that you can pull that sample and quickly cool it for checking. If the pH is too low or high, you want to know this while there is still time to do something about it. For the rest, if you find after the fact that your sample was a little high or low, don't worry. The beer will still taste good. Adjust your water treatment program for the next batch.

I prefer to get my brewing liquor drawn and measured ahead of time. The main reason I do this is that it eliminates the temptation to rush the filter. I use my fermenter as a large measuring/holding vessel for the sparge liquor, and I run the mash liquor into the mash mixer using the dipstick. If you don't have a mash mixer, use your kettle or whatever you plan to heat the water in. If the sparge liquor is to be treated with phosphoric acid, I do that also; it's one less thing to remember the next morning. I prefer to add treatments to the mash during mash-in, but I also prefer to calculate my mash liquor volume ahead of time so that I can have the water treatment salts ready.

EQUIPMENT PREP

It is very good practice, if possible, to set up your equipment the night before brew day. This will automatically enforce some review of equipment. You will notice whether anything has gotten dusty and needs a rinse-out. Gather up all the lengths of tubing that you will need, plus adapters, clamps, and tools, especially the all-important nut driver. If you have permanent tube or hose connections — especially a homebuilt heat exchanger — go over all of them and tighten as necessary. Set out all the ancillary equipment such as the air pump. Check the HEPA air filter to make sure it is dry and clean inside.

One thing you should not do ahead of time is plug in your pump. Develop the habit of plugging it in immediately before use, and unplugging it immediately after. When it is time to use it, always check the speed control or other switch to make sure it is in the off position before plugging in.

COLD LIQUOR

This only applies for those places and times when your tap water is too warm to cool the wort by itself.

If you are using a keg as a cold liquor back, you must remember to fill it with water and put it in the refrigerator 2 days before you brew. If you need or prefer to use ice water, then you need to either make or buy enough ice. Here is a rough guideline: The key number is the latent heat of fusion for water. It takes 80,000 calories (80KCal) to change 1 kilogram (2.2 pounds) of ice at 0°C (32°F) into 1 kilogram (1 liter) of water at the same temperature. I won't take you through all the calculations, but to apply these numbers to homebrewing, 4 gallons of water at 82°F plus 11.6 pounds of ice at 32°F, stirred together, will yield 5.4

gallons of cold liquor at 32°F. However, in order to get this result, the ice must melt completely, and the mixing vessel and ambient air temperature must also be 32°F. If it is warmer, then more ice and less water will be needed. If your water is cooler, then less ice will be needed, although a few degrees does not change the quantity very much.

My suggestion is to make or buy 12 to 15 pounds of ice for each 5 gallons of cold liquor. On brew day, make up the cold liquor during wort boil. Put the ice in a picnic cooler and add water to make 5 gallons total volume. Then stir (the bigger the ice cubes, the more stirring it will take). When most of the ice is melted, pull a water sample and take its temperature. If it is close to 32°F, add another 1 to 2 pints of water and stir some more. (Remember, ice will not flow through the heat exchanger. You need 5 gallons of liquid.) If not, then stir until all the ice is melted and check the water temperature. As long as it is 40°F or under you are fine. Keep the insulated lid on the cooler whenever you are not stirring.

Brew Day

Finally, it's time. If you have done your homework, the brewing will probably go pretty well. But there are some things you learn only by doing, things you have to get a feel for, and many specific brewing operations are like that. There will be a few bumps in the road, but you will produce fermentable wort that becomes drinkable beer.

MASHING LIQUOR AND MASHING-IN
I'll give alternative instructions for a mash/lauter tun, or a mash mixer.

Mash/Lauter Tun
You should already know how much water you will be using to mash in and what its strike, or starting, temperature should be. If your mash/lauter tun has a false bottom, then be sure your foundation water volume is included in your total.

For tempering the mash, you need to have an extra gallon of filtered brewing water at the ready. Hold half of it in a pitcher or jug and start bringing the other half to a boil on your kitchen stove. When it boils, cover and lower the heat to simmer.

The next step is to heat the volume of mash water to 10 degrees above the strike temperature using your brew kettle so that the water temperature will continue to climb for 1 to 2 minutes after shutting off the heat; hitting your target will get easier with practice. If you over-shoot, I suggest just stirring the water. The temperature will drop fairly fast with air-cooling. When the temperature is correct, transfer to the mash/lauter tun and cover. Allow it to sit for 10 minutes or more to pre-heat. During this time, the lauter tun walls will absorb heat from the water, lowering its temperature.

After preheating, stir and check the temperature, and adjust to strike-heat level by additions of cold or boiling water as necessary. Keep track of the additions, because once you have the strike temperature correct, you must remove a volume of water equal to the total of all the tempering additions you made. If you neglect to do this, the water-to-grist ratio, and therefore the mash temperature, will be higher than desired.

Finally, dump your grist and any water treatments into the mash tun and go to work with your paddle. There may be some balling: every wad of dry grist has to be broken up. However, be careful — you must avoid hitting the false bottom or manifold. You do not want to displace it or, heaven forbid, knock it apart. Eventually you will have the mash well mixed. Double-check the temperature and temper if necessary, then pull a small sample for a pH check, put the lid on, and let it stand for conversion. Stir after 30 minutes and then check the temperature. You may be surprised by how much heat has been lost. If you feel the need, add some boiling water to raise the temperature. Continue to rest for another 30 minutes. Then proceed with lautering.

Mash Mixer

For tempering the mash, have half a gallon of cold, filtered water available.

You should already have calculated your mash water volume. Round the figure up to the nearest quart.

Put the water into the mash mixer, cold. Turn the burner or element to high. After 10 minutes, stir the water and check the temperature. Thereafter, stir and check every few minutes until the water tempera-ture reaches 145 to 155°F. Turn off the heat. If you overshot and the temperature is higher than 155°F, stir in a little cold water (1 to 2 cups) to bring it down between 155 and 145°F. Precision is not needed here.

Dump in the grist and any water treatment, and stir with abandon. Go all the way to the bottom; there's no apparatus down there to worry about. Once you have the grist well mixed, turn on the heat at a medium to medium-high setting, and stir and check the temperature continuously (at least once a minute) until you are 2 degrees below target. At this point, turn off the heat or, if using an electric stove, move to an adjacent cold element. The temperature will continue to rise for a bit; keep stirring and see where it settles in. If within 1 degree of target, plus or minus, pull a sample for a pH check, then cover and let it sit. If lower, heat for another 30 to 60 seconds and recheck. If higher, stir in ½ to 1 cup cold water and recheck. Once it's in the range, put some insulation around it if you can. Even a few old towels or a blanket will help. After 30 minutes, stir and check, then reheat to target plus or minus 2 degrees.

After 1 hour, heat the mash once more, this time bringing it to around 170°F. This will compensate for the temperature drop during transfer. Transferring the mash to the lauter tun can be dangerous. You may wish to scoop some of the mash in with a pitcher before pouring the rest into the tun. Once the mash is in, cover the tun and let it settle 10 minutes, then proceed with lautering.

pH Check

You should have a small cup of ice water on hand. Put your sample container into it and let the sample cool to room temperature. That should only take a few minutes. This is a key step: all pH checks must be done on cooled samples. Even if you have a nice pH meter with automatic temperature compensation (ATC), it will still give an inaccurate reading at mash temperatures. The ATC circuitry compensates for the effects of temperature on the probe, but not on the chemistry of the mash. The pH values given in this book, and in standard brewing texts, are for readings taken on room temperature samples.

If the pH of the sample reads below 5.0, you should stir 1 to 2 grams of calcium carbonate into the mash and do another check. Repeat if necessary. A pH this low is extremely unlikely with pale or amber beer recipes — so unlikely, in fact, that I would recalibrate my meter and double-check before making any adjustments. Much more likely is a reading higher than desired, and in this case the simple remedy is to add 1 to 2 grams calcium chloride or calcium sulfate to the mash.

Foundation Water (When Using Mash Mixer)

If your lauter tun has a false bottom, then you must add hot sparge liquor as "foundation water" to a depth that just covers the false bottom before transferring the mash. This water is not counted as part of the mash liquor. It is necessary to ensure that the mash will "float" rather than pack down prior to vorlauf. This is unnecessary with a manifold.

During the Mash Conversion

At this point, there are two jobs you have to do besides keeping an eye on temperatures: heat the sparge liquor in the brew kettle and sanitize the heat exchanger. These can be combined if you wish to use hot liquor for sanitizing, as many commercial breweries do. With a good propane burner you can heat 6 gallons of water to 190°F in 30 minutes or less, then connect your hoses together and pump the hot water from the kettle into the heat exchanger output, out of the heat exchanger input, and then finally back to the kettle or directly into the hot liquor back. (This latter technique is the most efficient arrangement, though it may require a long hose.) Set a fairly low flow rate so that the pump-through takes at least 20 minutes. After sanitizing, spray the heat exchanger intake and output with Star San and cover them with foil until it is time to reconnect everything for knockout.

One small inconvenience with this method: if you have a CPVC thermowell on your heat exchanger, it will have to be left off and sanitized separately by soaking in a bowl of Star San. The CPVC and especially the nylon hose barbs are not rated for 190°F water.

If you prefer to use Star San or another chemical sanitizer, you need to set up a pathway with your pump fed by a bucket containing 1 gallon of solution. I use my grant, which has a ½-inch hose barb output. With a chemical sanitizer there is no need for a back-flush arrangement: the easiest method is to front-flush the Star San through the heat exchanger and collect it in your fermenter, which will need sanitizing anyway. I made up a small valve fitting that I attach to the heat exchanger output. When I have pumped most of the Star San through, I shut off the valve and stop the pump, then let the heat exchanger sit for 10 or 15 minutes before finishing the transfer and draining the heat exchangers. Then I rinse out the grant by hand and flush water through the pump body and heat exchanger, catching it in a plastic bucket (2 gallons is enough). Then I close the valve on the output of the heat exchanger, cover the input with foil, and leave it. I drain the heat exchanger shortly before knockout.

After sanitizing the heat exchanger you may be able to use the pump to move your sparge liquor from the kettle to the hot liquor back. I find that the sparge liquor needs to be about 185°F in the kettle, as it seems to lose about 15 degrees between the air cooling during transfer and heat absorption by the back itself. If your hot liquor back is elevated above the lauter tun, your pump may not want to lift the hot water that high. My pump tends to cavitate, or run empty — the symptoms are fast spinning and rattling noises — when I try to do this. Meanwhile, I do the transfer the hard way, and carefully: 3 gallons into the back, which I lift into position, then the remainder via bucket.

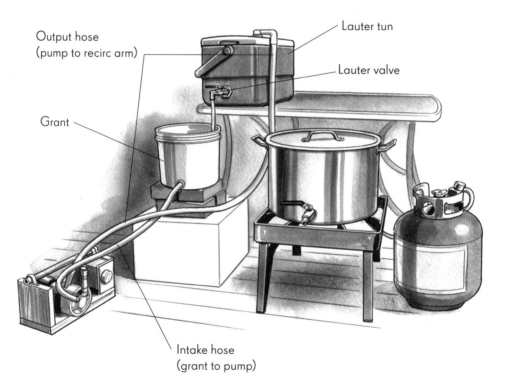

Lauter recirc. Another view of the author's brewery, with hoses arranged for recirculation of the cloudy wort.

LAUTERING

Lautering is divided into three steps: recirculation (or *vorlauf*), runoff, and sparge. Let's go over the details of implementing them.

Vorlauf

As mentioned before, prior to vorlauf you need to get your equipment in place. If you are going to do it manually, then the grant can be set inside the kettle. If you will be using the pump, get all the hoses connected together for your recirc loop. Run a length of vinyl tubing from the lauter tun output to the bottom of the grant. Also have a pint-size pitcher at hand. Open the lauter valve slightly, and when you have a steady but slow flow, start collecting into the pitcher and time how long it takes to fill. Ideally, for a lauter tun with a bottom area of 1 square foot (which is almost exactly the size of my lauter tun) you want a flow rate of 45 seconds per pint. For lauter tuns with smaller or larger bottom areas, flow should be set proportionately. Rapid runoff may seem like a good idea, but — especially with a false bottom — it often causes a stuck mash, where the grain bed packs too tightly and the flow slows to a trickle. If this happens, the only remedy is to shut the valve, stir up the mash, and start over. With manifolds, a rapid runoff usually makes it harder to get the wort clear, so go slowly!

When you first open the lauter valve, it is possible that the flow may stop after a few seconds because a piece of husk is blocking the valve. If this happens, open the valve until flow resumes, then immediately return it to the previous setting. Once I have found the correct opening for my desired runoff rate, I try to find something that I can use as a feeler gauge to measure the opening — a drill bit or a nail, anything that makes a snug fit in the gap between the base of the handle and the valve body.

The first principle of clarification is that you cannot go too far. I have often been cited as saying the opposite, but the remarks I made in *BrewingTechniques* magazine many years ago pertained to a rather unique situation at a large brewery with the most modern, mechanized lauter tuns and grain mills that have three sets of rollers. The brewers there found that they could filter wort through the grain bed as clear as finished commercial beer. Trust me, you will not encounter this. Your goal should be to get the wort as clear as you can. Depending on the grain bill, this might not be very clear, but a beginner should exercise patience and do a long, slow vorlauf. You may think the wort is "clear enough" after 5 minutes. Take a sample and set it aside, then continue to recirculate for another 10 minutes. Collect another sample and compare them. If they look the same, you have wasted a little time. If not, your beer will be better for it. I find with my lauter tun that it takes 10 to 15 minutes to get the wort as clear as possible. With a false bottom and/or a deeper bed, it would almost certainly take less time.

The mechanics of manual recirculation are quite simple. Keep bailing, being careful to pour the wort over the grain bed as gently as possible. At all costs you must avoid "digging a hole." The shallower the bed, the gentler your technique must be.

Recirculation with a pump is a bit more involved. First you need to have a vorlauf arm that will deliver a gentle flow of wort close to the bed surface. See the Projects chapter for more about this (page 194). The basic equipment setup is that wort flows by gravity into the grant. The grant feeds the input of the pump, and the pump returns the wort to the lauter tun via the recirc arm. Connect the hoses before you begin. You first need to get your runoff rate established, just as you would with manual vorlauf. When you have 3 to 4 inches of wort in the grant, you should prime the pump and start recirculating. Disconnect the pump output hose from the vorlauf arm and keep the end in your pitcher while you lower it to prime. This should enable you to catch any wort that spills out so you can return it to the grant.

When the pump appears to be primed, reattach the hose end to the vorlauf arm and turn on the pump. Set it immediately to a low setting and observe whether the wort is moving. If it's not, speed up the pump until you see the wort rising in the hose. If the wort will not move, shut off the pump and have another go at priming.

Once the wort is recirculating, use the speed control to adjust the flow rate so that the wort level in the grant stays fairly steady. Once you have that setting, you can try to "yo-yo" the wort level up and down a few times: this will help to pull some of the debris off the grant floor. However, you may find that varying the return rate this way in a thin grain bed can cause the wort to get cloudy. Once the flow slows down, the wort should clear up again.

If you find that a rapid return rate has "dug a hole" in the grain bed, you can do some gentle landscaping with a spoon or paddle to fill it in.

As the recirculation goes on, you should be able to observe the clarification of the wort in the runoff tube, and also in any samples you take. Be careful when getting samples not to pinch the tube shut: this is the same as closing the valve, which will "float" the filter bed and hurt clarity. The only time the lauter valve should be closed is in the case of a stuck mash, where the entire grain bed needs to be broken up anyway.

There is a large range of practice when it comes to outflow rates, by which I mean, the speed of wort flow from the lauter tun into the grant. The usual method is to start off slowly and gradually increase the outflow rate after the wort is clear. However, my experience with a manifold lauter tun and a thin grain bed indicates that *any* change in the outflow rate is likely to alter wort clarity for the worse. With a thin, loosely packed grain bed, speeding up the runoff will pull small trapped particles out of their matrix. On the other hand, slowing the runoff significantly may float the bed, with the same result. I find that it's better to start with a slow rate and hold it. With a false bottom lauter tun and/or a deeper grain bed, though, the conventional method will likely prove best.

Transition to Runoff and Sparge
Runoff is the period when the first wort is run into the kettle, prior to commencing the sparge. The grain bed should always be covered with liquid, so runoff time depends on the depth of wort above the grain bed when recirculation ends. With a picnic cooler lauter tun, the depth is only an inch or so and runoff may take only a minute.

Transition from recirculation to runoff is a critical operation, because you want to preserve the clarity of the wort. This means that there can be no disturbance in the outflow from the lauter tun, and if you are using a pump, no disturbance of the debris in the bottom of the grant.

In a manual vorlauf operation, transition is a simple process. Check to make sure the kettle valve is closed, then remove the grant from the kettle. The only tricks are that you must not (1) pinch the runoff tube shut, or (2) spill the grant contents into the kettle. As with other critical operations, a little practice ahead of time may help. When I did manual vorlauf I used a large but relatively shallow mixing bowl for a grant. This made transition easier than with a bucket. It also helped to have a wide, shallow kettle. After removing the grant, gently ladle the contents into the lauter tun. Let the wort level draw down to an inch or so, then begin sparging.

When using a pump, transition is a bit more complicated. First, before you begin, speed up the pump slightly and draw the level of wort in the grant down to only a couple of inches. Then, cut the pump speed back to minimum. This should stop recirculation and you should see the wort level drop in the output hose. Quickly check to make sure the kettle valve is closed. Then, pinch the hose near the end, pull it off the recirc arm, and push it onto the kettle valve. Crack the kettle valve open just enough that wort starts flowing into it. If the kettle sits at the same level as the grant, then you probably can control the level in the grant entirely with the kettle valve. However, in a kitchen brewery where the kettle sits on the stovetop, the kettle valve will likely have to be opened wide and you may have to adjust the pump speed to control the level in the grant. In either case the principle to observe is to keep a gentle, steady flow of wort from grant to kettle, with no abrupt changes in level or rate. This is important because you must not disturb the debris in the bottom of the grant. Especially while you are learning, be attentive. It is all too easy to get distracted, and before you know it the grant is empty — or overflowing. You would not be the first brewer to let that happen.

An alternative to making the transition by physically moving the hose is to fashion a branching tee with a pair of valves and put it in the output line of the pump. This reduces transition simply to shutting one valve while opening the other. However, it does not compensate for the height differential (if there is one) between the kettle and the lauter tun, so the kettle valve still has to be maneuvered. I have not implemented such a tee; it is more appropriate to a system with a permanent framework and hard piping. If you decide to do things this way, then make sure you crack the kettle valve open before you make the transition.

With a shallow grain bed and a grant in the line, runoff is likely to be very short. As soon as you have flow into the kettle, check the lauter tun and open the hot liquor valve if necessary. Then you can turn your attention back to equalizing the in- and out-flow of the grant.

Sparging

This is the simplest part of lautering. All that is required is to maintain an inch or so of water atop the grain bed, and, if using a pump, keep a steady level in the grant. I find that even with my sparge arm, which has only eight small holes, I still have to throttle back the hot liquor valve considerably. As the back empties, the valve may need to be opened slightly to maintain a steady sparge rate.

At some point during the sparge, you can begin heating the kettle. Ideally, you would like the kettle to come to a boil just as sparging ends, but it is hard to gauge this when you are starting out. With a runoff rate of 45 seconds per pint, sparging should take around 45 minutes. I suggest you fire the burner when you have about 3 gallons of wort in the kettle and see what happens. If you get a boil before all the wort is collected, just shut off the heat. Next time you can adjust to get the sparge and boil synchronized.

If you are using the kettle valve to control the wort level in the grant, then firing the kettle while sparging poses a hazard. From that point on, remember to only touch the valve handle using a mitt or a pot holder.

During sparge you should weigh out your hop additions. Also, if your kettle finings need hydration, this should be started now, as it may take an hour for them to dissolve. Don't get distracted from your main job though, which is keeping the water and wort levels correct in the lauter tun and grant, respectively. You also must monitor the level in the kettle using your dipstick. Depending on the evaporation rate they expect, most homebrewers collect between 6.5 and 7 gallons of wort in the kettle. They boil this down to 5.5 gallons in 60 to 90 minutes. Because of "shrinkage" — cold water is denser that hot water — that amounts to about 5.28 gallons of cooled wort. Add losses at knockout (the hop and trub pile) and fermenter (yeast), and that generally yields 5 gallons of beer.

MANAGING WORT COLLECTION AND BOILING THE WORT

It is not easy to determine in advance how much wort to collect. Boiling 7 gallons of water for 90 minutes will certainly tell you, but that's an expensive test to run. My suggestion is to collect 6.5 gallons for your first brew. This can almost always be boiled down to 5.5 gallons in 90 minutes or less. While you boil, watch your evaporation. If the wort level drops half a gallon in the first half hour, throw in your bittering hops and set your boil time to 75 minutes. After knockout you can add filtered water to the fermenter as needed to get the correct volume of wort. Then, the next time you brew you can plan for a shorter boil and/or more wort in the kettle. If, on the other hand, it looks like evaporation is going slowly, then see if you can increase the burner heat to get a more vigorous boil. It is hard to control the flame on most propane burners, but in the case of low evaporation you can at least try to turn up the gas.

Especially for your first few brews, it is a good idea to collect and quickly cool a sample of your "kettle full" wort. Then you can take a hydrometer reading, which will allow you to predict the gravity of your wort in the fermenter. The only place you can trip up here is over the volumes of hot versus cold wort; otherwise, it's a straight calculation.

For example, say you have 6.5 gallons of hot wort in the kettle, and you plan to boil down to 5.5 gallons hot, which will "shrink" to 5.28 gallons during cooling. First, multiply the 6.5 gallon number by 0.96, which will correct for the greater volume displaced by boiling hot liquids. This gives a figure of 6.24 gallons. Then read the gravity of your cooled wort sample. Say it's 1.039. *__The post-boil starting gravity of your wort should be 39 x 6.24 / 5.28 = 46, or 1.046.__* If that is significantly lower than you expected (four points or more), then you have two choices: (1) adjust the gravity of the wort upward by adding some light dry malt extract to the kettle, or (2) adjust your bitterness downward to match the lower gravity. This means recalculating your hop additions.

I do not recommend going longer than 90 minutes when boiling a pale wort, and really, 75 minutes is better. Wort darkens as it boils, and the darkening depends on time, not on evaporation rate. Amber and dark worts can go 2 hours if need be. My experience with my burner and kettle has mostly been at the other end of the scale: with a fresh cylinder of propane, I can boil off 1.5 gallons in 60 minutes.

Your goal should be to get a good rolling boil with the kettle lid removed. If your burner will not allow this, then you can use the kettle lid to increase the vigor of the boil. But if this is necessary then you will have to collect less wort in the kettle: as little as 6.25 to 6 gallons. The evaporation rate only needs to be 6 or 7 percent per hour, so the problem here is not a compromise of wort quality, but possible loss of extract. Collecting less wort means sparging less, which means leaving more sugar in the lauter tun.

During the boil you may have to adjust your burner to maintain a good rolling action. Here are some other things you may need to do:

▸ Make up cold liquor if you are using ice.
▸ Drain the lauter tun as much as possible. My routine is to remove the lid assembly and then the hose, and put a bucket into position below the valve and open it wide. With a manifold, it will help to prop the lauter tun at an angle so that it drains more completely. When you are doing this, also disconnect the grant from the pump. If the grant outlet has no valve, be careful not to spill wort. Put the hose ends into the bucket to minimize spillage, then dump the grant contents into the bucket.
▸ Connect the pump and its hoses for knockout. This is all on the hot wort side and sanitizing is not necessary. However, you should rinse

out the hoses and pump body before connecting them. Leave the output end of the heat exchanger closed until you have started whirlpool.

▶ Put a gallon of Star San solution in the fermenter, then attach the lid, shake, and roll it. Keep this up for several minutes. Then dump the solution into a bowl or bucket. Put the lid loosely on the fermenter and leave it, unrinsed, until final setup for knockout.

▶ Soak the cold wort hose and the thermowell tee in Star San until final setup for knockout, unless it is already clamped to the heat exchanger output. Do not immerse the thermometer, however.

▶ If you are going to be using cold liquor for cooling, then toward the end of the boil you should get the keg out of your refrigerator and move it, along with your carbon dioxide cylinder and all necessary hoses and fittings, into your brewery. Connect everything together so it's ready to go. Also at this time you can arrange the water output hoses of your heat exchangers to carry the water either to a drain or onto your lawn.

▶ One more thing you may want to do during the boil is to start rehydrating your yeast. Obviously, if you have the option of just pitching straight into the cooled wort, you don't need to bother with this. If you do need or wish to rehydrate, follow all timing instructions on the packet carefully. You can count on whirlpool to final setup to knockout taking half an hour your first time through, so you may want to put off the yeast work until knockout is under way. It is best to pitch wet yeast as soon as possible — even while it is still going into the fermenter. On the other hand, this is counterproductive — to put it mildly — if the wort temperature is at all off. I feel that you will have more than enough to think about during your first knockout, and it is better to delay pitching slightly rather than to let the yeast sit too long in warm water or risk shocking it in wort that is too cold.

Hopping Schedules

All the recipes in this book call for simple hopping schedules, with the first lot of hops (often called *kettle hops* or *bittering hops*) added 45 minutes before the end of the boil. This gives you some flexibility to adjust your boil time without changing the bitterness of the finished beer. Many brewers like to add some hops before the wort comes to a boil, because they dampen the initial foaming and reduce the danger of a boilover. Once you have an idea of how your kettle-burner combination behaves, you may want to incorporate first-wort hopping, as that practice is called, into your brewing. Online recipe calculators will allow you to do this while maintaining approximately the same bitterness level in the beer.

You should also be aware that the longer the hops are boiled, the more their volatile aromas are driven off with the steam, so even if the bitterness is the same, hop flavors may be diminished. You can compensate for this by introducing a third hop addition, at 10 or 15 minutes before the end of the boil.

The last lot of hops, for flavor and aroma, is usually called *finish hops*, and these are often added as the boil ends and whirlpooling starts. Because whirlpool and knockout times are much shorter in home breweries than in the average pub brewery, I usually add my finish hops 5 minutes before the end of the boil.

Recipes for some very popular beer styles include an addition of *dry hops*. For those of you not familiar with this term, dry hopping is the practice of adding hops after fermentation is over, either in the fermenter or, in the case of "real ale," in the serving cask. Hops added at this stage lend a very different sort of flavor and aroma to the beer. Most authorities contend that dry hops add no bitterness (I am not so sure about this), but they definitely add a large dose of aromatic hydrocarbons and other volatile substances that are vaporized and boiled off when hops are added to boiling wort. Dry hops are almost always listed as part of the hop bill in printed recipes, and they should be, but do not be confused: dry hopping is not part of the brew day routine.

Kettle Finings and Yeast Nutrient

Kettle finings are usually added 10 or 15 minutes prior to the end of the boil. If you are adding yeast nutrient, such as Servomyces, that also goes in shortly before the end of the boil. Follow the instructions that come with these ingredients and you'll be fine.

Whirlpool

If you have a gas burner, shutting it down will stop the rolling action of the boil almost immediately. Electric elements take longer. As soon as the wort stops rolling, you can commence with your whirlpool.

As noted earlier, whirlpooling is very easy in a home brewery. All you need to do is start the wort spinning with a stainless steel spoon.

The only technique required is to start slowly and then gradually build up speed. This will minimize splashing and the incorporation of air into the hot wort. Once the wort is spinning rapidly, pull the spoon out. There is no point in more stirring. Cover the kettle and let it sit while you do the final setup for knockout.

SETTING UP FOR KNOCKOUT

While the hop/trub pile is settling in the kettle, drain the heat exchanger of water and attach the thermowell and thermometer, if they are not already in place. Spray any hose ends and barbs with Star San before connecting them. Wash your hands and dip them in the bowl of Star San before you rinse out the fermenter. Spray a clean table or counter surface with Star San and set the lid on it, with the inside surface facing up. Then hold the fermenter upside down and spray clean water up into it. Move the water stream around, but do not touch the inside of the fermenter with the hose end. Only grip the rim of the fermenter bucket with your Star San–soaked hand. When the bucket is rinsed, set it upright for a minute while you pick up the lid and rinse it, then set the lid loosely on the fermenter and move it into position under the thermowell. Remove the cold wort tube from the Star San, rinse it briefly, then move the fermenter lid aside just enough so that you can push the tube onto the outlet barb of the thermowell. Finally, set the lid so that it covers as much of the fermenter as possible.

After rinsing out the fermenter, attach your water hose to the tap water input of the heat exchanger, unless you are doing single-stage cooling with cold liquor.

Now you need to open the kettle valve and get the pump primed. The wort hoses should already be attached for knockout. Try to get the pump body full while keeping the end of the hose elevated so that hot wort does not flow out. This can be a dangerous maneuver, and it is best to wear rubber gloves.

KNOCKOUT

These instructions assume you are using a two-stage heat exchanger. If not, then forgo the instructions that refer to tap water, but start your cold liquor flow before you start pumping wort. Also, you should have at least calibrated your cold liquor and wort flow by now. If not, then you are about to play a hand of five-card draw with a deck of jokers.

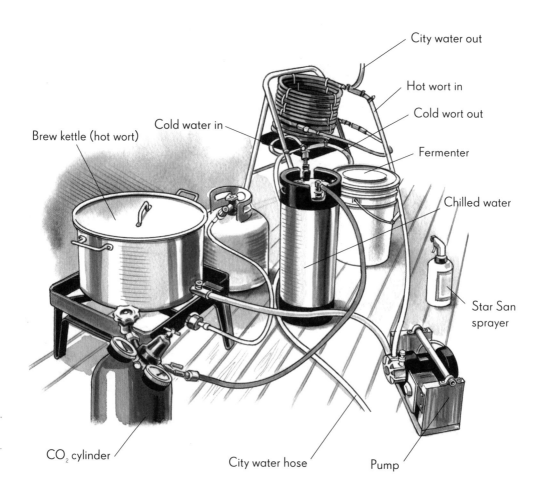

City water out

Hot wort in

Cold wort out

Cold water in

Brew kettle (hot wort)

Fermenter

Chilled water

Star San
sprayer

CO₂ cylinder

City water hose

Pump

Wort cooling. In the author's wort-cooling setup, hot wort is pumped from the brew kettle to the input of the city water heat exchanger, while city water is fed in from the opposite end. (The white hose snaking along the deck floor is the water hose.) Ice water is supplied by a keg of chilled water that is pushed by pressure from the carbon dioxide tank. Note the spray bottle of Star San on the right: it is never far away when handling cooled wort or beer. All hose ends, barbs, and so on are given a shot before connecting.

First, open the tap water valve and get a good flow rate going. I suggest 1.5 gallons per minute, but if you have not calibrated, just open the valve halfway or so. Next, start your pump and set the speed control to your mark, which should deliver a gallon every 2 to 2½ minutes. Then open the shutoff valve on your carbon dioxide tank and watch the temperature at the thermowell. Once wort starts making its way through, you should try to control the temperature by adjusting the flow of cold liquor. However, you must not exceed the maximum setting that you previously calibrated. If you do, the cold liquor keg will run out before all the wort is in the fermenter. If you see that your cold liquor flow is already near the maximum and the wort is still too warm, your next option is to increase the flow of tap water. However, once you reach a certain point — about three times the wort flow rate — further increases in tap water flow will scarcely affect the knockout temperature. If you are up against a maxed-out cold liquor rate and maxed-out (practically) tap water rate, then you must slow down the wort flow from the pump. This is your most powerful tool, and as long as your cold liquor holds out, you can always set a wort flow rate that will deliver the desired temperature. However, when you slow down the wort flow you must also slow down the cold liquor, so my suggestion would be to adjust wort flow to deliver 10 degrees below your knockout temperature, then cut back cold liquor flow until you are on target.

I wish I could give more detailed practical guidance on this worst-case scenario, but the fact is I have never encountered it with my system. With my homebuilt heat exchanger, described in detail in the Projects chapter (page 194), and 80°F tap water, I can knock out 70°F wort in 10 minutes and still have a gallon or so of cold liquor left in the keg. At slower rates even less is necessary. Nonetheless, you should be aware that any cooling system has limits. If you want to brew lagers in the summer, you need either a large cold liquor back or a powerful heat exchanger. Otherwise, your knockout times will be impractically long.

I am afraid all this talk about worst cases and limits makes heat exchanger operation look more difficult than it really is. Just to put it in perspective, here's a recap of the steps, in order:

STEP 1. Start tap water flow.

STEP 2. Start wort pump and set speed as calibrated.

STEP 3. Start cold liquor flow and adjust to maintain desired wort temperature.

That's it. That's all it takes to knock out. And as I noted, I have never had a problem. However, I do hope this discussion convinces you that calibration is worthwhile. I also hope it helps you understand why the homebrewer's boast of a 3-minute knockout rings hollow. In order to manage the flow rates and control the output temperature, you need time. The more slowly your thermometer reacts, the more time you need. I consider 10 minutes to be a practical minimum for wort knockout. Most commercial breweries take at least 20.

YEAST PITCHING AND AERATION

One interesting thing about dried yeast is the manufacturers' claim that wort aeration is not required. I have never had the nerve to test this. They don't say that aeration will hurt anything, so I always do it. In any case, it is necessary with liquid yeasts, whether that be a slurry from a brewery or previous batch, a tube or smack pack, or a starter made from one of those.

Assuming you are planning to aerate, you should wipe down the outside of the aerating tube with sanitizer, then plug in the pump before you put in the stone and as much of the tube as will go into the sanitizer bowl or bucket. The reason for doing things this way is that the inside of the air tube is sterile because the air is sterile filtered, so there is no need to get sanitizer into it and then worry about getting it out again. By running the pump you ensure that liquid is kept out while the exterior surfaces are sanitized.

Pitching itself is a simple operation and the only point that needs emphasis is — **think sanitary!**

Start by spraying a clean work surface with sanitizer. Once you have moved your covered fermenter into position for pitching, spray the lid and then leave it in place. If the yeast container is sealed, dip or spray the outside of it. Soak or wipe the stirring spoon with sanitizer for a few minutes, then dip your hands, rinse your hands and the container, and before touching anything else, open the yeast container. If the container is a smack pack you also have to dip the scissors and rinse them before use. With a dried yeast packet I still prefer to dip everything, but I blot the scissors and packet dry with paper towels before cutting it open. Once the yeast container is open, put down the cap or scissors and with your free hand, lift off the fermenter lid momentarily while you add the yeast.

If you are direct pitching dried yeast, sprinkle it on the wort surface and let it sit, loosely covered, until it is time to stir it in. The packets usually say half an hour. Once the yeast is stirred in, you can aerate if you wish. With slurry, quickly rinse off the stirring spoon and use it immediately, then insert the aerating stone — be sure it is resting on the bottom of the fermenter — and begin aerating. Half an hour is more than enough to saturate the wort with oxygen, assuming you get a good stream of fine bubbles through the wort.

Once the yeast is pitched, you can turn your attention to cleanup, but any time you need to break off and return to the wort, whether to stir in the dry yeast, remove the aerator or whatever, always wash your hands and arms in the sink with soap and water, rinse well, then spray anything you will be touching and, just before you lift the fermenter lid, dip your hands in sanitizer.

I prefer to get the fermenter capped and set in its place, with the air-lock attached, before I start digging out the lauter tun. Wet spent grains are full of bacteria. They also are surprisingly sticky, and I always get some on my clothes. There is no way I would stand over an open fermenter once I go to work on grain-out.

One tip for working with plastic fermenters (bucket or carboy): do not fill the airlock until you have moved the vessel to its station for fermentation. Otherwise, the flexing of the container will suck in water or sanitizer. The fermentation area should be somewhere away from drafts, doors, and windows, where the temperature is fairly steady and around 68 to 70°F, or whatever your chosen yeast prefers. This would rule out, for example, a closet with a heating/cooling duct running through it.

GRAVITY READING

I prefer to pull a sample of cooled wort and check the gravity before pitching yeast, but it can be done after pitching. My method makes it easier to assess the cold break in the sample jar.

This procedure is similar to yeast pitching, or any handling of the fermenter. All the equipment that touches the wort must be clean and sanitized. Spray the outside surface of the lid. Immerse the hydrometer and sample jar in Star San, dip your hands, then rinse the jar. Lift the lid with one hand while filling the jar with the other. Set the lid back on the bucket rim, set the jar in its base, and then rinse off the hydrometer, shake it, and insert into the jar. Spin it to dislodge bubbles, then take a reading, following the directions that came with the instrument. Some brewers routinely discard wort samples, but I feel that as

Cold break. Cooled wort in a test jar, just before pitching. Rapid cooling improves the formation of cold-break particles and gives a clearer, more stable beer.

long as everything is sanitary — including your hands — and kept that way, there is no need to do this. After reading, I dip my hands once more, then toss the wort back into the fermenter and proceed to pitch and aerate.

CLEANUP

Two rules: First, never leave cleanup of equipment for the next day. Only a dire emergency — childbirth, for example — should override this rule. Second, always start your cleanup with the heat exchanger, because that is critical. It is where the "cold side" of brewery operations begins, and therefore where the danger of infection begins.

You cannot let residue dry inside it. So, as soon as you have pitched your yeast, you must flush out the pump, hoses, and heat exchanger

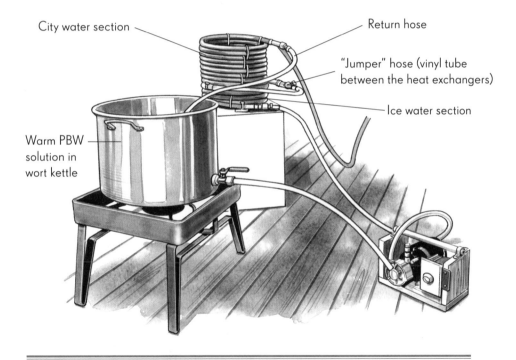

CIP back flush. The author's two-stage wort cooler setup for back-flush cleaning, using the kettle as a reservoir for cleaning solution. Note how the city water (upper) and ice water (lower) sections are connected by a length of vinyl tubing, with a second length used to return the solution to the kettle.

with tap water. Then remove the trub pile from the kettle, rinse it out, and set up to commence CIP. During CIP you can hand wash the mash mixer, grant, and any hoses or other equipment that may need it. The hot liquor back only needs to be drained.

As mentioned, I always leave the lauter tun until pitching and aeration are completed and the fermenter is put away. On a homebrewing scale, grain-out is really no trouble at all. Trust me. I normally just scoop out the spent mash with a plastic spoon. If your lauter tun has a manifold, you will find that nothing is as efficient as your own (gloved) fingers for digging out the bottom, around the pipes. Still, clearing out the last bits always requires a hose. After CIP of the heat exchanger, pump your cleaning solution into the lauter tun — through the recirc arm if you have one — and soak the manifold or false bottom for a while. Run a bit through the valve. I seldom disassemble the manifold, but it is important to rinse it thoroughly, along with the recirc arm and the rest of the lauter tun, after cleaning. Collect the used PBW solution in a bucket and dispose of it in the sink or toilet.

Spent grain disposal can be a bit of a headache. If you compost, or know someone who does, that is a good option. You may need to make allowances for the acidic nature of the spent grains — and whatever you do with them, they will soon get more acidic, as the bacteria get to work. There are few things more revolting than wet, two-day-old mash. Being no sort of gardener, I usually put the spent grains in a plastic trash bag and leave it in the rolling bin for the weekly pickup, but I have to admit that this results in a pool of foul-smelling liquid in the empty bin afterward. Lately I have taken to putting the bag of spent grains inside a bag mostly filled with normal kitchen refuse. That results in less residue and, hopefully, a less unpleasant experience for the poor guys who collect my garbage.

Fermentation Management

Every beginning brewer worries about fermentation. If they read on a yeast company website that ales should ferment out in 2 to 3 days, but their beer is still bubbling away after 4 days, they think something must be wrong. Not necessarily. Wort temperature has a tremendous impact, as does the yeast strain, wort composition and gravity, among other factors.

One thing I have found is that the dry-pitching method results in a slower start and a longer fermentation than rehydrating. Nonetheless,

Fermentis, a company that makes and sells yeast, recommends dry pitching. So do most homebrew shops. The reason for the recommendation is that it is easy to kill yeast during rehydration, so you have to be very careful with the water temperature. One shop owner told me that he has gotten many "no-fermentation" complaints from people who rehydrate, but none from those who simply sprinkle the yeast on top of the wort. I prefer to rehydrate, but I also recommend having a spare yeast packet on hand, just in case. The point here is, stay loose and don't panic.

A homebrewer with a single refrigerator has very little choice about fermentation temperature. Ambient is what you use. Fortunately that is just fine for most strains of ale yeast. Given normal pitch rates and (for liquid yeasts especially) proper aeration, most ales will show signs of fermentation in 8 to 12 hours. My personal deadline is 16 hours. If I don't see bubbling in the airlock by then, I figure it's time to panic. I always keep a packet of dry yeast on hand for this eventuality.

The more difficult question is, when is it time to crash cool? This is an irreversible decision. Ale yeasts go right to sleep when the temperature drops into the 40°F range — some can barely work even at 62°F — and once they conk, it is hard to wake them up again. You can estimate the vigor of fermentation by the bubbling of the airlock, but this is a very rough guide, and it tells you nothing about whether the attenuation was normal. That is why it is worthwhile to take a gravity reading before you put the fermenter into the fridge. You don't want to gamble on this. My rule of thumb is, if the airlock pretty much stops bubbling, take a gravity reading. If it's a little high, I'll give the beer a couple of more days. Otherwise, into the fridge it goes. If it's still high after a couple of more days, then there's a decision to make, and there are no easy guidelines here. Things that can be tried:

▶ Stir or shake the yeast back into suspension in hopes that it will get back to work. This seldom helps but might be worth a try. If you do this, be sure to sanitize your stirring implement.
▶ If the gravity is really high — 5 SG points or more over the maximum expected terminal point — I would consider pitching a packet of dried yeast. As long as the temperature is not too low, this will almost always work. Dried yeast is preferred because at this point you do not want to aerate the wort/beer. You probably want a neutral strain like US-05 or Nottingham that will not change the flavor profile of the beer very much.

- If the gravity is only a few points higher than expected — say, 1.015 when the yeast attenuation data would suggest a final gravity of 1.010 to 1.012, then you can choose to do nothing — in other words, crash cool the beer and proceed as usual. It will probably taste fine. However, you might want to look at your notes and see if you can figure out what happened. The usual causes of weak fermentations are low pitch rates, poor aeration, low temperatures and, more rarely, abnormal mash conditions that do not produce the normal ratio of simple sugars (i.e., the ones yeast can ferment) to complex carbohydrates.

Taking a gravity reading requires all the same attention to sanitation as yeast pitching. Immerse the hydrometer and jar in Star San and leave them until just before use. First, spray the lid, then pop the top off the airlock and remove the bubbler. Pull the airlock out of its O-ring, then spray down a clean table or countertop and dip the opener and your hands in Star San. Do not rinse off, but immediately pry off the lid. From this point procedure is the same as previously described.

CRASH COOLING

Crash cooling is a great help to clarification. It encourages the yeast to flocculate and drop out of suspension. At the same time it precipitates chill haze, which is basically an extension of the cold break. If chill haze is formed in the fermenter, it can be removed during filtration, or drop out with the yeast, helped along by the use of finings.

Assuming that your fermentation has been normal and terminal gravity has been reached after 8 days or less in the fermenter, crash cooling should be done immediately. Once the yeast stops fermenting it is prone to autolysis — feeding on itself — which can produce sulfur-like off-flavors. At cold temperatures this process is drastically slowed, which is another reason crash cooling produces cleaner-flavored beer. My suggestions are:

- FOR UNFILTERED BEER, leave the fermenter in the refrigerator at 40°F for 3 to 4 days before racking it into a carboy and adding finings. Put the carboy in the refrigerator and allow the beer to settle for 10 days or more before racking into the keg and carbonating.
- FOR FILTERED BEER, leave the fermenter in the refrigerator for a week before racking it into a keg for filtration.

RACKING FROM THE PRIMARY FERMENTER

Racking is a very simple procedure, especially if you have an Auto-Siphon. The biggest concern here is sanitation. Have a bowl and spray bottle of Star San on hand. All equipment, including the racking cane, hose, and receiving vessel, must be sanitized immediately before use. The easiest way to sanitize the racker and hose is to make up a gallon or so of Star San solution in a bucket, then siphon it into a large bowl, or your receiving vessel (carboy or keg). Do not neglect, though, to spray or immerse the exterior surfaces of your equipment. And don't forget

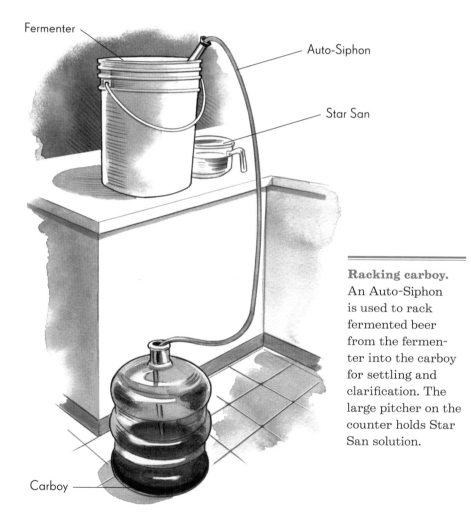

Racking carboy. An Auto-Siphon is used to rack fermented beer from the fermenter into the carboy for settling and clarification. The large pitcher on the counter holds Star San solution.

to keep your hands clean and sanitized as well! Another important rule is that an item is sanitary only until it touches something that is not. If your hose touches the floor, it is contaminated.

I prefer to sanitize a carboy by shaking, and then dumping the solution into my bowl. I always do a few quick rinses afterward, and I also rinse and shake out the racking arm and hose. This is not necessary, but I do it out of habit. As I said, the only sanitizers I consider truly no-rinse are Oxine and peracetic acid.

There are clips you can use to hold the racking arm in place against the wall of the bucket or the mouth of the carboy, but the Auto-Siphon requires two hands anyway. If you have crash cooled the beer as recommended, almost all the yeast will be firmly settled on the bottom and there is usually no reason not to set the cane tip right on the bottom. Put it against the wall, so you can tilt the bucket at the end of the racking process and recover as much (semi)clear beer as possible, while leaving all the dregs behind. However, if you want to be cautious, you can hold the racking arm off the bottom and slowly lower it as the level of beer drops in the bucket.

If you are racking into a carboy, all that's left is to stir in the finings, fit an airlock and stopper, and put it in the refrigerator. Oh, I almost forgot — and clean everything up. With your fermenting bucket you have the choice to soak or scrub — gently, with a sponge. Scrubbing takes less PBW, but there is a better chance of scratching. With the Auto-Siphon, be sure to wash the inside and outside of both tubes.

Racking from a settling tank/carboy into a serving keg is exactly the same operation as from a fermenting bucket into a carboy. After filling the keg, proceed immediately with carbonation, as outlined below.

Fining

If you want to use finings, you should stir them into the settling tank after racking. It never hurts to premix isinglass finings with a cup or so of beer, then add that to the settling tank. For two-step finings (Super-Kleer and the like) follow the instructions to the letter. For stirring, I just use my racking tube, after rinsing it off and sanitizing. There really is not much else to it. The biggest hassle is making up any dried finings ahead of time, and making sure they stay sanitary.

Filtration and Carbonation

Filtration is basically a process of using carbon dioxide pressure to push the beer out of one keg, through the filter, and into a second keg.

As with any brewing operation, the most important thing is to make sure that everything that touches the beer is clean and has been sanitized ahead of time. (Is there an echo in here?) The next most important, with fermented beer, is to minimize air pickup during filtration. These goals point to a tedious but straightforward prep routine.

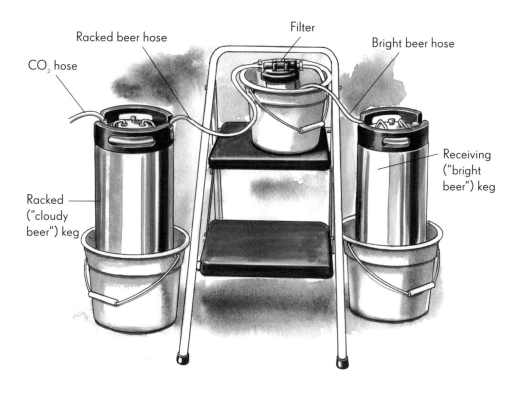

Filtering. A homebrew filter operation using a cartridge filter. Just off to the left is the carbon dioxide tank, which is used to push the beer out of the left-hand keg and through the filter.

The easiest way I have found to sanitize the filter, lines, and kegs, is to basically do a "prefilter run" using 40 ppm activated Oxine solution. The routine is as follows:

Step 1. Set everything up and put all equipment together as for the filter run. Make sure the gas valve on the regulator is closed. The racked beer keg connects to the input of the filter. The output plug of the bright beer keg connects to the output of the filter. Leave the keg lids off or hanging loose.

Step 2. Make up 5 gallons of activated Oxine solution in the racked beer keg. Set the carbon dioxide regulator to 6 PSI or whatever the filter instructions recommend. Put the lid on the keg and then open the gas valve on the regulator. Push the Oxine solution through the filter housing into the bright beer keg. At the end of the run turn the filter upside down to empty it as well as possible.

Step 3. When carbon dioxide starts bubbling up in the bright beer keg, detach the beer and gas hoses from the racked beer keg. Also detach the beer hose from the output of the filter. Put the lid on the bright beer keg, put the end of the beer hose in a bucket, then connect the gas hose and push the Oxine solution out of the keg into the bucket. When finished, disconnect the gas hose from the keg and close the regulator valve. Set the bucket of Oxine aside. Reattach the bright beer hose to the filter output.

Step 4. Now it's time to filter. Rack the cold beer out of the fermenter into the racked beer keg.

Step 5. Close up the keg and reconnect it to the gas. Leave the racked beer hose connected to the filter, but *not* to the keg.

Step 6. Purge the headspace of air. Adjust the regulator to 6 PSI. Then open the gas valve and pressurize the keg full of racked beer. Release the pressure by pulling on the ring attached to the relief valve. If the relief valve cannot be operated manually, you will have to disconnect the gas line and press down on the poppet of the gas plug. Repeat three times.

Step 7. With head pressure at zero, reconnect the racked beer line to the keg. Open the pressure relief valve on the bright tank and leave it that way until the filter run is over. Set the carbon dioxide pressure to the lowest value recommended by the filter instructions. Stop for a minute and double-check that everything is connected together just as it was when you sanitized the filter. Then open the gas valve and run the beer through the filter. If necessary, increase the pressure as the run goes along, but note the maximum pressure specified. The Filter Store states that the maximum is 35 PSI. With its 0.5-micron filter cartridge, filtration should take 10 to 15 minutes. I find that 6 PSI is enough to push the beer through the filter.

Step 8. When all the beer is in the bright keg, close the pressure relief valve. Disconnect the gas hose from the empty keg, set the regulator to 30 PSI, and attach the hose to the bright keg. Turn on the gas. Purge the headspace three times, but this time leave it pressurized after the last fill. Set it in the beer fridge and proceed to cleanup.

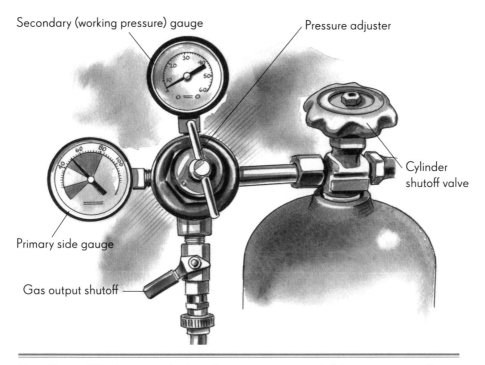

Secondary (working pressure) gauge

Pressure adjuster

Cylinder shutoff valve

Primary side gauge

Gas output shutoff

Regulator. The bar attached to the center screw of this two-gauge adjustable gas regulator makes it easy to adjust pressure. In this illustration, the regulator is set as low as possible, for filtration. Note the shutoff valve is open only partly to further reduce pressure.

Step 9. To clean a cartridge filter, make up 1 gallon of PBW solution in the bottom of a 5-gallon bucket. Disassemble the cartridge housing and clean by hand. Put the hoses and couplers in the solution to soak. Make sure they are filled. The cartridge itself is best cleaned by soaking. I leave it in the bucket for an hour, spinning and swirling it several times. To keep it submerged, I set a small plastic bucket over it — this is just heavy enough to hold it under. The Graver cartridge has a polypropylene mesh wrapped around the pleated element, and this protects it. If you have a cartridge without such a protective sheath, you will have to weight it down in some manner, but be careful not to bend or fold the pleats. While the cartridge is soaking, clean all hoses, racking arm, kegs, and fermenters by hand. On plastic, use nothing rougher than a sponge and avoid scrubbing. Let the PBW do the work. The best way to clean small tubes, including the dip tube in a corny keg, is to siphon or push solution through them, then stop the flow and leave them to soak a while.

CARBONATION AND SERVING

The usual methods of carbonating beer in the keg are:

▸ Let the beer sit under pressure in the keg until it has absorbed sufficient carbon dioxide from the headspace. This takes weeks with a full keg, because there is a large volume of beer relative to the small area of liquid-to-gas contact at the surface.

▸ Speed up the process by applying high pressure to the keg (around 30 PSIG) and shaking vigorously and repeatedly. This works. However, at my age, shaking a 5-gallon keg enough to dissolve the required amount of carbon dioxide is barely possible and definitely not desirable. Instead, I recommend the following:

▸ Install a tee fitting in your carbon dioxide gas line, and add a length of gas hose to the tee, then fit the end with a black (beverage) coupler rather than a gray (gas) coupler. To carbonate the beer, set your regulator to 30 PSIG, then attach the black gas coupler to the beverage coupler of your keg. You will hear carbon dioxide bubbling through the beer. When the bubbling stops, gently lift the relief valve ring to release some head pressure. That will bubble more gas up through the beer. When it stops, release a little more pressure.

There are no rules as to how many times to do this in order to get an acceptable level of carbonation. It all depends on the temperature of the beer — the colder it is, the more carbon dioxide it will absorb — and on your technique. If you are trying to carbonate freshly filtered beer, it will be warmer than fridge temp and you will have to go more cycles. For this reason, if possible, I prefer to put the keg in the fridge overnight after filtration, with 30 PSIG of carbon dioxide pressure on the beverage line. The next day I can often get the carbonation up to a palatable level by doing the release-bubbling cycle about ten times.

The question here of course is, how much carbonation should a beer have, and how do I know when I have hit it? The first part is pretty easy: for most light beers, about 2.7 volumes, or in other words, 2.7 liters of carbon dioxide dissolved in each liter of beer. For darker beers, go with a little less, say 2.4 to 2.5. Hefeweizens and some other wheat beers can go up to 3. Standard beer style specifications always include a carbonation level, so it is easy to get this information.

The second part is very difficult for a homebrewer. The standard instrument for measuring carbonation levels in beer is the Zahm and Nagel SS-60, which costs about as much as a bare-bones home brewery, all by itself. Recently Taprite has come out with a similar unit that I have seen priced about $\frac{1}{3}$ to $\frac{1}{4}$ of the Zahm and Nagel. If you go searching for one of these, be sure you are looking at the instrument for beer. There is a much cheaper one for soda pop, but it is not suitable. Also be aware that any carbonation tester requires you to waste at least 8 ounces of beer. The Zahm unit wastes at least a pint. My suggestion is to rely on your sense of taste. After carbonation, disconnect the gas from the product plug, lower regulator to normal dispense pressure, hook up the gas hose and beer dispense line as normal, and pull a small glass of beer. If it tastes under-carbonated, resume carbonating. If it tastes overly gassy, then disconnect the gas, release the head pressure, and set the keg in the fridge. Over the next day or so release head pressure several times, then taste a sample to see whether or not it is okay.

If it seems I'm indefinite and low-tech on this topic, it's because I am. But the fact is, those temperature-pressure carbonation charts that you can find everywhere on the Internet are accurate only once your beer has reached an equilibrium — in other words, is neither losing gas to the headspace nor absorbing gas from it — and only if you know those parameters. (In fact, a carbonation tester is basically a small sealed vessel with a thermometer and pressure gauge attached. You fill it with beer, shake it to achieve equilibrium, then read the carbonation level off a pressure-temperature chart. The reason you can't do this with a keg is that it is practically impossible to shake it enough to achieve equilibrium.) This suggests keeping an accurate thermometer in your fridge, with the probe in a glass of water, and also at some point checking your carbon dioxide gauge against one of known accuracy. Short of that, try to use a gauge that reads 30 PSIG full scale rather than 60, and that can be reset to zero if needed.

For serving beer, the options are laid out in the chapter on building your brewery (page 34). The only additional tips I have are:

First, make sure your glass is clean. No residue.

Second, always open the faucet full to pour beer. A half-open faucet will cause more foam, not less. If the beer is foaming too much, tip the glass and let the beer run down the side. If it is still foaming too much, check your serving temperature and check the gas system for leaks. Basically, excess foaming means that carbon dioxide is breaking out of solution somewhere, because there is an imbalance in the system. This imbalance can exist only because:

▸ The beer is warming up as it flows through the line. Remember solubility of gases in liquid decreases as temperature increases.
▸ There is insufficient restriction in the beer line. For instance, $^3/_{16}$-inch vinyl tubing has a restriction of about 3 PSI per foot, hence the recommendation of at least 5 feet of this size tubing for your dispense hose, and around 12 PSIG head pressure. Line restriction must always at least equal dispense pressure.
▸ Imbalance in the keg. In other words, the beer is over-carbonated either because the temperature has risen or head pressure has been lowered since the beer was carbonated.

The very worst thing you can do is to lower the head pressure: this will exacerbate the imbalance. On the contrary, try increasing head pressure by a few PSIG. If the problem is gas breakout in the keg, that will remedy it eventually. However, if the imbalance is caused by insufficient restriction in the beer line, then the only remedy is to increase it.

LINE CLEANING

I recommend cleaning your draft beer lines and faucets every 2 weeks. In fact, every week is better. PBW is good for this. My routine with my cobra head faucet is to make up 1 gallon of PBW in the keg, shake it around for a while, then turn the keg upside down and press on the carbon dioxide poppet valve to flush cleaner into it. Then I turn the keg upright, set it on a counter, and open the pressure relief. Finally, I push a short length of ⅜-inch tubing onto the end of the cobra head, flip it open, and start a siphon into a bucket on the floor. After a minute I shut off the valve and let everything soak for half an hour before resuming.

If you have a full-blown kegerator with a number of brass or stainless beer fittings and faucets, something stronger may be called for once in a while. You may want to use a mild caustic potash-based cleaner, such as BLC. Wear gloves and be careful. A number of online retailers sell inexpensive line-cleaning kits using a plastic pressure pump bottle to push the cleaner through the line. This is a wise investment once you move past the simple cobra-head faucet. The general routine is water flush, alkaline cleaner, followed by plenty of water. If you feel the need to use a sanitizer, Saniclean or Star San is probably easier on brass than Oxine. If the system is all plastic and stainless, then Oxine (100 ppm) would be my first choice.

6

ADVANCED
TECHNIQUES

This chapter is intended only as a brief introduction to the topics covered. Tens of thousands of words have been written about each one, and you'll find some of those works listed in the resources section (see page 255).

What I will do here is just report my experience with these techniques and offer some pointers that will help you avoid mistakes.

Yeast Propagation and Culturing

When you get to the point where you want to make exotic styles of beer, or just explore the possibilities and variations that a wide choice of yeasts can give you, then you will have to get into yeast propagation. This is especially true if you typically brew 10-gallon batches or larger. A single tube or activator pack of ale yeast is enough for pitching 5 gallons of normal-gravity wort; for a higher gravity or larger amount, it is inadequate. You will need to do at least one stage of propagation. For lager yeasts, two stages may be needed.

The usual homebrewing method of yeast propagation requires a 1- or 2-liter Erlenmeyer flask and some spare wort. In addition, many homebrewers buy or build a simple magnetic stir plate.

As to quantities, my recommendation for a 5-gallon batch of ale is to propagate your yeast in a liter of starter wort, no higher than 1.042 gravity. For lager beers to be pitched cold, as they should be, 2 liters. Best practice is two stages of propagation, first 500 milliliters, then 2 liters.

There are two problems with yeast propagation. The first is the danger of contamination during the process. This can be minimized by the use of sanitary techniques at every step of the operation. I recommend some practice before you "go live." A tutorial session with a person seasoned in the ways of yeast is good, but look askance at any advice to skip or shortchange standard methods. Your mentor may have just been lucky so far. I also advocate doing your propagation as far away as possible, both in time and space, from your malt milling and mashing-in operations. Here's a frightening number from one of my Siebel instructors: a million microorganisms per gram of malt dust. Still air is a good thing, unless you have a laminar flow hood. Microbes have no legs, so they cannot crawl into a flask, but they can hitchhike on any stray particle riding the air currents.

The second problem with propagation, which is less widely acknowledged, is that both the wort and the method create a flask of beer with, shall we say, a distinctive flavor profile, probably not one you want in your beer.

Most homebrewers use dry malt extract to make their propagation wort. I have already pointed out the drawbacks of extract wort, but frankly, for most homebrewers there is no practical alternative most of the time for creating a starter wort. If you do this, make a normal-to-low gravity, pale-colored wort, using the lightest extract you can find. Also, I recommend adding a hop pellet or two to the wort; this will suppress some types of bacteria. Not a panacea, obviously, but a help. Boil the wort for only 10 to 15 minutes. Cool it in the boiling vessel, covered with a sheet of foil, then leave the trub behind as you pour into the carefully sanitized flask. Keep all vessels covered as much as possible.

Sometimes it is possible to "steal" a liter of wort from a current brew. This avoids the problem of adding extract flavors to the final batch when you pitch; however, only light-colored, mildly hopped, low-to-normal gravity wort is suitable for this duty, especially if your intended beer fits this description, for example, a hefeweizen. Even where colors are similar, be cautious. An American Pale Ale wort might leave its mark on your Vienna lager.

The other half of the propagation odor problem is the method. Continuous agitation is generally recommended for maximum yeast growth; it is the whole idea behind the stir plate. The trouble is that it oxidizes the beer beyond recognition. The only possible remedies are intermittent shaking, which produces less yeast as well as less oxidation, or separating the yeast slurry from the beer as much as possible. The latter can be hard to achieve.

The simplest method of separation is to crash cool the flask for a couple of days to help the yeast floc out, and then decant as much smelly beer as possible. This is definitely worth doing, but the shape of the Erlenmeyer flask militates against a good separation when you try to decant it. As an alternative, you can fashion a miniature racking tube and hose out of small-diameter materials and carefully siphon off most of the liquid while leaving the yeast layer undisturbed in the upright flask. Yet another option would be to transfer the flask contents to a conical graduate (*Imhoff cone*) for chilling, settling, and decanting. Obviously both of these methods are fraught with danger and require great care with sanitation.

In my view, propagation is more difficult than yeast culturing, in the sense that contamination may not be immediately apparent. The "starter" may look and smell normal but still have enough bacteria or wild yeast to cause trouble down the road. Wild yeast, in particular, are often slow growers and do their damage late in the fermentation. By contrast, when you grow up a yeast colony from a single cell on a petri dish, it is pretty apparent whether your technique is good: if not, mold growth will tip you off. Morphology of the colony can help you distinguish culture yeast from interlopers, and then, of course, your first few small steps of propagation will tell you whether that cell was a good one. There are no magic shortcuts that homebrewers can take to simplify yeast banking and culturing. You simply have to pony up for the tools and materials required, and follow the same procedures that "real" microbiologists do. (I would proudly contend that a homebrewer who successfully maintains a bank of yeast strains *is* a real, practical microbiologist.)

Lager Brewing

Lager brewing is a bit more difficult than ale brewing, and it definitely requires more equipment, mainly of course a dedicated refrigerator fitted with a high-temperature thermostat that can hold temperatures from around 40 to 60°F. Such thermostats are available from most homebrew supply shops, in a range of prices. Lager yeast requires cold pitching and a slow, cold fermentation and maturation (lagering), in order to develop the flavor so beloved by the devotees of this beer family.

Cold pitching and fermentation means less growth in the fermenter, which in turn means that a larger volume of yeast must be pitched than would be typical of ales. (Although some ales, which are pitched colder than normal, also require a larger quantity of pitching yeast; I am thinking in particular of the famous Weihenstephan strain of hefeweizen yeast). My recommendation for 5 gallons of lager would be two packets of dry yeast, hydrated and then stepped down to pitch temperature with small additions of cold wort about 10°F at a time, at 10-minute intervals. I have already given a recommendation for liquid yeasts in the previous section.

As to pitching temperature, my general recommendation for dry yeast would be the bottom end of the fermentation temperature range, as stated on the packet; for example, if it says 10 to 15°C, pitch at 10°C (50°F). For a propagated slurry, pitch at 3 to 5 degrees *below* your target fermentation temperature. Manufacturers' instructions often call for pitching warmer and then dropping the temp; this requires a smaller quantity of pitching yeast, but in my experience, with several yeasts including the 308 and 34/70 Weihenstephan strains, it produces higher-than-desirable ester levels. (*Esters* are fruity aromatic compounds and are more typical of British and European ales.) Sorry to be the bearer of bad news, but once again, there are no easy dodges here. If you want your beer to taste like a lager, you have to handle it like one. The time for a temperature rise is toward the end of fermentation (say at about 65 percent apparent attenuation, which would be 1.019 for a 1.053 wort) in order to help the yeast eliminate diacetyl, which is a buttery aromatic that can overwhelm the more subtle aromas of a well-made lager.

Things you can do to help your yeast get going in the cold include adding yeast nutrient and giving it plenty of oxygen. It can be helpful to use oxygen rather than air, or to re-aerate a few hours after you pitch but before there are signs of fermentation.

One more observation on the subject of yeast behavior — and this goes for ale as well as lager — is that many characteristics are strain-specific. The 308 strain (sometimes called South German) will stop dead in its tracks around 50°F; other lager strains can ferment away at temps in the mid to high 40s. When you are trying to plan a lager fermentation, try to find information about your particular strain. Manufacturer's data sheets are a good place to start.

So, to sum up, my advice for a beginning lager brewer would be:

Step 1. Get a fermentation fridge. Then get a high-temp thermostat and calibrate it. You must know your temperatures when you are working with lager yeasts.

Step 2. Set knockout and pitch temp a few degrees colder than planned fermentation temperature.

Step 3. Pitch a lot of yeast, aerate twice, and use yeast nutrient in the wort.

Step 4. At 65 to 70 percent attenuation, set your thermostat up to around 60°F and let the beer ferment out at that temperature for a few days. This is the point to rack the beer into a carboy for lagering. A corny keg can also be used, but if you do this make up a pressure gauge fitting attached to a gas coupler to ensure pressure does not rise too high. Natural carbonation, developed during the secondary fermentation/lager phase, is traditional for lager beer, but filtration of carbonated beers is more difficult and requires maintaining counterpressure of 15 PSI or more in the whole system. (Both kegs plus filter cartridge — homebrew sheet filters are not designed for such pressure.)

Step 5.   Then start running the temp down, 3 degrees per day, until you reach 35°F. Let the beer mature ("lager") at 34 to 38°F for at least 3 weeks.

Step 6.   Filter and carbonate as usual. Yeast flavors are especially undesirable in lager beer, yet most lager yeasts are "powdery" and will drop out slowly. If you have time, lagers can drop quite bright on their own, but this typically requires at least 2 months in the keg. Still, if you want to try this, lay the keg on its side for maturation; that way the yeast will not be stuck on the bottom where it can be pulled out during pours.

You may have noticed that this whole section is about fermentation and I have not included a word about mashing. It is the fermentation that makes lager *lager*. Some people think that lagers must be or should be made using special mash methods. Maybe so, but the vast majority of German lagers these days are brewed using a simple, rapid-infusion method similar to the one outlined in the operations chapter (page 128). In any case, the next section will take a quick look at what those methods have to offer.

Step and Decoction Mashing

There are advantages to be gained from putting the mash through a series of rests at different temperatures. This method, called step mashing, allows you to exercise some control over the wort composition by selecting temperatures at which the various malt enzymes work most efficiently. Step mashing can enhance, for example, protein degradation, which should result in a clearer finished beer, because protein is a major component of chill haze.

That said, I must add a cautionary anecdote. As I mentioned previously, there was a time when Blackstone was contract brewing a couple of our beers. When we got into this, a good friend who is a very experienced, highly educated professional brewer, advised me to implement a protein rest for the contract beer. He felt this was important in order to get satisfactory haze stability in a bottled, all-malt beer, which would be subjected to swings of temperature and generally abused more than draft beer normally is. Needless to say I took his advice. The problem we found, though, was that the new mash program, while it probably did result in a more stable beer, also gave us a thinner mouthfeel (body) and a less malty palate. This is a general principle of brewing: change anything — be it in the materials or the tools or the process — and you change the beer, almost always in several ways. In this case we decided the change was, on the whole, for the worse. We went back to the single-infusion system we had always used (out of necessity) at the pub, and were able to get much closer to our desired flavor.

I would not discourage anyone from experimenting with step mashing. All you need is a mash mixer, which is one of the simplest and least expensive upgrades you can make to your home brewery. If you are looking to achieve greater clarity in your beer, a protein rest is worth a try. My suggestion would be to mix the mash at 122°F and let it stand for 30 minutes, then heat the mash into starch conversion range. Try to control the temperature rise so that it averages around 1.5 to 2°F per minute. You should probably set the starch conversion step a degree or so higher than for a single infusion, and you can shorten the stand a little as well — say 45 minutes instead of an hour.

My intention here is only to give you an introduction to the possibilities of step mashing. If you wish to explore the chemistry and methodology further, there are many articles and some books that cover it in detail (see the list in Resources).

More interesting than step mashing, at least to me, is its older and more complicated sibling, decoction mashing. This technique involves removing a portion of the mash from the tun, boiling it, and returning the boiled fraction to the main mash in order to achieve the temperature steps. It can be quite elaborate, and some decoction brewers boast about taking 4 hours or more to run their mash through the sequence of steps using three separate boils: the classic triple-decoction method.

You might think that as a career pub brewer, I would be even less interested in decoction than I am in step mashing. Not true. While it is far more difficult, decoction also offers more potential benefits, or at least alterations, compared to producing wort by the infusion technique.

I am not going to go into the "how-to" of this method at all. Fortunately, Greg Noonan has left us a great book, *New Brewing Lager Beer*, that covers the ground in detail and with much insight. I only wish to explain my own interest in the method, which, as noted, is rapidly losing ground in its country of origin. Despite its difficulties, decoction is fascinating because boiling the mash produces so many chemical and flavor changes. The net result is that you cannot even use the same grain bill as you would if you wanted to brew the same beer by infusion. Boiling caramelizes the malt sugars, giving a darker color and a richer flavor. As an example, to brew an Oktoberfest by infusion you would probably select a grain bill consisting of a mix of Vienna and light Munich malts, with some caramel malt thrown in for additional flavor and color. By contrast, to brew this style by decoction you would likely select a combination of pilsner and Vienna and/or light Munich malts, and eschew the caramel malt. I cannot get much more specific than that, because the schedule of decoctions obviously makes a large difference to the results.

I do want to lay one criticism to rest. Some people have claimed that decoction makes for a grainier, more astringent beer. They point to the indisputable fact that boiling the mash extracts a lot of tannins from the husks. Well, the proof is in the tasting. Decoction-mashed beers are in my experience among the smoothest and least astringent. The real danger with the method is scorching, which is all too easy when you boil by direct fire, as almost all homebrewers do. That will impart burnt flavors that are completely out of character for the classic beer styles associated with decoction mashing.

Bottling

Having lambasted bottling at the beginning of this book, I have to admit here that the practice has some uses. Generally these fall into two categories: convenience and flavor enhancement.

Convenience is the reason most homebrewers want to bottle. It is just too hard to lug around kegs of beer when you go to a picnic or a club meeting. So we end up buying a few cases of bottles and learning how to fill them under counterpressure. The technique is straightforward, and a simple filler is not that expensive. There are even plans on the Internet for bare-bones designs that can be put together quite cheaply, although I feel that the compromises that come with the low price are worthwhile only if you never intend to fill more than a few bottles at a time. Instead, I would recommend a standard single-bottle filler; I am particularly impressed by the Fermentap design, which utilizes a single valve to control gas and beer inflow. While still not foolproof, it should make for simpler operation than competitors that have two separate valves on the gas and beer lines. There are a number of videos online that take you through the steps of setting up and using these units. My *Homebrewing Guide* also has a fairly detailed step-by-step.

Blichmann has introduced a simpler alternative to the counterpressure filler called the Beer Gun. It is a well-made unit and offers the great advantage of one-hand operation. It permits carbon dioxide purging before filling, but the bottle is filled under atmospheric pressure, so it relies heavily on the low temperature of the beer and a lot of restriction in the beer hose to minimize foaming and carbonation loss. I consider it a satisfactory alternative, but I think bottle-to-bottle consistency, in fill level, carbonation level, and oxygen pickup, is harder to achieve than with the conventional two-handed fillers. It is, however, a great tool for quickly filling a few *growlers* (half-gallon jugs) or 2-liter soda bottles.

BOTTLE CONDITIONING

Now we come to the place where most people start their homebrewing: bottle conditioning. Every homebrewer is familiar with the routine of priming the batch of (unfiltered) beer and transferring it into bottles, which are then capped and stowed away for several weeks, or longer, to allow the bottle fermentation to work out and carbonate the beer. While I consider this exercise to be unnecessary and likely detrimental for most normal beer styles, I have to admit that it makes a difference in the flavor. To repeat myself: change anything, you change the beer. If you are making a beer where fermentation characteristics are a big component of the flavor profile, then up to the point where the yeast begins to autolyze, it can enhance that component. Thus, for many high-gravity, high-alcohol ales produced in Belgium, bottle conditioning is an integral part of their making, constituting the final step in the fermentation that produces those unique aromas. Thus, you will notice that a few of my recipes actually recommend bottle conditioning. Here a few suggestions about how best to implement it.

As I said, the basic technique of bottle filling is familiar to every homebrewer. The only special equipment required is a filler wand, which is a length of rigid plastic or stainless tubing with a spring-loaded valve on one end, and of course a capper. I prefer the benchtop capper design because it makes the job go a bit faster, but the two-handed models are completely satisfactory.

My first recommendation for implementing a bottle-conditioning operation is to pay great attention to sanitation. Even if you have brand-new bottles, at least rinse them out in a weak Oxine solution (40 ppm) and drain them upside down until it is time to start filling. A bottle tree is a handy accessory for this. If you use one, wash it off and spray it down with Star San before you start hanging the bottles on it. Likewise, be careful to spray the capper, especially the capping surfaces, and if you get beer foam on them, spray it off before you go on to the next bottle. Put the caps in a bowl of Oxine solution until ready for use.

I recommend making up the priming sugar as a syrup. For a 5-gallon batch, boil 2 cups of water, stir in the sugar (½ cup corn sugar for most ales, ¾ to 1 cup for highly carbonated beer such as hefeweizen), and cover while you rack the beer into the bottling tank.

For a bottling tank I prefer an open bucket, because it makes it easier to stir in the priming syrup and, if used, yeast or finings.

I recommend bottling the beer at 55 to 65°F. This means removing the fermenter from the refrigerator several hours prior to racking. The exact time depends on ambient temperature and on the material. For a plastic fermenter and normal room temperature of 70°F, it will take about 8 hours.

You need to consider whether you can harvest a few teaspoons of the yeast from the bottom of the fermenter and add that back into the racked beer in the bottling bucket to provide enough yeast for the bottle conditioning. By that I mean you need to decide whether you can trust that yeast to "wake up" and do its job. Almost always, it will; however, if you have doubts, you may want to rack the beer off into the bottling bucket ahead of time and "proof" the yeast by adding a small amount to a bottle or flask of the beer and adding a bit of sugar. Wait and see if it starts to ferment. This should take only a few hours if the beer is at room temperature.

If you doubt the viability of the yeast in the fermenter, the alternative is to use fresh yeast. This is simple with dried yeast; half a packet is plenty, sprinkled on the surface of the beer and then stirred in after half an hour. (Be sure to keep it covered in the meantime!) However, if you have used a liquid yeast culture especially suited for this style of beer, you probably want to use that same yeast for conditioning. That can get expensive; hence my recommendation to proof the yeast.

Finings can and should be used with powdery yeast strains: those are the ones that don't settle very well after fermentation. They require no reintroduction of yeast, but if you omit fining, the beer may never clarify in the bottle. Of course, for the cloudy wheat beer strains, this is a good thing.

Bottle-conditioned beers should be left at room temperature for several days. Thereafter a cool environment is preferable, although you may want to keep the temperature warm enough for the yeast to continue to work, slowly. One of the most fascinating aspects of bottle-conditioned beers is how the flavor changes as they age. Most always they reach a peak at some point, then autolysis sets in and they go downhill. Deterioration happens very quickly if the beer is stored at room temperature. My recommendation is that once you feel the beer has reached a peak, store it in a refrigerator as cold as possible to slow down the autolysis. And drink it up!

Cask-Conditioned Beer ("Real Ale")

This is a topic fraught with controversy. For its most ardent devotees, cask-conditioned ale inspires a fervor that can only be described as religious. ("Religious" as in, religious wars.) I don't doubt that, after reading what follows, some members of the real-ale fraternity will be aching to defenestrate me.

So, to defuse or diffuse as much as possible the wrath I know is coming my way, let me say two things straight off. First, I like real ale. Really like it. A cask-conditioned pale ale is a completely different taste experience from the filtered, highly carbonated variety. The difference is especially striking when you have both examples side by side and know that both came from the same batch. It is amazing how much difference the post-fermentation treatment and service presentation can make. What's more, when one makes this comparison with a beer style that was originally developed for cask conditioning — for example, classic British pale or mild ale — cask-conditioned beer clearly comes out the winner. Malt and hop flavors are far more evident, and they merge to make a truly memorable taste experience.

The second thing I have to say is, I am by no means an expert in real ale. I have not yet attempted to set up a cask cooler and beer engine in my home. Still, I have about 15 years' experience in the field, working in pubs where we kept real ale on tap and served it by the traditional method, hand pumped from a beer engine, at traditional service conditions. This is how I got the tasting experience I mentioned in the last paragraph. We typically would prepare one to three casks from each batch of pale ale, stout, or other suitable styles, then filter and carbonate the remainder and serve it through the regular draft taps.

I guess I had better back up now to give a brief description of cask-conditioned ale for readers who are not yet beer aficionados.

Basically, cask-conditioned ale is ale that is carbonated and served from the same cask. To this extent it resembles bottle-conditioned beer. It is different because (1) it is very lightly carbonated — casks cannot withstand carbon dioxide pressure, so the beer only retains whatever level of carbonation is possible at atmospheric pressure; and (2) it is served at cellar temperature — British cellar, that is — around 50 to 55°F. (It is an exaggeration bordering on calumny to say that the British drink "warm beer.")

A cask cooler in a brewpub. These casks are firkins (approximately 11 U.S. gallons). The wooden plug to the front is the keystone, with the coupler in place. When the cask is tapped the coupler is driven into the keystone with a mallet. The small plastic device on top of the keg, inserted into the center hole of the bung, is a cask breather. The cask cooler is fitted with an auxiliary thermostat to hold the temperature at 50°F.

Additionally, cask-conditioned ale is often dry-hopped, always with whole hops, right in the cask, to impart the freshest possible hop aroma and flavor. Also, it is never filtered. Some commercial bottle-conditioned beers are filtered, then deliberately dosed with yeast and primed for bottle conditioning. In fact, often a different yeast is used for bottle conditioning than was used for fermentation. Also, the beer is often deliberately left cloudy in the bottle. This is expected and desired with some continental wheat beers. On the other hand, cask ale, while unfiltered, is not expected to have a yeasty flavor, or to be cloudy. "Starbright" beer, as they describe it in England, is the ideal.

If you are interested in serving cask-conditioned ale in your home, then the first thing you need to do is take stock of your equipment. You will need, at a minimum, a cellar or refrigerator that you can keep at 50°F. Then you will need a cask or modified keg in which to condition and then serve the beer. Finally, you need a way to tap your cask.

One way homebrewers get into cask ale is to lightly modify a standard soda keg by cutting an inch off the long dip tube that goes to the bottom. This leaves space for the yeast and dry hops. My feeling is that this is too uncertain. You really need an upside-down "thimble" on the end of your dip tube if you want to be able to draw truly clear beer.

Because real ale is not pushed to the faucet by carbon dioxide pressure, there are only two ways to get it out of the vessel. One is to draw it off from a spigot inserted at one end of the cask or keg; the other way is to pump the beer out using a *beer engine*, which is a hand-powered pump. The beer engine is the most practical option for a commercial pub, and as far as I can tell, the only way to do it if you are using a modified corny keg for your cask. If you acquire a real cask — the *pin* (4.5 imperial gallons, or about 5.4 U.S. gallons) is the best size for homebrew — then you can fit it with a matching faucet and draw the beer by gravity.

Both options are expensive, and you need to do some research to decide which option will best fit your budget and your home draft system.

To achieve clarity, the only practical method is finings. Our usual method at the pub was to dose the finings, primings, and loose dry hops through the bunghole of the cask before filling it from the fermenter. The tap you fit into the *keystone* (end plug) of a cask is fitted with a screen to keep the hops and "floaters" out of the line. With a modified corny keg, you may need to put the hops in a mesh bag.

One final point, where my concern about defenestration comes in. Real ale is good for about 3 days when dispensed from an open cask, hence my recommendation of a cask breather, which allows you to maintain a blanket of carbon dioxide on top of the beer and thus extends its service life to that of a normal draft beer. A cask breather is just a simple check valve inserted in the central hole of the cask bung. It is fed by a carbon dioxide line regulated down to 1 PSI. You can do something similar with a modified corny keg. You may be violating the strict code of real ale service, but you will have good-tasting beer down to the last pint.

As for other practicalities: priming rates can and should be very low, no more than 2 tablespoons of corn sugar for a 5-gallon batch. Try dry hopping with 1 ounce of whole hops to start with. Not all styles require dry hopping, but pale ales benefit greatly. Keep the cask at low room temperature for a couple of days to ferment, then keep it in your cask cooler at 50 to 55°F during clarification and serving. Last and most important, never move a cask while you are tapping it. You will disturb the sediment and ruin the clarity. This obviously implies that if you use a real cask and drive the spigot into the keystone, you should let the beer settle back down for 24 hours before tapping.

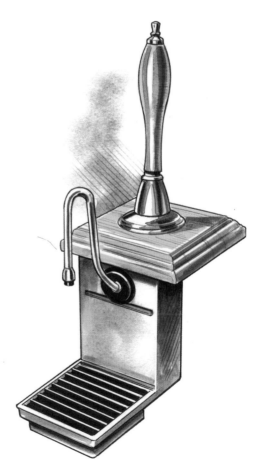

Beer engine. A classic hand pump for serving cask-conditioned ale.

PROJECTS

In building a home brewery, anyone, including me, falls into the trap of making false steps and wasting time, effort, and money. This chapter, which is filled with some of the projects I completed in the course of building my 5-gallon home brewery, should help you avoid such mistakes, whether you follow the directions to the letter or adapt them to suit the size and configuration of your system.

PROJECT I: LAUTER TUN AND HOT LIQUOR BACK

First of all, I must note that the project outlined here is not the one I started with. It is what I would have started with had I known then what I know now. My original idea was to build a mash/lauter tun that could be used for both sparging (*continuous* or *fly sparging*) and infusion rinsing (*batch sparging*). The outcome of that experiment is detailed in the appendix; suffice it to say I found I had built a fair lauter tun but that it could have been better if it had been built solely for that purpose. Hence the revisions presented here.

At the same time I built a hot liquor back based on the same picnic cooler and fittings, and I have not replaced that.

A NOTE ON THE HAYWARD BULKHEAD

This design is not original in any respect, but I have not seen a write-up on installing the Hayward bulkhead in a lauter tun. I resorted to it because it appears to be the only such fitting available at a size and price that make sense for a low-budget home brewery. All the same, it is almost grotesquely over-engineered for the use I put it to. If you look at the illustrations, I think you'll agree that the interior of the lauter tun looks pretty slick; the exterior looks pretty silly. Still, function has to come first, and this thing, plastic though it is, is strong enough to handle a brass ball valve with ease.

One thing you may not be aware of, if your acquaintance with plumbing is as casual as mine, is that CPVC comes in two specifications. The only type you see in the big-box home improvement stores is the copper pipe tube sizing, or CTS. This is light beige in color, and its outside diameters match copper pipe. The other is iron pipe tube sizing, or IPT, which matches the external diameters of iron plumbing pipe. PVC pipe is all IPT and comes in Schedule 40 and Schedule 80 grades. The difference is in the thickness of the wall and therefore the pressure rating and general ruggedness. They are distinguished by color: Schedule 40 is white whereas Schedule 80 is dark gray. Well, CPVC pipe and fittings are also made in Schedule 80 grade to the IPT dimensions. They are medium gray to distinguish them from both PVC and CTS-spec CPVC. This other branch of the CPVC family matches up well with PVC piping but not at all with CTS, and unfortunately, adapters are hard to come by. The Hayward bulkhead is a member of this tribe, and this is why you have to fashion an adapter.

CHOICE OF A PICNIC COOLER

I selected the 28-quart Coleman model 6277/79. This comes in two versions: one has a thin, uninsulated lid; the other, which I have seen only at Wal-Mart, has a thicker, insulated lid. This is preferable for a hot liquor back, because the lid is the main point of heat loss. However, the thinner lid is actually preferable for a lauter tun, because it is easier to fit with a recirc arm and a sparge arm. See that project on page 210.

A NOTE ON OTHER COOLERS: I prefer a cooler with a drain plug for the lauter tun. The plug is always placed very near the bottom. This makes cleanup simpler: after scooping out as much of the spent grain as you can, just open the drain plug and flush out the remains. I would not attempt to use the drain plug as the outlet for the manifold; the pipe fittings will cause interference with the manifold. Instead, place the bulkhead on the opposite side of the cooler.

Whatever cooler you select, make sure it has a flat outer wall so that the bulkhead will snug up properly. Try to find one that has a relatively small floor area for its capacity. My Coleman is almost 1 square foot, which is too big. With small mashes (8 pounds of grain or less), the grain bed is only about 4 inches deep. A depth of 6 to 8 inches is easier to work with. I get very good efficiency, and I have never had a stuck mash, but maintaining wort clarity requires a delicate touch. Unfortunately most coolers in the 5- to 7-gallon range have similar dimensions. The only exception is the tall beverage-cooler type, and fashioning a manifold for a round bottom is difficult. Coleman makes a square-shaped tall beverage cooler (5655C71), but it also has a few drawbacks. The draw-off is a spigot, designed for pouring drinks, which is not convenient for cleanout. It is also pricey.

Shopping List

☐ 2   Coleman 28-quart rectangular coolers:

     Model 6277/79

     Inside dimensions approximately 8½ x 16½ inches;

     working capacity approximately 6 gallons

☐   Schedule 80 CPVC fittings (all from McMaster-Carr)

     2   Hayward through-wall fittings (bulkhead) (Catalog #36895K831):

PIPE SIZE	HOLE DIAMETER	MAXIMUM WALL DEPTH	OVERALL LENGTH
½ inch	$1^3/_8$ inch	$2^5/_{64}$ inch	$3^3/_4$ inch

     2   ½-inch close nipples (Catalog #6810K12)

     2   ½-inch nipples 2-inch lg. (Catalog #6810K32)

☐   CPVC CTS pipe and fittings:

     1   10-foot length of ½-inch pipes

     5   ½-inch tees

     6   ½-inch elbows

     2   ½-inch couplers

     2   ½-inch slip x ½-inch FPT adapters

☐   Valve assemblies:

     2   ½-inch brass ball valves

     1   ½-inch NPT x ⅜-inch hose barb elbow, nylon (for lauter tun)

     1   ½-inch NPT x ½-inch hose barb elbow, nylon (for hot liquor back)

     1   roll Teflon pipe tape

☐   CPVC cement:

     1   (8-ounce) can Oatey FlowGuard Gold OneStep

Required Tools

- ☐ ³⁄₈-inch drive electric drill
- ☐ 1³⁄₈-inch hole saw
- ☐ Mini copper/plastic pipe cutter
- ☐ Hacksaw or rotary tool with cutting disc and arbor
- ☐ Phillips screwdriver
- ☐ Yardstick or square
- ☐ Vise grips
- ☐ Sandpaper or file
- ☐ Bench vise (optional but helpful)

ASSEMBLY

1. Remove both lids using a screwdriver.

2. Build the lauter tun first. If you find, during final assembly, that the bulkhead has been placed too low for a good fit, then you can make that cooler into your hot liquor back and use the second one for the lauter tun.

3. Cut CPVC for lauter tun. (Note: These lengths assume that you are following my recommendation for mating the bulkhead to the manifold. If you follow the method I used for my prototype, the measurements for a couple of pieces are slightly different. The measurements for the prototype are given in italics.)

   ▸ Three 14¼-inch pieces (collectors)

   ▸ One 12-inch piece (collector) *Prototype 12¼ inches*

   ▸ Six 1³⁄₁₆-inch pieces (connectors)

   ▸ One 1⅛-inch piece (connector) *Prototype ⅞ inch*

   ▸ One piece approximately 1 inch long (trial — see steps 12 and 13)

4. Without using glue, put manifold together as per photo. The longer connectors go on the short side of the manifold, spacing the pipes 1½ inches apart. The short connector goes into the branches of the fifth tee (draw-off tee) that sits at one end of the short collector pipe. Check to be sure that all pieces are pushed together as tightly as possible and that the spacing between the collector pipes is uniform and measures correctly. Then test fit in the cooler. It should lie flat on the bottom, be a snug fit lengthwise and with a space of about ¾ inch to 1 inch on either side.

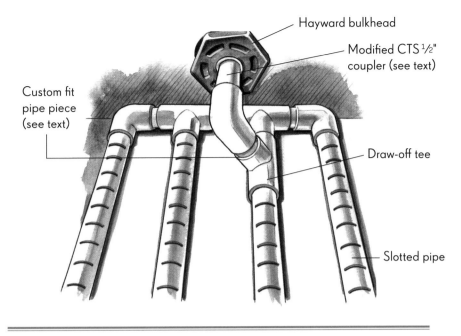

Labels on figure:
- Hayward bulkhead
- Modified CTS ½" coupler (see text)
- Custom fit pipe piece (see text)
- Draw-off tee
- Slotted pipe

Prototype adapter. Close-up of the interior of the lauter tun, showing how the manifold is connected to the Hayward bulkhead.

5. At this point you have to undergo the tedium of cutting the slots. A rotary tool is faster than a hacksaw, but I would not buy one just for this job. A bench vise is helpful for holding the pipes while cutting. I suggest some pieces of cardboard or cloth to protect the plastic. The slots go on the top*, about ½ inch apart. Start at either end of each collector, and mark about ¹⁄₁₆ inch from the joint. Then mark every ½ inch along the pipe. No need to be extremely precise; if you find that when you get to the middle, you have two slots marked within ¼ inch of each other, split the difference and make one slot. The most important thing to keep in mind while cutting is, don't go too deep. Cut only one-third the depth of the pipe, one-half at most. The deeper the cut, the more the pipe is weakened and the more easily it will break. You don't have to be fanatical: you can eyeball it, but keep the principle in mind.

*NOTE: *"Slots up" or "slots down" is debated among homebrewers who use a manifold lauter tun. I have tried both arrangements and have consistently gotten better extraction with the slots up. This is counterintuitive — you would think that placing the slots farther from the bottom would give poorer extract, especially with a thin grain bed. If you are curious, try it both ways and see what you find. I also found that the wort clears faster and stays clearer with the slots up.*

6. Prepare to drill the hole for the bulkhead (through-wall fitting). On the outside of the cooler, measure down about 8⅜ inches from the top edge. Because of the attachment point for the handle, you will have to measure down on either side and draw a line across. Use a Sharpie. The seam marks the center, so start your hole where the seam meets your line. Measure twice before you drill. Also remember, it's better to be a little too high than too low. Too high means that you'll have to cut a connector piece a little longer in order to reach; too low and you'll have to use the rescue method (see page 203).

7. Having carefully determined the spot for drilling, use a nail or the tip of a Philips screwdriver to make a dimple in the plastic. This will help keep the bit from wandering when you start the pilot hole. I suggest turning the cooler on end. It seems to make it easier to make a perpendicular cut. Be especially careful to keep the drill straight when you have gone through the outer plastic skin. As soon as the pilot bit penetrates the inside skin, stop. Finish the hole from the inside.

8. The photo shows a prototype with an improvised adapter that I made from a ½-inch CPVC coupler. The inside diameter is a perfect fit, obviously. The outside diameter is almost good, but some couplers are fatter in the middle and you need to file or sand down that region a bit, until the coupler can be pushed into the bulkhead. The other problem is that the coupler is ¼ inch too long. You need to cut that much off one end. I used a pipe cutter, then I pushed my shaved monstrosity, cutoff end first, into the bulkhead — it fit flush, as I hoped. Because of the possible gaps, I applied CPVC cement to the outside of the adapter before putting it in place.

9. The way I suggest you do it, which is much neater, is to modify a 2-inch Schedule 80 CPVC nipple. Basically you turn the NPT × NPT nipple into a shorter, NPT × unthreaded nipple. Measure and then cut off one threaded end, so as to leave a piece with one threaded end and a ⅝-inch section of unthreaded pipe. (I suggest using a hacksaw.) The unthreaded end will fit snugly into the bulkhead, leaving only the threads exposed. Screw the ½-inch CTS slip × FNPT adapter onto the nipple first, then push or (if necessary, with padding) tap it home. The adapter should butt right up against the bulkhead.

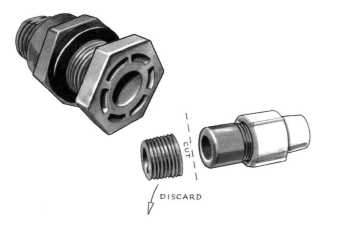

CUT

DISCARD

10. Mounting the bulkhead is self-explanatory. Be sure the inside surface is clean before you do it. Do not overtighten the nut. You can easily overtighten it with your bare hands; don't use a wrench.

11. Finally, wrap a close nipple with pipe tape and screw it into the valve body. At this point don't worry about getting it tight. Then wrap the other end of the nipple with tape and screw it into the bulkhead. Turn it until it starts feeling tight, then just bring it around until the handle is at the top. Now it's truth time: take the cooler outside, put 3 or 4 gallons of water in it, and check for leaks. If you find any, tighten up the offending joint.

12. At this point, you may want to do a trial fit. The last connector is the question here. With the manifold sitting flat in the bottom of the lauter tun, measure the distance between the elbow and the bulkhead. Add $7/8$ inch to that figure, mark it off on your pipe, and cut. Push it all the way into the elbow. Now comes the fun. You have to angle things and do some twisting, but you should be able to get it together. Once you do, you may think twice about your resolve to disassemble the whole thing for cleaning after every brew. However, you are not done yet.

13. Check to make sure that the manifold is lying flat on the bottom of the cooler, just as it did before you installed the bulkhead. Also check to see that it is centered from side to side. Try to adjust it so that it meets these conditions. If you can, you're almost done. You just need to check the joint between the draw-off tee and its elbow. They should be just about flush — almost no pipe showing between the fittings. If that is not the case, then you need to measure the gap as best you can, cut a longer piece, and try it. If you cannot get the manifold centered, the connector is too long. Cut another ⅛ inch shorter and try that. If you can't center it with a ⅞-inch connector and no gap between the tee and the elbow, you drilled your hole too low.

Bulkhead. The Hayward bulkhead with brass ball valve.

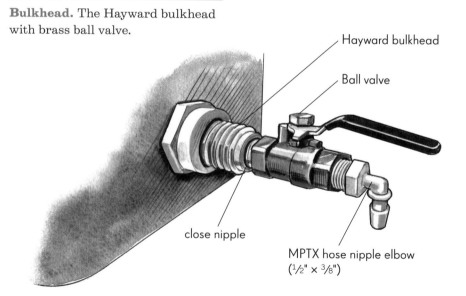

Hayward bulkhead

Ball valve

close nipple

MPTX hose nipple elbow
(½" × ⅜")

RECOVERING FROM A MISPLACED HOLE — HOW TO RESCUE YOUR MISDRILLED LAUTER TUN

This design is pretty lenient. Adjustments in the length of one connector will usually allow optimum alignment of the manifold. However, if, after installing yours, you just can't get things to sit right, then it's time for plan B. As long as the bulkhead does not interfere with the manifold, and the cooler does not leak with the valve installed and shut, this will do it.

The trick is to relocate the fifth tee (the one in line with the short collector pipe) from the end nearest the bulkhead to the opposite end. Then use a short length of high-temp tubing to connect the tee to the bulkhead. This arrangement gives you some slack so that even if the hole is well off-center, or somewhat too low on the wall, the lauter tun will still work just fine. You will need just a few extra pieces for this:

> 1 length of ⅝-inch inside diameter (I.D.) reinforced high-temp tubing,cut to make a straight run
>
> 2 hose clamps
>
> 4 spacing blocks to keep the manifold centered (I would use 1x1 hardwood stock to make these.)

This is a lot cheaper than a new cooler.

All you have to do is reverse the manifold end to end, rotate the fifth tee, measure, cut, and clamp the tubing, and — as the Brits say — Bob's your uncle.

The only drawbacks are:

▶ Cost — reason enough to avoid it if possible, in my book

▶ Grain-out is harder (tubing gets in the way)

▶ Can become off-center, as mentioned

▶ Doesn't look as slick as a "hard-piped" layout

PRINCIPLES OF MANIFOLD DESIGN

I am not going to go into the fluid dynamics of lautering here; frankly, I don't understand it well enough to do so, even if I wanted to. The best practical explanation I have found is an article by John Palmer (see Resources). But because most of you will not be building a lauter tun based on the same cooler that I used, a few guidelines for laying out your own design may be in order. Start with these rules:

▸ In a rectangular cooler, the slotted collector tubes run parallel to the long sides. The short connector tubes that run perpendicular to them should not be slotted.

▸ Collector tubes should be evenly spaced across the width of the cooler.

▸ The distance between the collector tubes should be no more than four times the outside diameter of each tube. Less is better. You can boil this down to: use as many collector tubes as will fit — but see the next point for an important qualification.

▸ The spacing from the outer collectors to the cooler wall should be half, or slightly more, of the distance between the tubes.

▸ Distance from slots (not pipes) is what counts in figuring distance to the short walls. It should be equal to the distance from the long sides, if possible.

These rules suggest a practical method for laying out your manifold. Start by figuring out how many collector tubes to use. First, measure the width of your cooler at the bottom. Then decide what size pipe you are going to use and acquire a few elbows and tees, and a length of pipe to measure. Assuming you are going to use ½-inch CTS CPVC pipe, as I suggest, you will find that the dimensions of the fittings dictate a minimum spacing between pipes of about 1¼ inches. Call that spacing **S**. Call the outside pipe diameter **D**. Call the number of pipes **N**. Then do a calculation, starting with three pipes:

The general formula is:

N x (S + D)

For ½-inch CPVC pipe, S + D = 1.875, so the calculation for three pipes is:

3 x 1.875 = 5.625

A cooler that narrow will likely be too small to use for a lauter tun. Suppose our cooler is 8½ inches across. Will four tubes work? Hmm . . .

4 x 1.875 = 7.5

You don't even have to calculate this one out, because 1.875 is less than 2, and the width is more than 8; obviously four tubes will fit. However, it's close enough that we can rule out 5, though you can do the calculation if you wish.

5 x 1.875 = 9.375

That's how wide your cooler needs to be for a five-pipe manifold — again, just to remind you, if and only if you are using standard American ½-inch CTS CPVC pipe and fittings.

Those who question the formula, because three collectors have only two spaces between them, should recall the fourth rule above. There has to be a distance of ½ S between each outside collector and the cooler wall. Put them closer and you will get channeling — that is, the liquid will flow faster near the walls of the lauter tun than it will in the center.

Okay, now that we know how many collector pipes to use, we need to determine the actual spacing. Again, a simple calculation. Here I use **A** for actual spacing and **W** for width of the cooler.

A = (W − ND) / N

(Or in English, subtract the total width of the pipes from the width of the cooler, then divide your answer by the number of pipes.)

For our example, that means **8.5 − 2.5 = 6** and **6 / 4 = 1.5**

Now it's just a matter of "cut and try" to determine the length of the connector pieces for the correct spacing.

BUILDING THE HOT LIQUOR BACK

After the lauter tun, the hot liquor back is a snap. You can put one together in less than an hour.

You don't need a manifold, obviously. All you need for the interior is:

Shopping List

- [ ] 1   Homemade threaded x unthreaded Schedule 80 pipe nipple, as for the lauter tun
- [ ] 1   ½-inch NPT female x ½-inch slip CPVC adapter
- [ ] 1   ⅝-inch connector
- [ ] 1   Elbow
- [ ] 1   Short piece of pipe for the draw-off tube (This you must cut to fit: you want it as close to the bottom as possible.)

ASSEMBLY

1. First, install the bulkhead. Then do a "dry fit" of all pieces, including the draw-off. Then cement in the gray pipe nipple. Clean the mating surfaces with rubbing alcohol. Follow the instructions on the cement can. Apply to both surfaces, but don't use too much. Cement the draw-off, elbow, and connector together. When the cement is set (give it 30 minutes), screw the adapter onto the threaded nipple, make sure it's tight, then cement the draw-off assembly to the adapter.

2. All that's left is installing the ball valve, as per the lauter tun.

HLB drawoff.
Close-up of the draw-off elbow in the hot liquor back. Note the small length of pipe snuggled as close to the bottom as possible. It permits almost complete emptying of the vessel without tipping.

THE HOMEMADE BULKHEAD ALTERNATIVE
This will save a few dollars, and it looks prettier on the outside of the vessel. But it is more trouble, as you will see.

Shopping List

- [ ] 1 ½-inch MIP x 2½-inch Watts A-838 brass pipe nipple (may need a different length for different coolers)
- [ ] 1 ½-inch Nibco #4703 CPVC slip to FPT adapter (equivalents are made by other companies)
- [ ] 1 ¾-inch I.D. x 1¼-inch O.D., 1¹⁄₁₆-inch slot I.D. neoprene grommet
- [ ] 1 1¹⁄₁₆-inch I.D. x 1¼-inch O.D. neoprene O-ring
- [ ] 2 or 3 ⅞-inch flat washers, ⅛ inch thick (These are hard to locate. Look for SAE flat washers at Lowe's, or try an auto parts store. I found some at my Ace Hardware. McMaster carries a pack of 25 [catalog #97669A23]. These are 0.048 inch thick, so you'll need more of them, but they allow finer adjustment.)
- [ ] 2 ½-inch PVC Schedule 40 couplers (You'll use only one, but you'll want to have a spare on hand.)

Required Tools

- [ ] 1⅛-inch hole saw
- [ ] ⅞-inch Forstner bit
- [ ] ⅜-inch or ½-inch chuck electric drill
- [ ] Cylindrical rasp bit or rattail file
- [ ] Combination square or yardstick

ASSEMBLY

1. Measure and mark the location of the bulkhead. Take the #4703 adapter and place it where it needs to go inside the cooler. This is in the center of one of the short walls. Orient it so the big end (hex nut) is against the wall. One of the hex sides must be parallel to the floor. Slide it down to where you want it. For a hot liquor back it can be near the bottom, as long as the adapter sits flush to the wall. For the lauter tun you first have to insert the manifold, then make sure the adapter is high enough that the connector pipe will go into it. In other words,

put together the whole assembly and do a trial fit. When you find the right spot, mark a pencil line across the top of the adapter. Now take the combination square, loosen the ruler (straight edge) a bit, and hook the handle over the lip of the cooler. Get the ruler flush with the wall and pull it down until the tip is on the pencil mark. Tighten it. That's your distance. Now turn the square around and mark a straight line on the outside cooler wall at this distance. You need to use a Sharpie on the outside wall; pencil will not take.

2. From the Sharpie line measure down the center seam of the cooler another $^{17}/_{32}$ inch. (The adapter is $1^{1}/_{16}$ inches across, flat to flat.) Mark a cross there. That's where you drill. Remember, a little too high is better than too low.

3. Drill the hole with the $1^{1}/_{8}$-inch hole saw; try to keep the bit parallel to the bottom of the cooler and squared up right to left. This is important. As soon as the tip of the pilot bit comes through the inside liner, stop drilling from the outside. *Do not cut into the inside wall!* Switch to the $^{7}/_{8}$-inch Forstner bit, and finish the hole by drilling from the inside.

4. Make the coupler into a reinforcing spacer. This piece is the key to getting a tight, leak-free seal. First, you have to remove the center ridge inside the coupler. Clamp it in a vise or otherwise hold it steady and use the rasp or file for this job. If using the rasp, be careful; don't remove any more material than necessary.

5. Now you have to cut the spacer to length. It should be about 1 inch for the Coleman cooler, but this is another instance of cut and try. From the outside, insert it in the hole and hold it flush against the inside liner. You may have to clear away a bit of insulation. Mark it all the way around with a pencil if possible. Then cut it off. I prefer to use a hacksaw for this because PVC is hard to cut with a pipe cutter. To get a straight cut start with four notches on the pencil line, all the way around the adapter. Then extend the cuts until they meet up. After cutting, sand or file the cut end if necessary, then insert it into the hole. The cut end should be flush with the outside wall of the cooler. If it is short, try again with your spare. (I did tell you to buy two!)

6. Assemble the bulkhead. First make sure the washer is in place inside the adapter, then screw it onto the pipe nipple as far as it will go. Do not use any pipe tape here. Be careful how much force you use; if you overtighten the adapter it will crack. (Fortunately, it's not very expensive.)

7. Then, slip the O-ring into the groove of the grommet and push the grommet down the open end of the pipe nipple until it is snug against the adapter. With the grommet in place, the threads on that end should be completely hidden. If this is not the case, then your adapter has not been screwed down fully onto the nipple. Fix this before going on.

8. Mount the bulkhead to the cooler. Wrap three layers of pipe tape around the exposed end of the nipple. Slip the nipple end of the bulkhead through the inside hole in the cooler wall and feed it through the spacer. Slide one washer over the threads and then screw on the ball valve until you see that the grommet is *slightly* deformed. This indicates that it is snug. If one washer does not allow you to snug up the bulkhead, unscrew the ball valve, remove the tape from the threads, rewrap, then slide on the second washer and retighten. Two should be enough unless your washers are thin. At this point you need to test the seal. Close the valve, fill the unit with water, and let it sit for a few hours to see if it leaks. Hint: Set it either outdoors or in a bathtub. Remember Murphy, the legislative chair of the ancient and honorable Order of Brewers.

9. If it passes the leak test, you are done. If not, you need to tighten the ball valve another half turn or so, and try again. If it leaks with cold water, it will leak worse with hot. However, with the proper number of washers and a good fit for the reinforcing spacer, it will seal well. In fact, the reason you need reinforcement is that the inside liner softens when hot, and may allow leakage. An unreinforced bulkhead will usually seal fine with cold water.

Now that you have your first CPVC plumbing project under your belt, you may want to tackle some of these other projects. All are optional in the sense that they are not required for brewing. You need a lauter tun, but you don't need a sparge arm, for example. The job can be done by hand.

PROJECT II: SPARGE ARM/RECIRC ARM

Modifying a thin Coleman cooler lid to hold the sparge and recirc arms freed me from constant bailing during vorlauf and sparging. Here is a brief step-by-step. Please refer to the illustrations.

Shopping List

- ☐ ⅝ inch hardwood dowels, 4 feet total length
- ☐ Stainless steel # 8 machine screws, ½ inch (for pipe hangers) and ¾ inch, for dowel frame
- ☐ Brass or stainless flat corner braces (4) and tees (4)
- ☐ ½ inch CPVC tubing, 12 elbows, 6 tees, 12 pipe hangers, 1 end cap
- ☐ ½ inch slip by female NPT CPVC adapters (2)
- ☐ ½ inch MNPT by ½ inch hose nipples
- ☐ ⅝ inch square hardwood dowel piece, 2 inches long
- ☐ Reflectix insulation and aluminum tape

Required Tools

- ☐ Electric drill and bit set
- ☐ ⅝-inch Forstner bit
- ☐ Tubing cutter
- ☐ Hand saw
- ☐ Utility knife

ASSEMBLY

1. Remove the cooler lid. Use a utility knife to cut away the inside liner.

2. Cut dowel pieces to form braces as in the picture. Screw the dowels to the lid, then attach to each other with the tee and corner braces.

3. Lay out the sparge arm and cut pipe pieces to fit. Consult the picture for suggested routing. Assemble the sparge arm and do a dry fit inside the lid. Mark where the hole for the pipe should go through the lid and drill with the Forstner bit. Drill 8 ⁵⁄₆₄-inch holes in the sparge arm. See the picture for placement. Assemble the arm and clamp in place with hangers.

(Instructions continue on page 214.)

CUTAWAY OF FINAL DESIGN

After the inside part of the lauter tun lid has been cut away (below right) with a utility knife, the wooden frame, sparge arm, and recirc arms are fitted to the lid.

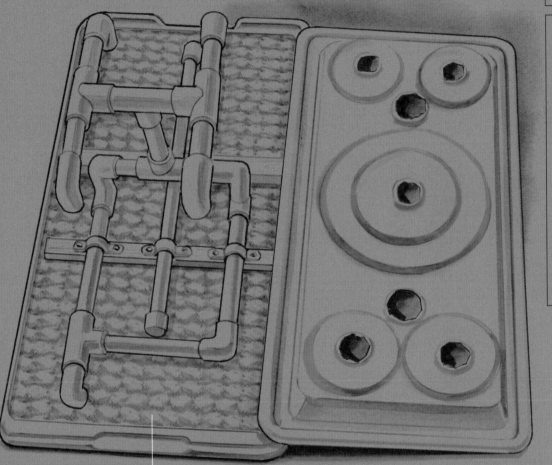

Reflective insulation

SPARGE ARM AND SINGLE RECIRC ARM IN PROTOTYPE

The inside part of this cooler lid has been cut away, and a wooden frame, sparge arm (drilled straight pipe), and a prototype recirc arm have been fitted inside. In practice, the single-outlet recirc arm gave too much flow and "dug a hole" in the thin grain bed of the lauter tun, making clarification difficult and slow. Hence the final design with four outlets, which distributes the flow and gives rapid clearing.

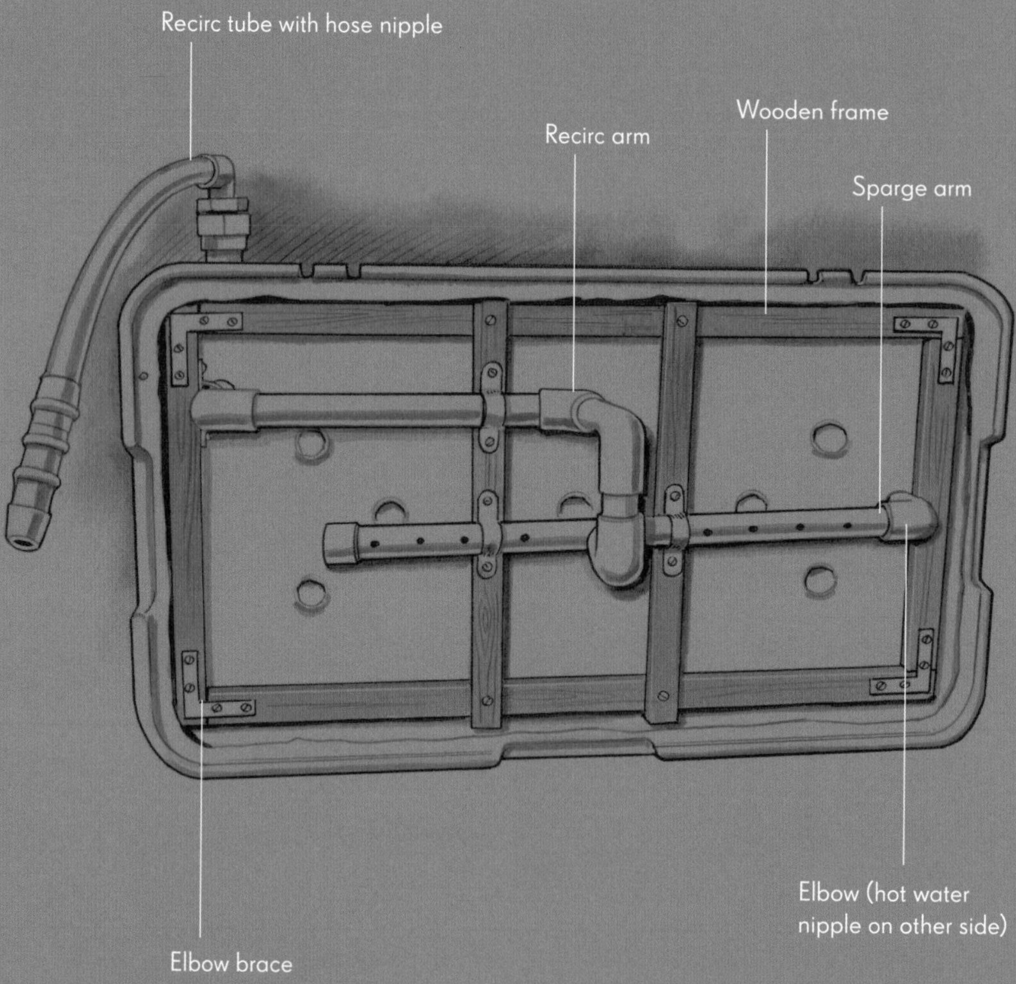

Recirc tube with hose nipple

Recirc arm

Wooden frame

Sparge arm

Elbow brace

Elbow (hot water nipple on other side)

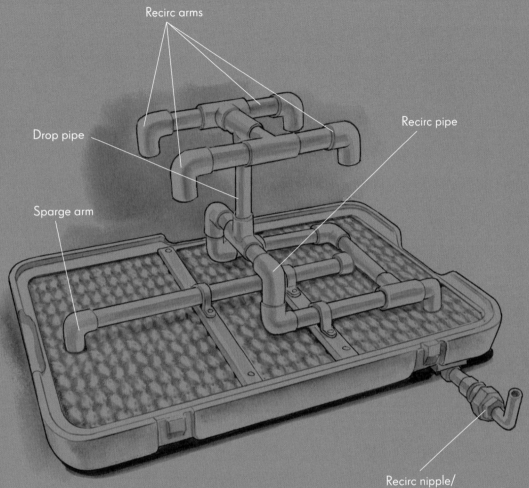

Recirc arms

Recirc pipe

Drop pipe

Sparge arm

Recirc nipple/
adapter fitting

SPARGE-RECIRC ARMS IN
FINAL DESIGN

The final design of the lauter tun lid, fitted
with bubble-foil insulation. The recirc arm
has four outlets to distribute the wort over
the surface of the grain bed.

4. Lay out the recirc arm and cut pipe pieces to fit. Assemble, dry fit, and drill as in step 3. Note where the mounting block goes, cut it from the square dowel, and screw it into place. Finally, put it in place and clamp it down. Attach the slip-NPT adapters and hose barbs.

5. Insulate with 3 or 4 layers of Reflectix, overlapping the cuts from one layer to the next.

NOTES ON THE DESIGN

The sparge arm is not my first. I found that 15 holes were too many. At full valve open, with the bottom of the hot liquor back sitting 2½ inches higher than the top of the lauter tun, eight holes will deliver 5 gallons of water in 10 minutes, which is three times faster than necessary. At normal sparge rates (i.e., 5 to 6 gallons of water in 30 to 40 minutes), they stream rather than dribble, as the first one did. Everybody's layout will be different, but remember, you can always drill more holes.

The H-shaped drop pipe assembly is the recirc arm. Originally it had only one outlet point, as you can see in the sparge arm picture showing the frame. I found that when recirculating fast, the outflow would disturb the grain bed and the wort would run cloudy. That led to the more elaborate final design. By distributing the wort to four points, the flow is much slower. It delivers a very gentle stream of wort near the surface. I cut a set of drop pipes of different lengths, and checked the height of the four drop points with different volumes of water in the lauter tun. It was a tedious way to spend an afternoon, but it enables me to select a pipe that will put the wort outflow just above the surface of the mash, whatever the volume.

The recirc arm does not need to be removed for sparging; the holes for the sparge arm are drilled on either side of the recirc arm tee and the streams do not splash off it. The four recirc outputs are all well away from the lauter tun walls; one thing I learned from my pub brewing is that dropping the wort down the side of the lauter tun causes problems with clarity during vorlauf and sometimes digs a channel that leads to uneven drainage. The sparge liquor can be delivered anywhere near the center, because there should always be 1 inch of water on the top of the grain during the sparge. And because it is just hot water, exposure to air does not matter. A fixed height for the sparge arm is no problem.

I have seen designs in which vorlauf wort and sparge liquor are delivered through the same arm, one very much like my recirc arm. This is just fine, but because of the way my brewery equipment is arranged, it was more convenient to put the hot liquor inlet at one end of the lid and the vorlauf inlet at the other, hence the choice of separate delivery plumbing.

Using a spray arm to deliver recirculated wort is bad, for two reasons: First, you will have to disassemble the spray arm to clean it. Second, and more important, it will aerate the hot wort. This is bad brewing practice.

None of the joints in this assembly is glued. If they start leaking, I will glue them, but I prefer to leave nonpressure joints unglued as long as they don't leak. This makes it possible to disassemble for cleaning and to reuse fittings, should I ever decide I want to modify the design.

Thinking of how things were at the pub, I first considered cutting a hole in the lid so I could look inside to check the liquid level on the grain. Then I started sketching a hinged door, wondering how I could make it big enough to reach in and cut the surface of the bed. All that is unnecessary here, of course, because the lid can just be lifted at one end for a peek or (briefly) set aside to do a cut. Homebrewing really is easier.

As I said, this is a prototype. On my next sparge arm project, I might consider using square plastic stock (HDPE or polypropylene) from McMaster-Carr instead of the wooden doweling. Also, if I found myself with a lid that was not amenable to retrofitting with a frame, I would get a piece of 1×2-foot sheet plastic (also available from McMaster), cut it to size, and mount the frame on that.

PROJECT III: GRANT

The grant in the illustration is as simple as can be. There is no need for a valve, because you can connect it to the input of your pump before beginning vorlauf. Of course, if you are recirculating the wort manually, you don't need an outlet at all. Just get a white 2-gallon HDPE bucket, and you're all set.

For use with a pump, I prefer a 1-gallon or smaller grant. With a larger one, it is easy to run so much wort in that the surface of the grain bed is exposed.

The outlet of my grant is made up of a ¼-inch through-wall fitting from McMaster Carr (catalog #8671T23), which requires a ⅝-inch Forstner bit for the hole. The other piece is a ¼-inch MPT × ½-inch hose barb adapter, available from McMaster (but only in packs of 10) and elsewhere. You also will need a ⅝-inch flat neoprene washer or two, as McMaster does not package these with the fitting. I found some at Ace Hardware.

Home brewery grant.
A home brewery grant
is easy to fabricate.

PROJECT IV: TWO-STAGE HEAT EXCHANGER

Before you start buying parts, take time to study this project. There are lots of plans out there for making heat exchangers using copper fittings, and you may want to consider them. My choice was dictated by the price of brass compression fittings, and the firm resolve, going back many years, that I will never solder copper again. If you share my feelings about soldering, then this CPVC-based design is the cheapest alternative. However, before you decide to build a homemade tube-in-shell heat exchanger, read through this section carefully. A pair of small plate heat exchangers, or a single high powered one, is a very nice upgrade.

The basic components of my design are a 50-foot coil of ⅜-inch copper refrigeration tubing, a medium-quality ⅝-inch I.D. 50-foot garden hose from anywhere, and four homemade CPVC tees, easily made up with basic fittings and a few feet of pipe. The only unusual or hard-to-find piece is the compression fitting that makes a tight seal where the copper tubing protrudes from the tee. This fitting (you'll need four of them) is the Genova Geno-Grip 53010, which you might be able to find at a local plumbing supply. The cheapest source I found online was Hardware World. This is the only CPVC fitting I know designed to make a watertight joint between ⅜-inch copper tubing and ½-inch CPVC, which is what you need to do.

Shopping List

- ☐ 1   50-foot coil of ⅜-inch copper refrigeration tubing
- ☐ 1   medium-quality ⅝-inch I.D. 50-foot garden hose
- ☐ 4   homemade CPVC tees
- ☐ 2   ½-inch FNPT adapters
- ☐ 4   Genova Geno-Grip 53010

ASSEMBLY

1. To begin building the heat exchangers, follow the picture to put all four tees together. Cut three lengths of pipe about 2½ inches long for each tee. Glue them into the four tees. One heat exchanger will be connected to a garden hose, so you can leave two of the ends of each tee for that unit as is. The other tees, for the smaller unit, will be attached to ⅜-inch vinyl tubing, so the side arm of each of those tees requires a ½-inch FNPT adapter and, eventually, a hose barb adapter. One of the straight-through arms of each tee has to be fitted with a Geno-Grip. Most of the work of installing this happens later, but for now you need to disassemble them and glue the slip joint piece to the pipe stub. When you take them apart, be sure to keep each set of parts together, and keep the parts in order. Also, do not throw away the instructions. While you will not be doing this fitting "by the book," they are still useful.

2. Next comes the gross work of putting the exchangers together. Start with your hose. Unroll it and lay it out as straight as you can. Leave about 6 inches on the female end and cut. Measure off 30 feet and cut. Measure 15 feet more and cut again. Now you have a 30-foot length, a 15-foot length, a 6-inch female stub, and a short piece of about 5 feet with a male end.

3. Unroll the copper coil. This will take longer and be more difficult. Don't make any sharp bends as you uncoil it. Once you have the length uncoiled, try to straighten the most obvious curves. Now it's time to start inserting the copper into one of the long pieces of hose. You can do this by yourself, but having another person on hand is a big help. Slide the hose over one end of the copper and start pulling and pushing it along. Keep going until the copper reemerges from the end of the hose, and then slide it along another 18 inches or so. Then take your pipe cutter and cut off the copper at the other end, leaving the same length sticking out. Now repeat the process with the other length of hose and the remaining copper. You will have a few feet of copper left over when you make the second cut.

4. Now you have to coil them up. For this you need a form of some sort. I used a 5-gallon bucket, and for this step a second person is almost essential. One person has to hold one end of the hose assembly against

COLD WATER HEAT EXCHANGER   CITY WATER HEAT EXCHANGER

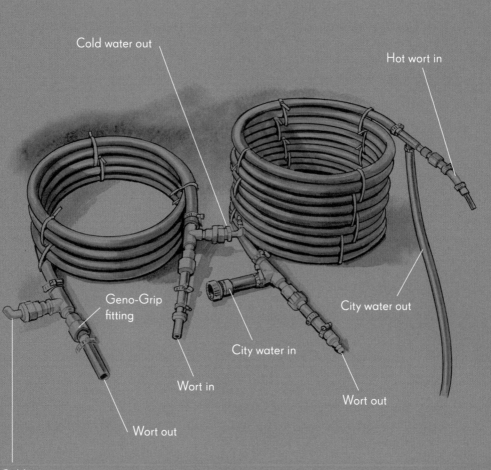

Cold water out

Hot wort in

Geno-Grip
fitting

City water in

Wort in

City water out

Wort out

Wort out

Cold water in

TWO-STAGE HEAT EXCHANGER

Building a two-stage heat exchanger like the
author's requires some effort, but its effectiveness in cooling wort is undeniable.

the form, down near the bottom, while the other person takes the other end and begins walking around the form. As he or she walks, both people must try to keep the copper from shifting position inside the hose. It will want to pull into one end. The person near the bucket has to keep pushing the hose tight against the form, and make sure the coils stack firmly on top of one another. The goal is to get the entire length coiled and still have 8 inches or more of copper sticking out each end.

5. Once you have the coils made, all that's left is to slip the tees onto the ends and clamp them down, and finally, attach the water connections and complete the installation of the Geno-Grips.

6. Here's the lowdown on installing the Geno-Grip onto one end of your tees: the pieces have to go on in the same order, with the same orientation, as shown in the instruction sheet. However, in your case you are inserting (have inserted, actually) the copper tube from the wrong end. So you cannot just push it into the Geno-Grip and tighten it down. You will have to "massage" the little metal grip ring by taking a small pair of needle-nose pliers, and bending each tang a little so that the ring will slip over the copper tube. Once you have completed this chore, lubricate the copper with a bit of Petrol-Gel, and slip the O-ring over the end. Work it down the tube. Finally, you will have to push it into the groove where it is supposed to sit. You will need to use your fingernails, or perhaps a Popsicle stick or something similar. I seriously advise against metal. You must make sure it is fully seated all the way around. This is what makes the seal. Then come the remaining pieces, in order. Screw the cap down, hand-tight only, and you should have a watertight seal.

7. You can see in the picture that I clamped a short piece of reinforced ³⁄₈-inch vinyl tubing to each end of the copper tube. This serves as a female connector for any sort of adapter I want to attach, depending on configuration. However, these stub ends have proved to be a weak point of the design: the copper tubing is smooth and therefore slippery. The hose must be clamped down firmly or it will slip off, and it most likely will do it when there is a hose full of wort pulling on it. Don't assume that a tight hose clamp will stay tight. Go around these joints with a nut driver before every brew session and tighten as needed.

PROJECT V: THERMOWELL

I am not a big fan of thermowells in kettles and lauter tuns, but you absolutely must have a thermowell fitted to the outlet of your heat exchanger. The illustration on page 222 shows a homemade thermowell that I put together from CPVC. It will accept a thin-stemmed, inexpensive digital or dial thermometer, and it mates up easily to a homemade tube-in-shell two-stage heat exchanger.

ASSEMBLY

1. It is fairly self-explanatory. The part that makes it work is a small nylon compression fitting (from McMaster-Carr, catalog #5533K433). This is made to fit ⅛-inch O.D. tubing. Your thermometer stem may be a little bigger than that. You will also need a ½-inch male to ⅛-inch female stainless bushing. McMaster also sells these. Alternatively, you can do it with nylon, but you will need two: ½ to ¼, and ¼ to ⅛.

2. To insert the thermometer, you will probably have to drill out the fitting. Fully loosen the compression nut, then get out the ⅛-inch bit and drill through. It should go easily. Then check to see if your thermometer stem will fit. If not, drill with the next larger drill bit and check again. Somewhere up the line it will fit. Then you can tighten the compression nut, screw the assembly into the bushing and screw the bushing into the thermowell.

3. The beauty of this little item is that the thermometer can be easily removed for other duties. However, I suggest you leave it in line during the back-flush CIP, then unscrew the bushing and take a look at it.

THERMOWELL

Close-up of the thermowell in operation, fitted with a small digital thermometer. At the bottom of the illustration is the rim of the fermenting bucket, with its lid placed to provide as much cover as possible. The silicone hose is carrying hot wort to the intake of the upper (city water) heat exchanger. The other wort hose connects the upper unit to the lower (ice water) unit.

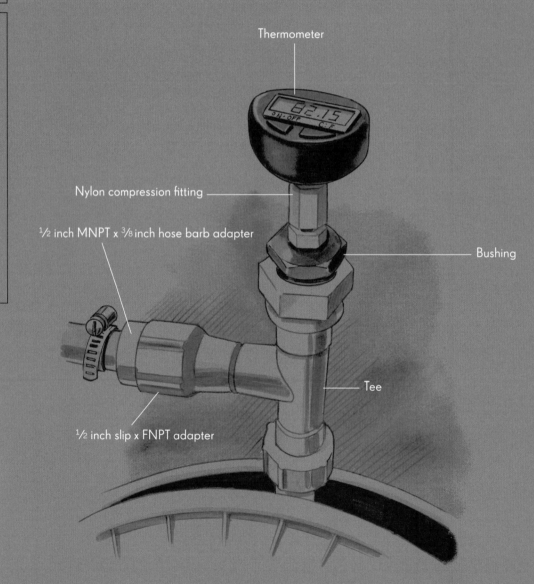

Thermometer

Nylon compression fitting

½ inch MNPT x ⅜ inch hose barb adapter

Bushing

Tee

½ inch slip x FNPT adapter

PROJECT VI: PUMP SPEED CONTROL

All magnetic-drive circulating pumps are centrifugal in operation, meaning they can be throttled back by placing a valve on the outlet side. So why bother with an electronic speed control? Well, there are several reasons:

▸ **First,** because it is easier to make small adjustments to flow rate than it is with a valve. Trust me on this one. I spent my working life coaxing and massaging pump output valves.

▸ **Second,** an output valve and its associated plumbing are — relative to the tiny pump — large and heavy, and can stress the pump body or even crack it. I would only "hard plumb" a valve to a March pump output if I had constructed a framework for it to which I could clamp the pipes and take the load off the pump body. The only exception would be a pump with a metal body.

▸ **Third,** if your pump has hose barbs molded into the pump body, rather than NPT threading, a speed control is the only viable option. And even if you have to fit hose barb adapters the speed control will be simpler to implement than a properly supported ball valve.

In sum, I think ball valves are all right in a rack system where all the piping is permanently mounted to the frame. Otherwise, a speed control is better. And for certain applications — such as lauter pumps — speed controls are the preferred solution even in microbreweries.

So, what is involved in fitting your pump with a speed control? Very little, actually. The photo shows the carrying platform I put together for my pump, with the speed control mounted alongside in a standard electrical outlet box. The fan speed control is a Lutron FS-5F that I found at Lowe's. Leviton makes an equivalent model. Be sure you get a simple, old-fashioned one with a control knob — not a slider — that is rated for 5 amps. You will also need a power cord. If you have a spare electronics power cable, you can cut the female end off, slit the outer insulation and pull out and strip the wires. Other items you'll need include wire nuts, screws, a box, and a face panel. The wiring is clearly explained in the sheet that comes with the controller.

SAFETY

The biggest objection to speed controllers is the old and very true adage that water and electricity don't mix. Nonetheless, breweries have been installing electric pumps for a hundred years, and electrocutions are extremely rare. This is not to say caution is not called for — only that there are effective measures you can take. They fall into three classes:

▸ **First,** shield the pump motor. I go into this a bit in my pump discussion in chapter 3 (page 66). Being fortunate enough to have a pump with a TEFC motor, this is taken care of for me. Brewers with open-frame motors sometimes install the whole pump unit in a plastic toolbox, which provides good protection from splashes. One objection to this is that there will be heat buildup in the box during long pump runs. Other, less drastic shielding can be improvised from sheet metal or even a plastic soda bottle. The main thing is to shield the vent slots on the motor from possible drips falling into them from above.

▸ **Second,** shield the speed control. One way is to mount a metal or plastic piece around the controller box. Another, which I did, is to wrap the control unit itself in some silicone tape before installing it in the box, use more tape for a gasket for the front cover, and then seal the box openings with silicone caulk. None of these measures is perfect. The main thing is to try to protect the controller box from splashes from above, just as with the motor.

▸ **Third,** fit the outlet or power cable with a ground fault circuit interrupter (GFCI). These items are often fitted to the power cords of hair dryers; GFCIs are usually built into the outdoor and bathroom outlets of modern homes as well. Other outlets are not usually protected. You can find aftermarket GFCI units at any hardware store that will plug into a standard outlet and provide the same protection. It will instantly cut off power if current is leaking to ground, as it would if water got into the pump motor.

I almost forgot the most basic precaution. Always use a three-prong power cable with a three-prong outlet, forget adapters to "get around" a two-prong outlet issue, and be sure to properly wire the bare or green ground wires in your box. If you try to operate an electric motor without proper grounding, you are asking for a shock and will probably get one. Take my word for it.

PUMP SPEED CONTROL

Attaching a simple speed control box to your pump allows you to make the small adjustments that end up making a big difference in your homebrewing operation.

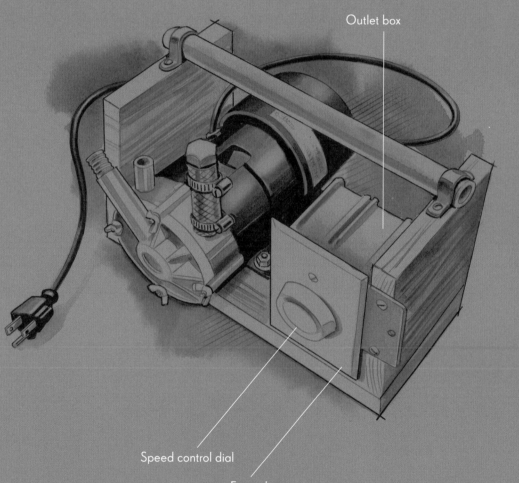

Outlet box

Speed control dial

Face plate

8

A HANDFUL
OF RECIPES

I am not presenting recipes for every classic beer style here. These recipes are mostly for popular ale styles that are easy to brew and therefore suitable for beginning all-grain brewers.

A note on hopping: Because hop bitterness (alpha) varies, the best way to state hop quantities is in Bitterness Units, abbreviated BU. This is the product of the hop weight (in ounces) multiplied by the alpha content (in percent) for whole leaf hops. For pellets, the resulting number is multiplied by 1.2 because pellets yield more bitterness than whole.

Example: **1 ounce Cluster hop pellets @ 5 percent alpha = 5 × 1.2 (pellet correction) = 6 BUs**

Remember that hop quantities are suggestions for a first trial. Utilization varies a great deal from one system to another, and so does taste. All gravities are calculated based on 90 percent extract efficiency, which is what I get from the lauter tun described in the Projects chapter (page 194).

3-RINGS AMERICAN BLONDE ALE

Starting in the Colonial era, American breweries in the Northeast brewed ale. Even in the 1950s most of them were still at it, offering another option to customers who wanted something a bit more distinctive than the top-selling light lagers. This recipe harkens back to those brews, most now long gone, along with the companies that made them, and salutes the rare survivors along with new breweries who are reviving the style.

Some of the East Coast ales are, and were, fermented with lager yeast, but others, including the famous Ballantine, were fermented with ale yeast, at least in their heyday. This is one instance in which authenticity is actually easier for a homebrewer than following the modern trend, especially because US-05/Wyeast 1056/Chico Ale Yeast is a direct descendant of the old Ballantine strain.

Level: Basic
MAKES 5 GALLONS

GRAIN BILL

6.5 pounds North American two-row pale malt

1 pound flaked maize

HOP BILL

KETTLE HOPS: Cluster 5 BU
(45 minutes before end of boil)

FINISH HOPS: Cluster 4 BU
(5 minutes before end of boil)

YEAST: Safale US-05, Danstar Nottingham

OTHER: Water treatments (gypsum or calcium chloride for mash; phosphoric acid for sparge liquor); kettle coagulant, yeast nutrient

PROCEDURE

1. Weigh out the grains. Mill the malt. Do NOT mill the flakes.

2. Calculate the hop quantities and weigh out.

3. Calculate the sparge and mash water quantities. Treat the water as appropriate for pale beers. (See Homebrewing Operations, page 128.)

4. The mash-in temperature is 151°F.

5. Let the mash stand for 1 hour at 151–149°F. Mash pH should be 5.2–5.5.

6. Recirculate until wort is clear, then run off and sparge. Wort collection should take at least 50 minutes.

7. Collect 6.5–7 gallons of wort in the kettle.

8. Boil the wort for 60–90 minutes to reduce volume to 5.5 gallons (hot). Add coagulant and nutrient to the kettle 10 minutes before the end of boil.

9. Postboil wort pH should be 5.0–5.3. OG should be 1.046–1.048.

10. Chill to 70°F and pitch yeast per package instructions. Ferment out at 68–70°F. Time should be no more than 6 days. Check final gravity; it should be 1.010–1.012. Crash cool in refrigerator for 5 to 7 days, then filter into keg and carbonate.

OLD TIMEY PORTER

This recipe has to be classed as a brown porter, even though it is too dark, too malty, and too hoppy for the style. The problem is, it does not fit any better in any of the other style categories. One rationale for classifying it as a porter is that historically, brown porters were heavier in pre-Prohibition times. On the other hand, I very much doubt that any porter brewed in the nineteenth century, on either side of the Atlantic, had a grain bill or a flavor much like this brew. The hopping is high, but the beer does not taste bitter; the caramel and raisin flavors ensure that malt predominates.

I would not suggest this recipe for a first all-grain brew, but once you have a bit of experience and can predict gravities pretty well, it is certainly worth brewing.

Level: Basic
MAKES 5 GALLONS

GRAIN BILL

7.5 pounds North American pale two-row malt

12 ounces flaked barley

8 ounces medium Crystal malt 50-60 degrees Lovibond (Muntons or Simpsons)

6 ounces Dingemans Special B malt

4 ounces chocolate malt, Belgian or British, around 400 degrees Lovibond

HOP BILL

KETTLE HOPS: Centennial 5 BU (45 minutes before end of boil)

FLAVOR HOPS: Willamette 7 BU (30 minutes before end of boil)

YEAST: Safale US-05

OTHER: Calcium carbonate, other water treatments for dark beer if required; kettle coagulant, yeast

PROCEDURE

1. Weigh out the grains. Mill the malt. Do NOT mill the flaked barley.

2. Calculate the hop quantities and weigh out.

3. Calculate the sparge and mash water quantities. Treat the water as appropriate for dark beers. (See Homebrewing Operations, page 128.)

4. The mash-in temperature is 153°F.

5. Let the mash stand for 1 hour at 153–150°F. Mash pH should be 5.2–5.5.

6. Recirculate until wort is clear, then run off and sparge. Wort collection should take at least 50 minutes.

7. Collect 6.5–7 gallons of wort in the kettle.

8. Boil the wort for 60–90 minutes to reduce volume to 5.5 gallons (hot). Add coagulant and nutrient to the kettle 10 minutes before the end of boil.

9. Postboil wort pH should be 5.0–5.3. OG should be 1.054–1.058.

10. Chill to 70°F and pitch yeast per package instructions.

11. Ferment out at 68–70 F. Time should be no more than 6 days. Check final gravity; it should be 1.012–1.015. Crash cool in refrigerator for 5 to 7 days, then filter into keg and carbonate.

Y-NOT PORTER

This is a far lighter bodied and milder porter, typical of Eastern United States breweries. Most of those porters are fermented with lager yeast, but I am calling for American ale yeast, partly for the sake of tradition, but mostly to make it easier to brew.

Level: Basic
MAKES 5 GALLONS

GRAIN BILL

6   pounds North American pale two-row malt

1   pound flaked maize

8   ounces Caramel 40 malt

3   ounces Black Patent malt

HOP BILL

KETTLE HOPS: Willamette 3 BU (45 minutes before end of boil)

FLAVOR HOPS: Cluster 3 BU (30 minutes before end of boil)

YEAST: Safale US-05 or Danstar Nottingham

OTHER: Water treatments (calcium carbonate, others for dark beer), kettle coagulant, yeast nutrient

PROCEDURE

1. Weigh out the grains. Mill the malt. Do NOT mill the flakes.

2. Calculate the hop quantities and weigh out.

3. Calculate the sparge and mash water quantities. Treat the water as appropriate for dark beers. (See Homebrewing Operations, page 128.)

4. The mash-in temperature is 151°F.

5. Let the mash stand for 1 hour at 151–149°F. Mash pH should be 5.2–5.5.

6. Recirculate until wort is clear, then run off and sparge. Wort collection should take at least 50 minutes.

7. Collect 6.5–7 gallons of wort in the kettle.

8. Boil the wort for 60–90 minutes to reduce volume to 5.5 gallons (hot). Add coagulant and nutrient to the kettle for 10 minutes before the end of boil.

9. Postboil wort pH should be 5.0–5.3. OG should be 1.047–1.049.

10. Chill to 70°F and pitch yeast per package instructions.

11. Ferment out at 68–70°F. Time should be no more than 6 days. Check final gravity; it should be 1.010–1.012. Crash cool in refrigerator for 5 to 7 days, then filter into keg and carbonate.

A basic recipe for a classic style; there are thousands of variations. Final gravity will vary depending on the yeast chosen. If brewed to a higher gravity, the beer becomes an ESB ("extra special bitter"); hops must be increased to compensate, of course.

Level: Basic
MAKES 5 GALLONS

GRAIN BILL

7   pounds Maris Otter Malt

4   ounces Crystal 60 British malt

HOP BILL

KETTLE HOPS: English Fuggles or Willamette 7 BU (45 minutes before end of boil)

FINISH HOPS: East Kent Golding 4 BU (end of boil)

YEAST: Safale S-04, Muntons, or Wyeast 1968

OTHER: Water treatments (calcium sulfate or chloride, phosphoric acid, others for amber beer), kettle coagulant, yeast nutrient

PROCEDURE

1. Weigh out the grains. Mill the malt.

2. Calculate the hop quantities and weigh out.

3. Calculate the sparge and mash water quantities. Treat the water as appropriate for amber beers (I recommend treating sparge liquor with phosphoric acid to lower pH, as for light beers; mash treatment as necessary for correct pH. See Homebrewing Operations, page 128.)

4. The mash-in temperature is 150°F. Stir well; British pale malt is very dry and prone to balling.

5. Let the mash stand for 1 hour at 150–148°F. Mash pH should be 5.2–5.5.

6. Recirculate until wort is clear, then run off and sparge. Wort collection should take at least 50 minutes.

7. Collect 6.5–7 gallons of wort in the kettle.

8. Boil the wort for 60–90 minutes to reduce volume to 5.5 gallons (hot). Add coagulant and nutrient to the kettle for 10 minutes before the end of boil.

9. Postboil wort pH should be 5.0–5.3. OG should be 1.044–1.046.

10. Chill to 70°F and pitch yeast per package instructions.

11. Ferment out at 68–70°F. Time should be no more than 6 days. Check final gravity; it should be 1.010–1.014. Crash cool in refrigerator for 5 to 7 days. I recommend this beer be fined rather than filtered; cask or bottle conditioning is the best presentation. For cask, dry hop with ½ to one ounce East Kent Goldings whole hops.

ENGLISH BROWN ALE

Another classic, this recipe is for the "Northern" style, which is higher gravity, maltier, and lighter in color, with the roasted flavor of chocolate malt. Crisp Chocolate malt has a softer flavor than some other brands, which is why I prefer it.

Level: Basic
MAKES 5 GALLONS

GRAIN BILL

7   pounds British mild ale malt

8   ounces Crystal 50-60 British malt

4   ounces Crisp Pale Chocolate Malt

HOP BILL

KETTLE HOPS: English Fuggles or Willamette 7 BU (45 minutes before end of boil)

YEAST: Safale S-04, Muntons, or Danstar Nottingham

OTHER: Water treatments (calcium carbonate, others for dark beer), kettle coagulant, yeast nutrient

PROCEDURE

1. Weigh out the grains. Mill the malt.

2. Calculate the hop quantities and weigh out.

3. Calculate the sparge and mash water quantities. Treat the water as appropriate for dark beers. (See Homebrewing Operations, page 128.)

4. The mash-in temperature is 150°F.

5. Let the mash stand for 1 hour at 150–147°F. Mash pH should be 5.2–5.5.

6. Recirculate until wort is clear, then run off and sparge. Wort collection should take at least 50 minutes.

7. Collect 6.5–7 gallons of wort in the kettle.

8. Boil the wort for 60–90 minutes to reduce volume to 5.5 gallons (hot). Add coagulant and nutrient to the kettle 10 minutes before the end of boil.

9. Postboil wort pH should be 5.0–5.3. OG should be 1.046–1.048.

10. Chill to 70° F and pitch yeast per package instructions.

11. Ferment out at 68–70°F. Time should be no more than 6 days. Check final gravity; it should be 1.010–1.012. Crash cool in refrigerator for 5 to 7 days, then filter into keg and carbonate.

OATMEAL STOUT

One of my favorites, this is full of flavor yet not too heavy for a session. This is an American variation. A note on roast barley — make sure you get a black-roasted variety. Some maltsters put out lighter-colored roasted barleys, and these simply will not do.

Level: Basic
MAKES 5 GALLONS

GRAIN BILL

- 7.5 pounds North American two-row pale malt
- 12 ounces flaked oats
- 8 ounces caramel 60 malt
- 7 ounces roast barley 450–550 degrees Lovibond

HOP BILL

KETTLE HOPS: Northern Brewer or Centennial 8 BU (45 minutes before end of boil)

YEAST: Safale US-05 or Danstar Nottingham

OTHER: Water treatments (calcium carbonate, others for dark beer), kettle coagulant, yeast nutrient

PROCEDURE

1. Weigh out the grains. Mill the malt. Do NOT mill the flakes.

2. Calculate the hop quantities and weigh out.

3. Calculate the sparge and mash water quantities. Treat the water as appropriate for dark beers. (See Homebrewing Operations, page 128.)

4. The mash-in temperature is 152°F.

5. Let the mash stand for 1 hour at 152–150°F. Mash pH should be 5.2–5.5.

6. Recirculate until wort is clear, then run off and sparge. Wort collection should take at least 50 minutes.

7. Collect 6.5–7 gallons of wort in the kettle.

8. Boil the wort for 60–90 minutes to reduce volume to 5.5 gallons (hot). Add coagulant and nutrient to the kettle 10 minutes before the end of boil.

9. Postboil wort pH should be 5.0–5.3. OG should be 1.054–1.056.

10. Chill to 70°F and pitch yeast per package instructions.

11. Ferment out at 68–70°F. Time should be no more than 6 days. Check final gravity; it should be 1.012–1.015. Crash cool in refrigerator for 5 to 7 days, then fine if you wish or just settle in a carboy for 7 to 14 days before kegging and carbonating. In my view there is no point in filtering a stout.

DRY (IRISH) STOUT

This stout is lighter bodied and far drier than oatmeal stout. The commercial stuff is made using a high-tech process that includes a carefully controlled lactic-acid fermentation. As close as most homebrewers can come is to use one of the liquid yeast cultures listed here as alternatives; they add a layer of complexity to the flavor.

Level: Basic

MAKES 5 GALLONS

GRAIN BILL

6.5 pounds North American two-row pale malt

12 ounces flaked barley

8 ounces roast barley 450–500 degrees Lovibond

HOP BILL:

KETTLE HOPS: Northern Brewer or Brewers Gold 10 BU (45 minutes before end of boil)

YEAST: Danstar Nottingham, or Wyeast 1084/White Labs WLP004

OTHER: Water treatments (calcium carbonate, others for dark beer), kettle coagulant, yeast nutrient

PROCEDURE

1. Weigh out the grains. Mill the malt. Do NOT mill the flakes.

2. Calculate the hop quantities and weigh out.

3. Calculate the sparge and mash water quantities. Treat the water as appropriate for dark beers. (See Homebrewing Operations, page 128.)

4. The mash-in temperature is 152°F.

5. Let the mash stand for 1 hour at 152–150°F. Mash pH should be 5.2–5.5.

6. Recirculate until wort is clear, then run off and sparge. Wort collection should take at least 50 minutes.

7. Collect 6.5–7 gallons of wort in the kettle.

8. Boil the wort for 60–90 minutes to reduce volume to 5.5 gallons (hot). Add coagulant and nutrient to the kettle 10 minutes before the end of boil.

9. Postboil wort pH should be 5.0–5.3. OG should be 1.054–1.056.

10. Chill to 70°F and pitch yeast per package instructions.

11. Ferment out at 68–70°F. Time should be no more than 6 days. Check final gravity; it should be 1.012–1.015. Crash cool in refrigerator for 5 to 7 days, then fine if you wish or just settle in a carboy for 7 to 14 days before kegging and carbonating. In my view there is no point in filtering a stout.

AMERICAN PALE ALE

The granddaddy. These days every brewer tries to put his own stamp on this style, usually by a combination of the newer American hop varieties. I think it's hard to improve on a simple blend of Cascade and Centennial.

To get a typical American aroma, I recommend dry hopping with 1.5 to 2 ounces of Cascade or Centennial pellets in the primary fermenter. Do this when fermentation has just about ended, and let the beer sit for 36 to 48 hours at room temperature afterward. If you can be very sanitary about it, a couple of stirs during this rest will help extract more hop aroma into the beer. Then crash cool and proceed as usual with racking and filtration.

Level: Basic
MAKES 5 GALLONS

GRAIN BILL

8   pounds North American two-row pale ale malt

8   ounces caramel 40 malt

HOP BILL

KETTLE HOPS: Centennial 8 BU (45 minutes before end of boil)

FINISH HOPS: Cascade 10 BU (5 minutes before end of boil)

DRY HOPS: Cascade 1.5 ounces (in fermenter)

YEAST: Safale US-05, Danstar Nottingham

OTHER: Water treatments (calcium chloride or sulfate, phosphoric acid, others for amber beer), kettle coagulant, yeast nutrient

PROCEDURE

1. Weigh out the grains. Mill the malt.

2. Calculate the hop quantities and weigh out.

3. Calculate the sparge and mash water quantities. Treat the water as appropriate for amber beers. (See notes on English Pale Ale on page 235 and Homebrewing Operations, page 128.)

4. The mash-in temperature is 151°F.

5. Let the mash stand for 1 hour at 151–149°F. Mash pH should be 5.2–5.5.

6. Recirculate until wort is clear, then run off and sparge. Wort collection should take at least 50 minutes.

7. Collect 6.5–7 gallons of wort in the kettle.

8. Boil the wort for 60–90 minutes to reduce volume to 5.5 gallons (hot). Add coagulant and nutrient to the kettle 10 minutes before the end of boil.

9. Postboil wort pH should be 5.0–5.3. OG should be 1.051–1.053.

10. Chill to 70°F and pitch yeast per package instructions.

11. Ferment out at 68–70°F. Time should be no more than 6 days. Check final gravity; it should be 1.010–1.012. Dry hop and let stand for 48 hours. Crash cool in refrigerator for 5 to 7 days, then filter and carbonate.

TEXAS BROWN ALE

A darker, sweeter relative of American Pale Ale, not really very much like the English original. Dry hopping is optional.

Level: Basic
MAKES 5 GALLONS

GRAIN BILL

8 pounds North American two-row pale ale malt

8 ounces caramel 60 malt

4 ounces chocolate malt

HOP BILL

KETTLE HOPS: Centennial 8 BU (45 minutes before end of boil)

FINISH HOPS: Cascade 8 BU (5 minutes before end of boil)

DRY HOPS: Cascade 1 ounce — optional (in fermenter, see notes above)

YEAST: Safale US-05, Danstar Nottingham

OTHER: Water treatments (calcium carbonate, others for dark beer), kettle coagulant, yeast nutrient

PROCEDURE

1. Weigh out the grains. Mill the malt.

2. Calculate the hop quantities and weigh out.

3. Calculate the sparge and mash water quantities. Treat the water as appropriate for dark beers. (See Homebrewing Operations, page 128.)

4. The mash-in temperature is 153°F.

5. Let the mash stand 1 hour at 153–150°F. Mash pH should be 5.2–5.5.

6. Recirculate until wort is clear, then run off and sparge. Wort collection should take at least 50 minutes.

7. Collect 6.5–7 gallons of wort in the kettle.

8. Boil the wort for 60–90 minutes to reduce volume to 5.5 gallons (hot). Add coagulant and nutrient to the kettle 10 minutes before the end of boil.

9. Postboil wort pH should be 5.0–5.3. OG should be 1.051–1.053.

10. Chill to 70°F and pitch yeast per package instructions.

11. Ferment out at 68–70°F. Time should be no more than 6 days. Check final gravity; it should be 1.011–1.013. Dry hop and let stand for 48 hours. Crash cool in refrigerator for 5 to 7 days, then filter and carbonate.

KOLSCH

This German Blonde Ale's name actually refers to the Rhineland district around Cologne, so anything brewed elsewhere should be referred to as "Kolsch-style." You can make something resembling a Kolsch using a neutral ale yeast such as US-05, but the most authentic results require a liquid strain such as White Labs WLP003 or Wyeast 2565. If choosing one of these yeasts, carefully read the information on the yeast lab website and decide whether you can manage the fermentation without investing in a second beer refrigerator.

Level: Basic
MAKES 5 GALLONS

GRAIN BILL

8 pounds North American pale two-row malt

HOP BILL

KETTLE HOPS: Liberty or Glacier 4 BU (45 minutes before end of boil)

FINISH HOPS: Liberty 6 BU (5 minutes before end of boil)

YEAST: Danstar Nottingham, Safale US-05, or liquid yeast (see notes above)

OTHER: Water treatments (gypsum or Calcium chloride for mash; phosphoric acid for sparge liquor); kettle coagulant, yeast nutrient

PROCEDURE

1. Weigh out the grains. Mill the malt.

2. Calculate the hop quantities and weigh out.

3. Calculate the sparge and mash water quantities. Treat the water as appropriate for pale beers. (See Homebrewing Operations, page 128.)

4. The mash-in temperature is 150°F.

5. Let the mash stand for 1 hour at 150–148°F. Mash pH should be 5.2–5.5.

6. Recirculate until wort is clear, then run off and sparge. Wort collection should take at least 50 minutes.

7. Collect 6.5–7 gallons of wort in the kettle.

8. Boil the wort for 60–90 minutes to reduce volume to 5.5 gallons (hot). Add coagulant and nutrient to the kettle for 10 minutes before the end of boil.

9. Postboil wort pH should be 5.0–5.3. OG should be 1.048–1.050.

10. Chill to 70°F and pitch yeast per package instructions.

11. Ferment out at 68–70°F. Time should be no more than 6 days. Check final gravity; it should be 1.009–1.011. Crash cool in refrigerator for 5 to 7 days, then filter into keg and carbonate.

HEFEWEIZEN (GERMAN WHEAT ALE)

The wheat is not the dominant flavor in this beer; it's the yeast. The German wheat beer yeasts produce fruity and spicy (clove) flavor in abundance. The beer is intentionally left cloudy. High carbonation is the rule.

Watch your runoff with this one. The rice hulls will help with the lauter. Also, as noted in the advanced techniques chapter (page 180), watch your fermentation temperatures, especially if using the Weihenstephan strain (Wyeast 3068/WLP300). A starter is recommended, along with a cool pitch and fermentation. One rule of thumb is that pitch and fermentation temperature should not add up to more than 30°C; in other words, if you pitch at 12°C (54°F), ferment at 18°C (65°F). If you cannot manage these temperatures, you might prefer to try a different strain, such as Wyeast 3333/WLP380. However, this beer requires control of fermentation temperatures in order to get consistent results.

Level: Advanced
MAKES 5 GALLONS

GRAIN BILL

4   pounds red wheat malt

4   pounds North American two-row pale malt

8   ounces rice hulls

HOP BILL:

KETTLE HOPS: Liberty or Hallertau Mittelfruh 5 BU (45 minutes before end of boil)

YEAST: See notes above

OTHER: Water treatments (gypsum or Calcium chloride for mash; phosphoric acid for sparge liquor); kettle coagulant, yeast nutrient

PROCEDURE

1. Weigh out the grains. Mill the malt. Do NOT mill the rice hulls.

2. Calculate the hop quantities and weigh out.

3. Calculate the sparge and mash water quantities. Treat the water as appropriate for pale beers. (See Homebrewing Operations, page 128.)

4. The mash-in temperature is 151°F.

5. Let the mash stand for 1 hour at 151–149°F. Mash pH should be 5.2 – 5.5.

6. Recirculate until wort is clear, then run off and sparge. Wort collection should take at least 50 minutes.

7. Collect 6.5–7 gallons of wort in the kettle.

8. Boil the wort for 60–90 minutes to reduce volume to 5.5 gallons (hot). Add coagulant and nutrient to the kettle 10 minutes before the end of boil.

9. Postboil wort pH should be 5.0–5.3. OG should be 1.047–1.049.

10. See recipe notes above for pitching recommendations.

11. See recipe notes above for fermentation temperatures. Time should be no more than 9 days if an adequate quantity of yeast is pitched. Check final gravity; it should be 1.011–1.013. Crash cool in refrigerator for 5 to 7 days, then rack into keg and carbonate. Alternatively, beer can be primed and bottle conditioned.

PILSNER

This is the only lager recipe in this book. Please read the Advanced Techniques chapter (page 180) before attempting this; you can make excellent pilsner using single-infusion mashing, but fermentation temperature control is vital. I recommend Wyeast 2124/WLP830 or Wyeast 2308/WLP838 yeast strains. The former tends to give a more tart, sulfury note; the latter emphasizes malt character. Of the dry yeasts, the Saflager W-34/70 would be my first choice. For hops, Saaz is still my favorite, although the German Spalt, French Strisselspalt, and Polish Lublin varieties also work well. Forget American hops or any sort of high-alpha variety.

Level: Advanced
MAKES 5 GALLONS

MALT BILL

6 pounds North American two-row pale malt (about 2 degrees Lovibond)

2.5 pounds North American pilsner malt (about 1.3 degrees Lovibond)

HOP BILL

KETTLE HOPS: Saaz 6 BU (45 minutes before end of boil)

FINISH HOPS: Saaz 9 BU (end of boil)

YEAST: See notes above, along with the lager brewing section of chapter 6 (page 183).

OTHER: Water treatments (gypsum or Calcium chloride for mash; phosphoric acid for sparge liquor); kettle coagulant, yeast nutrient

PROCEDURE

1. Weigh out the grains. Mill the malt.

2. Calculate the hop quantities and weigh out.

3. Calculate the sparge and mash water quantities. Treat the water as appropriate for pale beers. (See Homebrewing Operations, page 128.)

4. The mash-in temperature is 151°F

5. Let the mash stand for 1 hour at 151–149°F. Mash pH should be 5.2 – 5.5.

6. Recirculate until wort is clear, then run off and sparge. Wort collection should take at least 50 minutes.

7. Collect 6.5–7 gallons of wort in the kettle.

8. Boil the wort for 60–90 minutes to reduce volume to 5.5 gallons (hot). Add coagulant and nutrient to the kettle for 10 minutes before the end of boil.

9. Postboil wort pH should be 5.0–5.3. OG should be 1.047–1.049.

10. See recipe notes above for pitching recommendations.

11. See Advanced Techniques chapter for fermentation temperatures and procedure. Final gravity should be 1.011–1.013. After cold storage period (lagering), filter and carbonate.

APPENDIX

Infusion Rinsing ("Batch Sparging")

At various points in this book I make references to infusion rinsing, so I owe you a brief explanation of it. It has become very popular among homebrewers, and if you read any homebrewers web forums or recent books, you will undoubtedly run across the term "batch sparging," which I consider a less accurate name for this procedure.

So, first off, what is batch sparging? Basically, it is an adaptation of a centuries-old brewing method that has almost completely disappeared from commercial practice. That does not mean it is a bad idea. The pipe manifold lauter tun, which is also very popular among homebrewers, is an adaptation of the old Anheuser-Busch Strainmaster that was phased out in the 1980s. Nonetheless, the design remains viable for homebrewers. The drawbacks of the Strainmaster — slightly lower efficiency and difficult grain removal — are not significant on the homebrew scale.

So, how about infusion rinsing? It is a revival of the old parti-gyle brewing method, wherein a single mash was used to make three different beers. Here's how it was done.

The mash was mixed and, after conversion, the first wort was drawn off until the bed was very well drained. This wort was boiled and fermented separately to make a strong beer. Next, the mash/lauter tun was infused with hot water and stirred well, then a second batch (gyle) was drawn off, and again boiled and fermented separately. This batch was of normal beer strength. Then the mash was infused once more and a third gyle was drawn off; this became (often with the addition of some sugar) "small beer."

Homebrewers revived the practice of parti-gyle brewing as a way of making strong, high-gravity brews without wasting so much of the extract that would otherwise be discarded with the spent grain. At the same time, a number of brewing enthusiasts looked critically at the sparging process and advocated either eliminating or curtailing it, as a way of reducing astringent-tasting tannins in the finished beer. These trends led to the creation of the infusion rinse, which is basically identical to parti-gyle brewing except that, most often, only two gyles are drawn off and then are blended together to produce a single beer. Hence the name *batch sparging*.

The attraction of batch sparging is its obvious simplicity: no need to manage the flow of hot water over the grain bed. No worries over cracking or channeling. It also removes the concern about oversparging, which is running off until the wort gravity drops close to zero, with an attendant rise in pH and tannin extraction. In fact, because the gravity of the second gyle is almost always above the rule-of-thumb cutoff point (1.008–1.010) at which extraction of tannins becomes an issue, there is no need for pH adjustments to the sparge water. A further bonus, potentially, is speed, because there is no need to slow down wort collection in order to maximize extract. Once the wort is clear, you can run it off as fast as you like.

Sounds pretty good, right? It sounded good to me, and when I went back into homebrewing my plan was to pretty much leave water chemistry behind by using Five Star "5.2" and infusion rinsing. However, I was concerned about loss of extract. I realized that efficiency would depend greatly on how dry I could drain the bed during the first runoff. I also was concerned about aeration of the wort during the infusion. So I decided to build a mash/lauter tun with a manifold: that, I thought, would allow me to do both infusion and conventional sparging, and then compare results.

The first problem I ran into was that "5.2" did not work as well as I had hoped. On my first brew, it brought the mash pH down, but not as far as expected. I've made great beers when the mash pH was as high as 5.5, and this brew was 5.4, so this was not a crushing blow. (As noted elsewhere, after my first brew I decided to discontinue it, for other reasons.) I also found that my efficiency was lower than expected, because I could not collect as much first wort as predicted. Most of the infusion-rinsing information I had read suggested that the water retention rate of a well-drained mash was about 1 pint for every 1 pound of grain. I found, with my lauter tun, that it was nearer to a quart. This meant that the difference in efficiency between the two methods was greater than anticipated. I had to lengthen the kettle boil by 45 minutes in order to get the gravity I wanted; obviously that meant less beer.

I also found that, at least with my equipment, the infusion-rinsing cycle takes longer than conventional lautering, and it is physically harder. Breaking up the compacted grain mass during the second infusion takes more time and effort than mashing-in. There is also the risk, not to be underestimated, of knocking apart the manifold. I did this on my second mash. I was not sure what had happened until runoff was over, but I knew something was wrong because the second run never cleared as well as it should. That was the last straw.

I fully expect the advocates of infusion rinsing to go through this narrative point by point and explain that these were all just "rookie mistakes" that could be easily corrected; that some of them have nothing to do with the choice of sparge method but are specific to the materials and equipment I chose; and that by the time you get half a dozen brews under your belt, batch sparging is a simple and repeatable procedure capable of producing excellent beer. No argument here, all true, with only one qualifier: if you want to try infusion rinsing, build a dedicated oversize lauter tun with a braided stainless steel "pigtail" or a strainer screen collector (e.g., the KettleScreen or Bazooka Screen) rather than a manifold, and make sure it is tightly clamped in place.

However, the same is true of conventional (continuous) sparging. By the time you have done half a dozen brews you have it down — especially with a properly designed pipe manifold, which is far less prone to stuck mashes or uneven drainage than a false bottom. As for the tannin issue, I contend, based on my own tasting, that this is a matter of paying attention to your process and managing it. Infusion rinsing is a perfectly good alternative, but it is not a panacea. Wort quality, including clarity and pH, is vital to making good beer. No lautering method will guarantee it.

RESOURCES

Books

Burch, Byron. *Brewing Quality Beers*, 2nd ed. Joby Books, 1992
A clear, straightforward introduction to extract brewing.

Classic Beer Styles series, Brewers Publications.
Books on most all the classic styles of beer, written by authors with a great range of backgrounds. Many are excellent.

Daniels, Ray. *Designing Great Beers*. Brewers Publications, 1996.
Excellent reference on recipe formulation.

de Clerck, Jean. *A Textbook of Brewing*. 2 vols. Siebel Institute of Technology, 1994.
Reprint of the 1957 translation. Volume 1 is still relevant and full of insight. Not a must-read, but a fascinating look back at craft brewing before it had that name.

Fix, George. *Principles of Brewing Science*, 2nd ed. Brewers Publications, 1999.
Every serious brewer needs to read this book.

Fix, George and Laurie Fix. *An Analysis of Brewing Techniques*. Brewers Publications, 1997.
Apparently out of print, but worth seeking out.

Line, Dave. *Big Book of Brewing*, 2nd ed. Fox Chapel Publishing, 2011.
Just back in print, the first book to bridge the gap between commercial brewing and homebrewing.

Miller, Dave. *Dave Miller's Homebrewing Guide*. Storey Publishing, 1995.
My semiadvanced homebrewing book. Gets into brewing science a bit.

Noonan, Gregory J. *New Brewing Lager Beer*, rev ed. Brewers Publications, 2003.
Another must-read. Don't be misled by the title; even if you are an ale-or-nothing person, this book is invaluable.

Palmer, John J. *How to Brew*. Brewers Publications, 2006.
The best up-to-date, all-around introduction to homebrewing.

Papazian, Charlie. *The Complete Joy of Homebrewing*, 3rd ed. HarperCollins, 2003.
A classic reference, oriented toward malt extract recipes. Charlie is founder of the American Homebrewers Association.

Online Reading and References

"A Better Brew" by Burkhard Bilger
www.newyorker.com/
reporting/2008/11/24/081124fa_fact_
bilger
Philosophy of brewing, a *New Yorker* (November 24, 2008) piece focused on "extreme beers." The author is a fan, but he gives space to the classical perspective.

Alzheimer's Myths
Alzheimer's Association
www.alz.org/alzheimers_disease_
myths_about_alzheimers.asp
Aluminum brew kettles

Brewing Water Chemistry Calculator
Brewer's Friend
www.brewersfriend.com/
water-chemistry
Especially useful for "building" brewing liquor from RO water. The other calculators on this website are also worth exploring.

Danstar
Lallemand Inc.
www.danstaryeast.com
Yeast information

Fermentis
www.fermentis.com
Home brewing yeast information

"Fluid Dynamics — A Simple Key to the Mastery of Efficient Lautering" by John J. Palmer and Paul Prozinski
www.brewingtechniques.com/library/
backissues/issue3.4/palmer.html
Lauter Tun Design. Republished from *Brewing Techniques* July/August 1995.

Force Carbonation Chart
Kegerators.com
www.kegerators.com/carbonation-table.
php

Home Brewing Yeast Strain Guide
Wyeast Laboratories
www.wyeastlab.com/hb_yeaststrain.cfm

Homebrew Yeast Strain Descriptions
White Labs
www.whitelabs.com/beer/homebrew_
strains.html

Hop Varieties
Hopsteiner
www.hopsteiner.com/varieties
Hopsteiner breaks down the varieties by the nation or region of the world, with a separate PDF for each variety.

***Hop Variety Handbook,* by Hopunion LLC, 2011.**
www.hopunion.com/17_
hopvarietyhandbook.cfm
A very convenient all-in-one e-booklet. Every brewer should have a copy.

**"Jon Plise Demonstrates
Our MoreBeer Counter
Pressure Bottle Filler"**
More Beer
http://morebeer.ning.com/video/
jon-plise-demonstrates-our
Counterpressure bottle filling video.
This is a vendor's website, but the
video is first rate. Only one criticism:
The presenter recommends Star San
for soaking and sanitizing the bottles.
I think Oxine is a better option.

Malt
Brewers Supply Group
www.brewerssupplygroup.com/Malt.
html
This page links to information and
specification pages for a number of
malt companies' products.

Malt
The Country Malt Group
www.countrymaltgroup.com/malt.asp
More links to data on malt from a
number of malting companies.

Malting 101, Technical Presentations
Briess Malt & Ingredients Co.
www.brewingwithbriess.com/
Malting101/Technical_Presentations.
htm
"Beyond Lovibond — Understanding
Beer Color" by Bob Hansen and
"Practical Milling for the Craft
Brewer" by Bob Hansen. Information
on beer color and malt milling.

Metric Conversions
www.metric-conversions.org

Nelson's Beer Quick-Calculator
Build A Beer
www.buildabeer.org/beerquickcalc.php

Tech Center
Cargill Incorporated
www.cargill.com/food/na/en/products/
malt/malt-specialty-products-group/
TechCenter
Links to information and specifications
on the lines of malt Cargill makes
or imports.

Water Quality Report
Metropolitan Government
of Nashville and Davidson
County, Tennessee
www.nashville.gov/water/qualityrpt.asp

Water Quality Report
Water Department,
City of Lubbock, Texas
http://water.ci.lubbock.tx.us/
waterqualityreport.aspx

"Yeast Propagations and Maintenance: Principles and Practices"
Maltose Falcons
www.maltosefalcons.com/tech/
yeast-propagation-and-maintenance-
principles-and-practices

Yeast Propagation and Culturing
Homebrew club websites and online
forums are a wonderful, but dangerous,
resource. The quality of information
varies wildly. However, this article is
by Maribeth Raines, a microbiologist
whose interest in homebrewing has
contributed greatly to its advancement.

Supplies and Equipment

Ace Hardware Corporation
866-290-5334
www.acehardware.com
General hardware, tools, and supplies

Bayou Classic Burner
Barbour International, Inc.
800-736-8028
www.thebayou.com

BetterBottle
High-Q, Inc.
800-435-4585
www.better-bottle.com
Carboys

Bio-Cide International, Inc.
800-323-1398
www.bio-cide.com
Oxine

Blichmann Engineering, LLC
www.blichmannengineering.com
Therminator plate heat exchanger and beer gun

Brewers Supply Group
800-374-2739
www.brewerssupplygroup.com
Malt

Briess Mal & Ingredients Co.
800-657-0806
www.briess.com
Malt and adjuncts

Cargill Incorporated
www.cargillfoods.com
Malts, including imported lines

The Coleman Company, Inc.
800-835-3278
www.coleman.com
Picnic coolers

Copper Tubing Sales
336-285-5364
www.coppertubingsales.com
Copper refrigeration tubing

Country Malt Group
www.countrymaltgroup.com
Domestic and imported malt and other ingredients

Crosby & Baker Ltd.
508-636-5154
http://crosby-baker.com
Homebrew equipment and supplies, as well as malts, wholesale only

Culligan Water
952-933-7200
www.culliganwater.com
RV-500 or RV-600 water filter

Danstar
Lallemand Inc.
www.danstaryeast.com
Yeast

Fermentap
800-942-2750
http://fermentap.com
Botter filler and other supplies and equipment, wholesale only

Fermentis
www.fermentis.com
Yeast

Fermtech Ltd.
519-570-2163
www.fermtech.ca
Auto-siphon

The Filter Store
800-828-1494
www.filterstore.com
Water filters

Five Star Chemicals &
Supply, Inc.
800-782-7019
www.fivestarchemicals.com
*Phosphate buffers, PBW, Star San,
and Saniclean*

Foxx Equipment Company
www.foxxequipment.com
Draft beer equipment, wholesale only

Graver Technologies
302-731-1700
www.gravertech.com
Filters

Hanna Instruments
800-426-6287
www.hannachecker.com
pH meters

Harbor Freight Tools
800-444-3353
www.harborfreight.com

Hardware World
800-385-8320
www.hardwareworld.com
Genova Geno-Grip 53010

Hayward
hflow@haywardnet.com
www.haywardflowcontrol.com
Bulkhead

The Home Depot
800-466-3337
www.homedepot.com
General hardware, tools, and supplies

Hopsteiner
212-838-8900
www.hopsteiner.com
Hops, wholesale only

Hopunion, LLC
509-453-4792
www.hopunion.com
Hops, wholesale only

Kegs.com Ltd.
SABCO
www.kegs.com
Refurbished kegs

Lallemand, Inc.
www.lallemand.com
Yeast

LD Carlson Company
800-321-0315
www.ldcarlson.com
*Brewing supplies and equipment,
including malts, wholesale only*

LOGIC, Inc.
608-658-2866
www.ecologiccleansers.com
Straight-A

Lowe's
800-445-6937
www.lowes.com
General hardware, tools, and supplies

March Manufacturing
847-729-5300
www.marchpump.com
Pumps

McMaster-Carr
609-689-3415
www.mcmaster.com
*All sorts of plumbing and other parts
for homebrew equipment projects*

Rahr Malting Co.
952-445-1431
www.rahr.com
Malts

Taprite Mfg., Inc.
800-779-8488
www.taprite.com
Draft beer dispense and test equipment

White Labs Inc.
303-530-046
www.whitelabs.com
Yeast

William's Brewing
www.williamsbrewing.com
Weldless pot and cooler fittings

Wyeast Laboratories, Inc.
www.wyeastlab.com
Yeast

Zahm and Nagel Co., Inc.
800-216-1542
www.zahmnagel.com
Carbonation tester

INDEX

Page numbers in *italic* indicate photos or illustrations; page numbers in **bold** indicate charts.

Other Storey Titles You Will Enjoy

BY THE SAME AUTHOR

Dave Miller's Homebrewing Guide.
A simple yet complete overview of homebrewing that is clear
enough for the novice but thorough enough for the brewmaster.
368 pages. Paper. ISBN 978-0-88266-905-2.

CloneBrews, **2nd edition, by Tess and Mark Szamatulski.**
One hundred and fifty recipes to brew beer that
tastes just like premium commercial brands.
440 pages. Paper. ISBN 978-1-60342-539-1.

The Homebrewer's Answer Book, **by Ashton Lewis.**
Hundreds of brewing problems solved by *Brew
Your Own* magazine's Mr. Wizard.
432 pages. Flexibind. ISBN 978-1-58017-675-0.

The Homebrewer's Garden, **by Joe Fisher & Dennis Fisher.**
Easy instructions for setting up your first trellis; growing your own
hops, malt grains, and brewing herbs; and brewing with recipes created
specifically for homegrown ingredients.
192 pages. Paper. ISBN 978-1-58017-010-9.

North American CloneBrews, **by Scott R. Russell.**
Recipes to duplicate your favorite American and Canadian beers at home.
176 pages. Paper. ISBN 978-1-58017-246-2.

Tasting Beer, **by Randy Mosher.**
The first comprehensive guide to tasting, appreciating, and
understanding the world's best drink — craft beers.
256 pages. Paper. ISBN 978-1-60342-089-1.

These and other books from Storey Publishing are available
wherever quality books are sold or by calling 1-800-441-5700.
Visit us at *www.storey.com*.